Data Engineering with Python

Work with massive datasets to design data models
and automate data pipelines using Python

Paul Crickard

BIRMINGHAM—MUMBAI

Data Engineering with Python

Commissioning Editor: Sunith Shetty

Acquisition Editor: Reshma Raman

Senior Editor: Roshan Kumar

Content Development Editor: Athikho Sapuni Rishana

Technical Editor: Manikandan Kurup

Copy Editor: Safis Editing

Project Coordinator: Aishwarya Mohan

Proofreader: Safis Editing

Indexer: Tejal Daruwale Soni

Production Designer: Alishon Mendonca

First published: October 2020

Production reference: 1231020

Published by Packt Publishing Ltd.

Livery Place

35 Livery Street

Birmingham

B3 2PB, UK.

ISBN 978-1-83921-418-9

www.packt.com

Packt.com

Subscribe to our online digital library for full access to over 7,000 books and videos, as well as industry leading tools to help you plan your personal development and advance your career. For more information, please visit our website.

Why subscribe?

- Spend less time learning and more time coding with practical eBooks and videos from over 4,000 industry professionals

- Improve your learning with Skill Plans built especially for you

- Get a free eBook or video every month

- Fully searchable for easy access to vital information

- Copy and paste, print, and bookmark content

Did you know that Packt offers eBook versions of every book published, with PDF and ePub files available? You can upgrade to the eBook version at packt.com and as a print book customer, you are entitled to a discount on the eBook copy. Get in touch with us at customercare@packtpub.com for more details.

At www.packt.com, you can also read a collection of free technical articles, sign up for a range of free newsletters, and receive exclusive discounts and offers on Packt books and eBooks.

Contributors

About the author

Paul Crickard is the author of *Leaflet.js Essentials* and co-author of *Mastering Geospatial Analysis with Python*, and is also the Chief Information Officer at the Second Judicial District Attorney's Office in Albuquerque, New Mexico.

With a master's degree in political science and a background in community and regional planning, he combines rigorous social science theory and techniques to technology projects. He has presented at the New Mexico Big Data and Analytics Summit and the ExperienceIT NM Conference. He has given talks on data to the New Mexico Big Data Working Group, Sandia National Labs, and the New Mexico Geographic Information Council.

About the reviewers

Stefan Marwah has enjoyed programming for over ten years, which led him to undertake a bachelor's degree in computer science from the reputable Monash University. During his time at the university, he built a mobile application that detected if an elderly person had Alzheimer's disease with help of natural language processing, speech recognition, and neural networks, which secured him an award from Microsoft. He has experience in both engineering and analytical roles that are rooted in his passion for leveraging data and artificial intelligence to make impactful decisions within different organizations. He currently works as a data engineer and also teaches part-time on topics around data science at Step Function Coaching.

Andre Sionek is a data engineer at Gousto, in London. He started his career by founding his own company, Polyteck, a free science and technology magazine for university students. But he only jumped into the world of data and analytics during an internship at the collections department of a Brazilian bank. He also worked with credit modeling for a large cosmetics group and for start-ups before moving to London. He regularly teaches data engineering courses, focusing on infrastructure as code and productionization. He also writes about data for his blog and competes on Kaggle sometimes.

Miles Obare is a software engineer at Microsoft in the Azure team. He is currently building tools that enable customers to migrate their server workloads to the cloud. He also builds real-time, scalable backend systems and data pipelines for enterprise customers. Formerly, he worked as a data engineer for a financial start-up, where his role involved developing and deploying data pipelines and machine learning models to production. His areas of expertise include distributed systems, computer architecture, and data engineering. He holds a bachelor's degree in electrical and computer engineering from Jomo Kenyatta University and contributes to open source projects in his free time.

Packt is searching for authors like you

If you're interested in becoming an author for Packt, please visit `authors.packtpub.com` and apply today. We have worked with thousands of developers and tech professionals, just like you, to help them share their insight with the global tech community. You can make a general application, apply for a specific hot topic that we are recruiting an author for, or submit your own idea.

Table of Contents

6

Building a 311 Data Pipeline

Section 2: Deploying Data Pipelines in Production

7

Features of a Production Pipeline

8

Version Control with the NiFi Registry

9
Monitoring Data Pipelines

10
Deploying Data Pipelines

11
Building a Production Data Pipeline

Section 3: Beyond Batch – Building Real-Time Data Pipelines

Appendix

Other Books You May Enjoy

Index

Preface

Data engineering provides the foundation for data science and analytics and constitutes an important aspect of all businesses. This book will help you to explore various tools and methods that are used to understand the data engineering process using Python.
The book will show you how to tackle challenges commonly faced in different aspects of data engineering. You'll start with an introduction to the basics of data engineering, along with the technologies and frameworks required to build data pipelines to work with large datasets. You'll learn how to transform and clean data and perform analytics to get the most out of your data. As you advance, you'll discover how to work with big data of varying complexity and production databases and build data pipelines. Using real-world examples, you'll build architectures on which you'll learn how to deploy data pipelines.

By the end of this Python book, you'll have gained a clear understanding of data modeling techniques, and will be able to confidently build data engineering pipelines for tracking data, running quality checks, and making necessary changes in production.

Who this book is for

This book is for data analysts, ETL developers, and anyone looking to get started with, or transition to, the field of data engineering or refresh their knowledge of data engineering using Python. This book will also be useful for students planning to build a career in data engineering or IT professionals preparing for a transition. No previous knowledge of data engineering is required.

What this book covers

Chapter 1, What Is Data Engineering, defines data engineering. It will introduce you to the skills, roles, and responsibilities of a data engineer. You will also learn how data engineering fits in with other disciplines, such as data science.

Chapter 2, Building Our Data Engineering Infrastructure, explains how to install and configure the tools used throughout this book. You will install two databases – ElasticSearch and PostgreSQL – as well as NiFi, Kibana, and, of course, Python.

Chapter 3, Reading and Writing Files, provides an introduction to reading and writing files in Python as well as data pipelines in NiFi. It will focus on **Comma Seperated Values (CSV)** and **JavaScript Object Notation (JSON)** files.

Chapter 4, Working with Databases, explains the basics of working with SQL and NoSQL databases. You will query both types of databases and view the results in Python and through the use of NiFi. You will also learn how to read a file and insert it into the databases.

Chapter 5, Cleaning and Transforming Data, explains how to take the files or database queries and perform basic exploratory data analysis. This analysis will allow you to view common data problems. You will then use Python and NiFi to clean and transform the data with a view to solving those common data problems.

Chapter 6, Project – Building a 311 Data Pipeline, sets out a project in which you will build a complete data pipeline. You will learn how to read from an API and use all of the skills acquired from previous chapters. You will clean and transform the data as well as enrich it with additional data. Lastly, you will insert the data into a warehouse and build a dashboard to visualize it.

Chapter 7, Features of a Production Data Pipeline, covers what is needed in a data pipeline to make it ready for production. You will learn about atomic transactions and how to make data pipelines idempotent.

Chapter 8, Version Control Using the NiFi Registry, explains how to version control your data pipelines. You will install and configure the NiFi registry. You will also learn how to configure the registry to use GitHub as the source of your NiFi processors.

Chapter 9, Monitoring and Logging Data Pipelines, teaches you the basics of monitoring and logging data pipelines. You will learn about the features of the NiFi GUI for monitoring. You will also learn how to use NiFi processors to log and monitor performance from within your data pipelines. Lastly, you will learn the basics of the NiFi API.

Chapter 10, Deploying Your Data Pipelines, proposes a method for building test and production environments for NiFi. You will learn how to move your completed and version-controlled data pipelines into a production environment.

Chapter 11, Project – Building a Production Data Pipeline, explains how to build a production data pipeline. You will use the project from *Chapter 6* and add a number of features. You will version control the data pipeline as well as adding monitoring and logging features.

Chapter 12, Building an Apache Kafka Cluster, explains how to install and configure a three-node Apache Kafka cluster. You will learn the basics of Kafka – streams, topics, and consumers.

Chapter 13, Streaming Data with Kafka, explains how, using Python, you can write to Kafka topics and how to consume that data. You will write Python code for both consumers and producers using a third-party Python library.

Chapter 14, Data Processing with Apache Spark, walks you through the installation and configuration of a three-node Apache Spark cluster. You will learn how to use Python to manipulate data in Spark. This will be reminiscent of working with pandas DataFrames from *Section 1* of this book.

Chapter 15, Project – Real-Time Edge Data – Kafka, Spark, and MiNiFi, introduces MiNiFi, which is a separate project to make NiFi available on low-resource devices such as Internet of Things devices. You will build a data pipeline that sends data from MiNiFi to your NiFi instance.

The *Appendix* teaches you the basics of clustering with Apache NiFi. You will learn how to distribute data pipelines and some caveats in doing so. You will also learn how to allow data pipelines to run on a single, specified node and not run distributed while in a cluster.

To get the most out of this book

You should have a basic understanding of Python. You will not be required to know any existing libraries, just a fundamental understanding of variables, functions, and how to run a program. You should also know the basics of Linux. If you can run a command in the terminal and open new terminal windows, that should be sufficient.

Software/hardware covered in the book	OS requirements
Python 3.x	Windows, macOS X, and Linux (any)
Spark 3.x	Linux
NiFi 1.x	Windows, macOS X, Linux
PostgreSQL 13.x	Windows, macOS X, Linux
ElasticSearch 7.x	Windows, macOS X, Linux
Kibana 7.x	Windows, macOS X, Linux
Apache Kafka 2.x	Linux, macOS X

If you are using the digital version of this book, we advise you to type the code yourself or access the code via the GitHub repository (link available in the next section). Doing so will help you avoid any potential errors related to the copying and pasting of code.

Download the example code files

You can download the example code files for this book at `https://github.com/PacktPublishing/Data-Engineering-with-Python`. In case there's an update to the code, it will be updated on the existing GitHub repository.

We also have other code bundles from our rich catalog of books and videos available at `https://github.com/PacktPublishing/`. Check them out!

Download the color images

We also provide a PDF file that has color images of the screenshots/diagrams used in this book. You can download it here: `http://www.packtpub.com/sites/default/files/downloads/9781839214189_ColorImages.pdf`.

Conventions used

There are a number of text conventions used throughout this book.

`Code in text`: Indicates code words in text, database table names, folder names, filenames, file extensions, pathnames, dummy URLs, user input, and Twitter handles. Here is an example: "Next, pass the arguments dictionary to `DAG()`."

A block of code is set as follows:

```
import datetime as dt
from datetime import timedelta
from airflow import DAG
from airflow.operators.bash_operator import BashOperator
from airflow.operators.python_operator import PythonOperator
import pandas as pd
```

Any command-line input or output is written as follows:

```
# web properties #
nifi.web.http.port=9300
```

Bold: Indicates a new term, an important word, or words that you see on screen. For example, words in menus or dialog boxes appear in the text like this. Here is an example: "Click on **DAG** and select **Tree View**."

> **Tips or important notes**
> Appear like this.

Get in touch

Feedback from our readers is always welcome.

General feedback: If you have questions about any aspect of this book, mention the book title in the subject of your message and email us at customercare@packtpub.com.

Errata: Although we have taken every care to ensure the accuracy of our content, mistakes do happen. If you have found a mistake in this book, we would be grateful if you would report this to us. Please visit www.packtpub.com/support/errata, selecting your book, clicking on the Errata Submission Form link, and entering the details.

Piracy: If you come across any illegal copies of our works in any form on the internet, we would be grateful if you would provide us with the location address or website name. Please contact us at copyright@packt.com with a link to the material.

If you are interested in becoming an author: If there is a topic that you have expertise in, and you are interested in either writing or contributing to a book, please visit authors.packtpub.com.

Reviews

Please leave a review. Once you have read and used this book, why not leave a review on the site that you purchased it from? Potential readers can then see and use your unbiased opinion to make purchase decisions, we at Packt can understand what you think about our products, and our authors can see your feedback on their book. Thank you!

For more information about Packt, please visit packt.com.

Section 1: Building Data Pipelines – Extract Transform, and Load

This section will introduce you to the basics of data engineering. In this section, you will learn what data engineering is and how it relates to other similar fields, such as data science. You will cover the basics of working with files and databases in Python and using Apache NiFi. Once you are comfortable with moving data, you will be introduced to the skills required to clean and transform data. The section culminates with the building of a data pipeline to extract 311 data from SeeClickFix, transform it, and load it into another database. Lastly, you will learn the basics of building dashboards with Kibana to visualize the data you have loaded into your database.

This section comprises the following chapters:

- *Chapter 1, What is Data Engineering?*
- *Chapter 2, Building Our Data Engineering Infrastructure*
- *Chapter 3, Reading and Writing Files*
- *Chapter 4, Working with Databases*
- *Chapter 5, Cleaning and Transforming Data*
- *Chapter 6, Building a 311 Data Pipeline*

1
What is Data Engineering?

Welcome to *Data Engineering with Python*. While data engineering is not a new field, it seems to have stepped out from the background recently and started to take center stage. This book will introduce you to the field of data engineering. You will learn about the tools and techniques employed by data engineers and you will learn how to combine them to build data pipelines. After completing this book, you will be able to connect to multiple data sources, extract the data, transform it, and load it into new locations. You will be able to build your own data engineering infrastructure, including clustering applications to increase their capacity to process data.

In this chapter, you will learn about the roles and responsibilities of data engineers and how data engineering works to support data science. You will be introduced to the tools used by data engineers, as well as the different areas of technology that you will need to be proficient in to become a data engineer.

In this chapter, we're going to cover the following main topics:

- What data engineers do
- Data engineering versus data science
- Data engineering tools

What data engineers do

Data engineering is part of the big data ecosystem and is closely linked to data science. Data engineers work in the background and do not get the same level of attention as data scientists, but they are critical to the process of data science. The roles and responsibilities of a data engineer vary depending on an organization's level of data maturity and staffing levels; however, there are some tasks, such as the extracting, loading, and transforming of data, that are foundational to the role of a data engineer.

At the lowest level, data engineering involves the movement of data from one system or format to another system or format. Using more common terms, data engineers query data from a source (extract), they perform some modifications to the data (transform), and then they put that data in a location where users can access it and know that it is production quality (load). The terms **extract**, **transform**, and **load** will be used a lot throughout this book and will often be abbreviated to **ETL**. This definition of data engineering is broad and simplistic. With the help of an example, let's dig deeper into what data engineers do.

An online retailer has a website where you can purchase widgets in a variety of colors. The website is backed by a relational database. Every transaction is stored in the database. How many blue widgets did the retailer sell in the last quarter?

To answer this question, you could run a SQL query on the database. This doesn't rise to the level of needing a data engineer. But as the site grows, running queries on the production database is no longer practical. Furthermore, there may be more than one database that records transactions. There may be a database at different geographical locations – for example, the retailers in North America may have a different database than the retailers in Asia, Africa, and Europe.

Now you have entered the realm of data engineering. To answer the preceding question, a data engineer would create connections to all of the transactional databases for each region, extract the data, and load it into a data warehouse. From there, you could now count the number of all the blue widgets sold.

Rather than finding the number of blue widgets sold, companies would prefer to find the answer to the following questions:

- How do we find out which locations sell the most widgets?
- How do we find out the peak times for selling widgets?
- How many users put widgets in their carts and remove them later?
- How do we find out the combinations of widgets that are sold together?

Answering these questions requires more than just extracting the data and loading it into a single system. There is a transformation required in between the extract and load. There is also the difference in times zones in different regions. For instance, the United States alone has four time zones. Because of this, you would need to transform time fields to a standard. You will also need a way to distinguish sales in each region. This could be accomplished by adding a location field to the data. Should this field be spatial – in coordinates or as well-known text – or will it just be text that could be transformed in a data engineering pipeline?

Here, the data engineer would need to extract the data from each database, then transform the data by adding an additional field for the location. To compare the time zones, the data engineer would need to be familiar with data standards. For the time, the **International Organization for Standardization (ISO)** has a standard – **ISO 8601**.

Let's now answer the questions in the preceding list one by one:

- Extract the data from each database.

- Add a field to tag the location for each transaction in the data

- Transform the date from local time to ISO 8601.

- Load the data into the data warehouse.

The combination of extracting, loading, and transforming data is accomplished by the creation of a data pipeline. The data comes into the pipeline raw, or dirty in the sense that there may be missing data or typos in the data, which is then cleaned as it flows through the pipe. After that, it comes out the other side into a data warehouse, where it can be queried. The following diagram shows the pipeline required to accomplish the task:

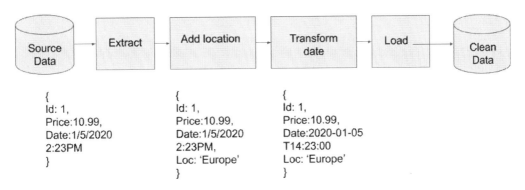

Figure 1.1 – A pipeline that adds a location and modifies the date

Knowing a little more about what data engineering is, and what data engineers do, you should start to get a sense of the responsibilities and skills that data engineers need to acquire. The following section will elaborate on these skills.

Required skills and knowledge to be a data engineer

In the preceding example, it should be clear that data engineers need to be familiar with many different technologies, and we haven't even mentioned the business processes or needs.

At the start of a data pipeline, data engineers need to know how to extract data from files in different formats or different types of databases. This means data engineers need to know several languages used to perform many different tasks, such as SQL and Python.

During the transformation phase of the data pipeline, data engineers need to be familiar with data modeling and structures. They will also need to understand the business and what knowledge and insight they are hoping to extract from the data because this will impact the design of the data models.

The loading of data into the data warehouse means there needs to be a data warehouse with a schema to hold the data. This is also usually the responsibility of the data engineer. Data engineers will need to know the basics of data warehouse design, as well as the types of databases used in their construction.

Lastly, the entire infrastructure that the data pipeline runs on could be the responsibility of the data engineer. They need to know how to manage Linux servers, as well as how to install and configure software such as Apache Airflow or NiFi. As organizations move to the cloud, the data engineer now needs to be familiar with spinning up the infrastructure on the cloud platform used by the organization – Amazon, Google Cloud Platform, or Azure.

Having walked through an example of what data engineers do, we can now develop a broader definition of data engineering.

> **Information**
>
> Data engineering is the development, operation, and maintenance of data infrastructure, either on-premises or in the cloud (or hybrid or multi-cloud), comprising databases and pipelines to extract, transform, and load data.

Data engineering versus data science

Data engineering is what makes data science possible. Again, depending on the maturity of an organization, data scientists may be expected to clean and move the data required for analysis. This is not the best use of a data scientist's time. Data scientists and data engineers use similar tools (Python, for instance), but they specialize in different areas. Data engineers need to understand data formats, models, and structures to efficiently transport data, whereas data scientists utilize them for building statistical models and mathematical computation.

Data scientists will connect to the data warehouses built by data engineers. From there, they can extract the data required for machine learning models and analysis. Data scientists may have their models incorporated into a data engineering pipeline. A close relationship should exist between data engineers and data scientists. Understanding what data scientists need in the data will only serve to help the data engineers deliver a better product.

In the next section, you will learn more about the most common tools used by data engineers.

Data engineering tools

To build data pipelines, data engineers need to choose the right tools for the job. Data engineering is part of the overall big data ecosystem and has to account for the three Vs of big data:

- **Volume**: The volume of data has grown substantially. Moving a thousand records from a database requires different tools and techniques than moving millions of rows or handling millions of transactions a minute.

- **Variety**: Data engineers need tools that handle a variety of data formats in different locations (databases, APIs, files).

- **Velocity**: The velocity of data is always increasing. Tracking the activity of millions of users on a social network or the purchases of users all over the world requires data engineers to operate often in near real time.

Programming languages

The lingua franca of data engineering is **SQL**. Whether you use low-code tools or a specific programming language, there is almost no way to get around knowing SQL. A strong foundation in SQL allows the data engineer to optimize queries for speed and can assist in data transformations. SQL is so prevalent in data engineering that data lakes and non-SQL databases have tools to allow the data engineer to query them in SQL.

A large number of open source data engineering tools use **Java** and **Scala** (Apache projects). Java is a popular, mainstream, object-oriented programming language. While debatable, Java is slowly being replaced by other languages that run on the **Java Virtual Machine (JVM)**. Scala is one of these languages. Other languages that run on the JVM include **Clojure** and **Groovy**. In the next chapter, you will be introduced to **Apache NiFi**. NiFi allows you to develop custom processors in Java, Clojure, Groovy, and **Jython**. While Java is an object-oriented language, there has been a movement toward functional programming languages, of which Clojure and Scala are members.

The focus of this book is on data engineering with Python. It is well-documented with a larger user base and cross-platform. Python has become the default language for data science and data engineering. Python has an extensive collection of standard libraries and third-party libraries. The data science environment in Python is unmatched in other languages. Libraries such as `pandas`, `matplotlib`, `numpy`, `scipy`, `scikit-learn`, `tensorflow`, `pytorch`, and `NLTK` make up an extremely powerful data engineering and data science environment.

Databases

In most production systems, data will be stored in **relational databases**. Most proprietary solutions will use either **Oracle** or **Microsoft SQL Server**, while open source solutions tend to use **MySQL** or **PostgreSQL**. These databases store data in rows and are well-suited to recording transactions. There are also relationships between tables, utilizing primary keys to join data from one table to another – thus making them relational. The following table diagram shows a simple data model and the relationships between the tables:

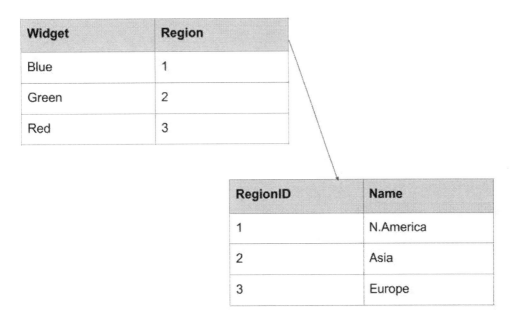

Widget	Region
Blue	1
Green	2
Red	3

RegionID	Name
1	N.America
2	Asia
3	Europe

Figure 1.2 – Relational tables joined on Region = RegionID.

The most common databases used in data warehousing are **Amazon Redshift**, **Google BigQuery**, **Apache Cassandra**, and other NoSQL databases, such as **Elasticsearch**. Amazon Redshift, Google BigQuery, and Cassandra deviate from the traditional rows of relational databases and store data in a columnar format, as shown:

Widget	Region
Blue	1
Green	2
Red	3

Widget	Blue
	Green
	Red
Region	1
	2
	3

Figure 1.3 – Rows stored in a columnar format

Columnar databases are better suited for fast queries – therefore making them well-suited for data warehouses. All three of the columnar databases can be queried using SQL – although Cassandra uses the Cassandra Query Language, it is similar.

In contrast to columnar databases, there are document, or NoSQL, databases, such as Elasticsearch. Elasticsearch is actually a search engine based on **Apache Lucene**. It is similar to **Apache Solr** but is more user-friendly. Elasticsearch is open source, but it does have proprietary components – most notably, the X-Pack plugins for machine learning, graphs, security, and alerting/monitoring. Elasticsearch uses the Elastic Query **DSL** (**Domain-Specific Language**). It is not SQL, but rather a JSON query. Elasticsearch stores data as documents, and while it has parent-child documents, it is non-relational (like the columnar databases).

Once a data engineer extracts data from a database, they will need to transform or process it. With big data, it helps to use a data processing engine.

Data processing engines

Data processing engines allow data engineers to transform data whether it is in batches or streams. These engines allow the parallel execution of transformation tasks. The most popular engine is **Apache Spark**. Apache Spark allows data engineers to write transformations in Python, Java, and Scala.

Apache Spark works with Python DataFrames, making it an ideal tool for Python programmers. Spark also has **Resilient Distributed Datasets** (**RDDs**). RDDs are an immutable and distributed collection of objects. You create them mainly by loading in an external data source. RDDs allow fast and distributed processing. The tasks in an RDD are run on different nodes within the cluster. Unlike DataFrames, they do not try to guess the schema in your data.

Other popular process engines include **Apache Storm**, which utilizes spouts to read data and bolts to perform transformations. By connecting them, you build a processing pipeline. **Apache Flink** and **Samza** are more modern stream and batch processing frameworks that allow you to process unbounded streams. An unbounded stream is data that comes in with no known end – a temperature sensor, for example, is an unbounded stream. It is constantly reporting temperatures. Flink and Samza are excellent choices if you are using Apache Kafka to stream data from a system. You will learn more about Apache Kafka later in this book.

Data pipelines

Combining a transactional database, a programming language, a processing engine, and a data warehouse results in a pipeline. For example, if you select all the records of widget sales from the database, run it through Spark to reduce the data to widgets and counts, then dump the result to the data warehouse, you have a pipeline. But this pipeline is not very useful if you have to execute manually every time you want it to run. Data pipelines need a scheduler to allow them to run at specified intervals. The simplest way to accomplish this is by using **crontab**. Schedule a cron job for your Python file and sit back and watch it run every X number of hours.

Managing all the pipelines in crontab becomes difficult fast. How do you keep track of pipelines' successes and failures? How do you know what ran and what didn't? How do you handle backpressure – if one task runs faster than the next, how do you hold data back, so it doesn't overwhelm the task? As your pipelines become more advanced, you will quickly outgrow crontab and will need a better framework.

Apache Airflow

The most popular framework for building data engineering pipelines in Python is **Apache Airflow**. Airflow is a workflow management platform built by Airbnb. Airflow is made up of a web server, a scheduler, a metastore, a queueing system, and executors. You can run Airflow as a single instance, or you can break it up into a cluster with many executor nodes – this is most likely how you would run it in production. Airflow uses **Directed Acyclic Graphs (DAGs)**.

A DAG is Python code that specifies tasks. A graph is a series of nodes connected by a relationship or dependency. In Airflow, they are directed because they flow in a direction with each task coming after its dependency. Using the preceding example pipeline, the first node would be to execute a SQL statement grabbing all the widget sales. This node would connect downstream to another node, which would aggregate the widgets and counts. Lastly, this node would connect to the final node, which loads the data into the warehouse. The pipeline DAG would look as in the following diagram:

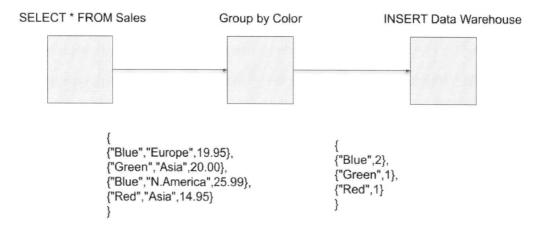

Figure 1.4 – A DAG showing the flow of data between nodes. The task follows the arrows (is directed) from left to right

This book will cover the basics of Apache Airflow but will primarily use Apache NiFi to demonstrate the principles of data engineering. The following is a screenshot of a DAG in Airflow:

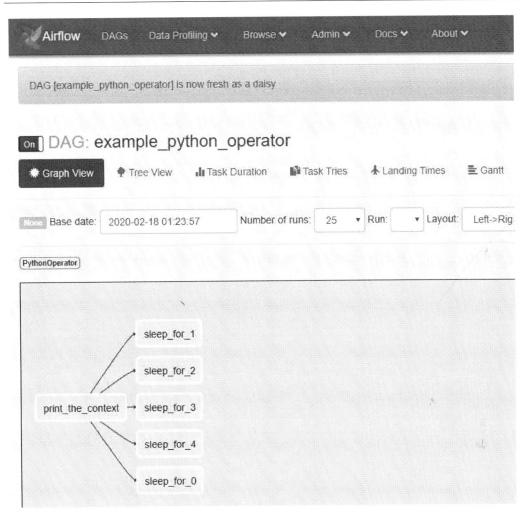

Figure 1.5 – The Airflow GUI showing the details of a DAG

The GUI is not as polished as NiFi, which we will discuss next.

Apache NiFi

Apache NiFi is another framework for building data engineering pipelines, and it too utilizes DAGs. Apache NiFi was built by the National Security Agency and is used at several federal agencies. Apache NiFi is easier to set up and is useful for new data engineers. The GUI is excellent and while you can use Jython, Clojure, Scala, or Groovy to write processors, you can accomplish a lot with a simple configuration of existing processors. The following screenshot shows the NiFi GUI and a sample DAG:

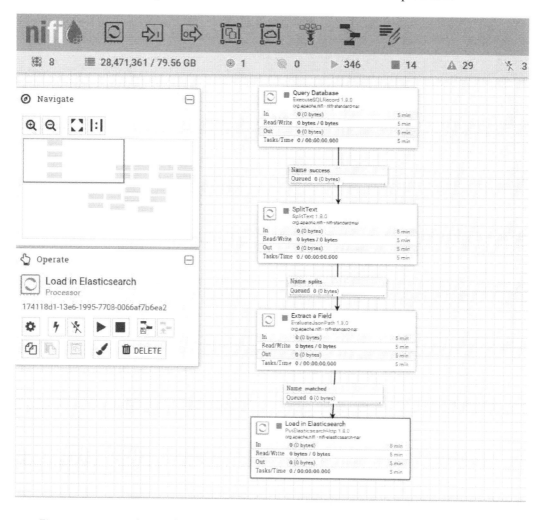

Figure 1.6 – A sample NiFi flow extracting data from a database and sending it to Elasticsearch

Apache NiFi also allows clustering and the remote execution of pipelines. It has a built-in scheduler and provides the backpressure and monitoring of pipelines. Furthermore, Apache NiFi has version control using the NiFi Registry and can be used to collect data on the edge using MiNiFi.

Another Python-based tool for data engineering pipelines is Luigi – developed by Spotify. Luigi also uses a graph structure and allows you to connect tasks. It has a GUI much like Airflow. Luigi will not be covered in this book but is an excellent option for Python-based data engineering.

Summary

In this chapter, you learned what data engineering is. Data engineering roles and responsibilities vary depending on the maturity of an organization's data infrastructure. But data engineering, at its simplest, is the creation of pipelines to move data from one source or format to another. This may or may not involve data transformations, processing engines, and the maintenance of infrastructure.

Data engineers use a variety of programming languages, but most commonly Python, Java, or Scala, as well as proprietary and open source transactional databases and data warehouses, both on-premises and in the cloud, or a mixture. Data engineers need to be knowledgeable in many areas – programming, operations, data modeling, databases, and operating systems. The breadth of the field is part of what makes it fun, exciting, and challenging. To those willing to accept the challenge, data engineering is a rewarding career.

In the next chapter, we will begin by setting up an environment to start building data pipelines.

2
Building Our Data Engineering Infrastructure

In the previous chapter, you learned what data engineers do and their roles and responsibilities. You were also introduced to some of the tools that they use, primarily the different types of databases, programming languages, and data pipeline creation and scheduling tools.

In this chapter, you will install and configure several tools that will help you throughout the rest of this book. You will learn how to install and configure two different databases – PostgreSQL and Elasticsearch – two tools to assist in building workflows – Airflow and Apache NiFi, and two administrative tools – pgAdmin for PostgreSQL and Kibana for Elasticsearch.

With these tools, you will be able to write data engineering pipelines to move data from one source to another and also be able to visualize the results. As you learn how to build pipelines, being able to see the data and how it has transformed will be useful to you in debugging any errors. As you progress, you may no longer need these tools, but other roles and users you will support may require them, so having a basic understanding of the tools will be useful.

The following topics will be covered in this chapter:

- Installing and configuring Apache NiFi
- Installing and configuring Apache Airflow
- Installing and configuring Elasticsearch
- Installing and configuring Kibana
- Installing and configuring PostgreSQL
- Installing pgAdmin 4

Installing and configuring Apache NiFi

Apache NiFi is the primary tool used in this book for building data engineering pipelines. NiFi allows you to build data pipelines using prebuilt processors that you can configure for your needs. You do not need to write any code to get NiFi pipelines working. It also provides a scheduler to set how frequently you would like your pipelines to run. In addition, it will handle backpressure – if one task works faster than another, you can slow down the task.

To install Apache NiFi, you will need to download it from `https://nifi.apache.org/download.html`:

1. By using `curl`, you can download NiFi using the following command line:

    ```
    curl https://mirrors.estointernet.in/apache/
    nifi/1.12.1/nifi-1.12.1-bin.tar.gz
    ```

2. Extract the NiFi files from the `.tar.gz` file using the following command:

    ```
    tar xvzf nifi.tar.gz
    ```

3. You will now have a folder named `nifi-1.12.1`. You can run NiFi by executing the following from inside the folder:

```
bin/nifi.sh start
```

4. If you already have Java installed and configured, when you run the status tool as shown in the following snippet, you will see a path set for JAVA_HOME:

```
sudo bin/nifi.sh status
```

5. If you do not see JAVA_HOME set, you may need to install Java using the following command:

```
sudo apt install openjdk-11-jre-headless
```

6. Then, you should edit `.bash_profile` to include the following line so that NiFi can find the JAVA_HOME variable:

```
export JAVA_HOME=/usr/lib/jvm/java11-openjdk-amd64
```

7. Lastly, reload `.bash_profile`:

```
source .bash_profile
```

8. When you run for the status on NiFi, you should now see a path for JAVA_HOME:

```
paulcrickard@pop-os:~$ sudo nifi*/bin/nifi.sh start

Java home: /usr/lib/jvm/java-1.11.0-openjdk-amd64
NiFi home: /home/paulcrickard/nifi-1.11.3

Bootstrap Config File: /home/paulcrickard/nifi-1.11.3/conf/bootstrap.conf
paulcrickard@pop-os:~$ 
```

Figure 2.1 – NiFi is running

9. When NiFi is ready, which may take a minute, open your web browser and go to `http://localhost:8080/nifi/`. You should be seeing the following screen:

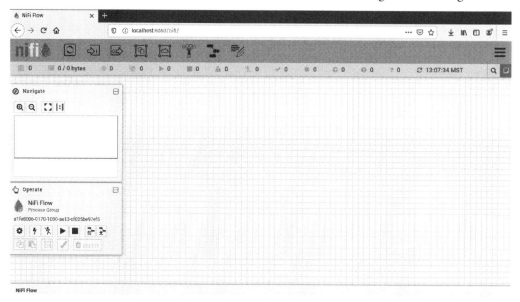

Figure 2.2 – The NiFi GUI

In later chapters, you will learn about many of the available configurations for NiFi, but for now, you will only change the port NiFi runs on. In `conf/nifi.properties`, change `nifi.web.http.port=8080` under the `web properties` heading to `9300`, as shown:

```
# web properties #
nifi.web.http.port=9300
```

If your firewall is on, you may need to open the port:

```
sudo ufw allow 9300/tcp
```

Now, you can relaunch NiFi and view the GUI at `http://localhost:9300/nifi/`.

A quick tour of NiFi

The NiFi GUI will be blank because you have not added any processors or processor groups. At the top of the screen are the component toolbar and the status bar. The component toolbar has the tools needed for building a data flow. The status bar, as the title suggests, gives an overview of the current status of your NiFi instance:

Figure 2.3 – NiFi component toolbar and status bar

The tool you will use the most is the **Processor** tool. The other tools, from left to right, are as follows:

- **Input Port**
- **Output Port**
- **Processor Group**
- **Remote Processor Group**
- **Funnel**
- **Template**
- **Label**

With these limited tools, you are able to build complex data flows.

A NiFi data flow is made up of processors, connections, and relationships. NiFi has over 100 processors all ready for you to use. By clicking the **Processor** tool and dragging it on to the canvas, you will be prompted to select the processor you would like to use, as shown in the following screenshot:

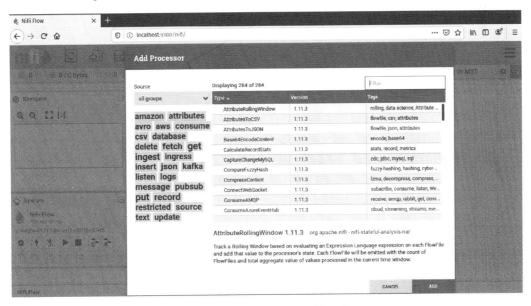

Figure 2.4 – Processors you can add to the canvas

Using the search bar, you can search for GenerateFlowFile. Select the processor and it will be added to the canvas. This processor will allow you to create FlowFiles with text. Drag the **Processor** tool to the canvas again. Using the search, select PutFile, then select the processor. This processor will save the FlowFile to disk as a file. You should now have a canvas as in the following screenshot:

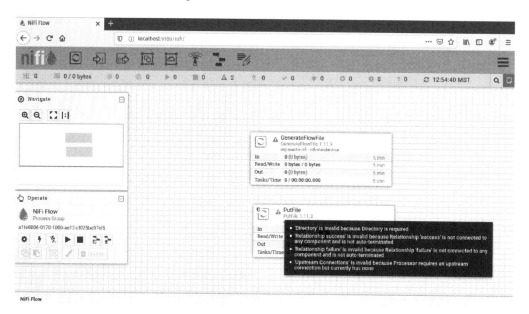

Figure 2.5 – Processors added to the canvas – with errors

When you add the processors, there will be a caution symbol in the left corner of the box. They have not been configured, so you will get warnings and errors. The preceding screenshot shows that the PutFile processor is missing the Directory parameter, there is no upstream connection, and the relationships for success and failure have not been handled.

To configure the processor, you can either double-click on the processor or right-click and select **Properties**. The following screenshot shows the properties for the processor:

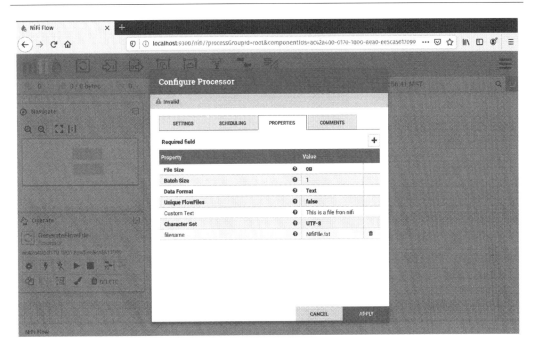

Figure 2.6 – Configuring the GenerateFlowFile processor

The following steps should be followed to configure a processor:

1. You must have a value set for any parameters that are bold. Each parameter has a question mark icon to help you.

2. You can also right-click on the processes and select the option to use.

3. For `GenerateFlowfile`, all the required parameters are already filled out.

4. In the preceding screenshot, I have added a value to the parameter of **Custom Text**. To add custom properties, you can click the plus sign at the upper-right of the window. You will be prompted for a name and value. I have added my property filename and set the value to **This is a file from nifi**.

5. Once configured, the yellow warning icon in the box will turn into a square (stop button).

Now that you have configured the first processor, you need to create a connection and specify a relationship – a relationship is usually on success or failure, but the relationship types change based on the processor.

To create a connection, hover over the processor box and a circle and arrow will appear:

1.   Drag the circle to the processor underneath it (`PutFile`).

     It will snap into place, then prompt you to specify which relationship you want
     to make this connection for. The only choice will be **Success** and it will already
     be checked.

2.   Select **OK**. Lastly, right-click on the `GenerateFlowFile` processor and select
     Run.

The red square icon will change to a green play button. You should now have a data flow
as in the following screenshot:

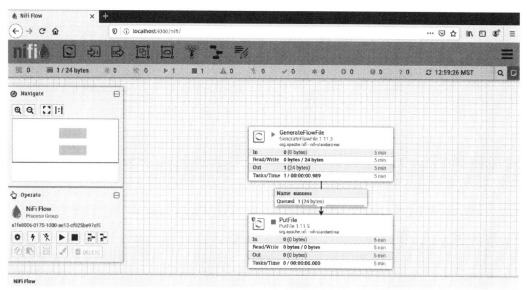

Figure 2.7 – Data flow half running

Between the two processor boxes, you can see the queue. It will show the number of
FlowFiles and the size. If you right-click on the queue, you will see a list of the FlowFiles
and you can get details about each one, see their contents, and download them. The
following screenshot shows the list view of FlowFiles in a queue:

Figure 2.8 – List of FlowFiles in the queue

You can view the details of the flow and the contents. The details view has two tables – details and attributes. From the **DETAILS** tab, you will see some of the NiFi metadata and have the ability to view or download the FlowFile. The **ATTRIBUTES** tab contains attributes assigned by NiFi and any attributes you may have created in the data pipeline. The **DETAILS** tab is shown in the following screenshot:

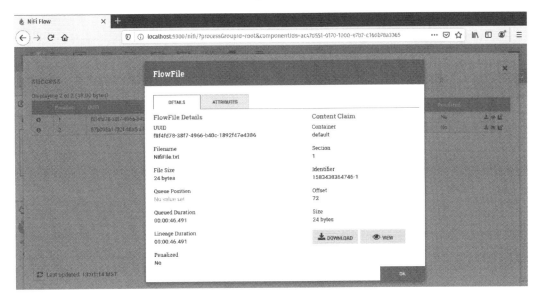

Figure 2.9 – Details of a FlowFile

From the **DETAILS** tab, if you select to view the FlowFile, you will see the contents in the window. This works best for text-based data, but there is also an option to view the FlowFile in hex format. There is also the option to display raw or formatted text. The following screenshot shows the raw FlowFile data, which is just a simple text string:

Figure 2.10 – Contents of a FlowFile

The `PutFile` process saved the FlowFile as a file on your machine at `opt/nifioutput`. The location can be specified in the configuration of the processor. If you do not have root privileges, you can change the location to your home directory. You now have a complete data flow. It is not a very good data flow, but it will generate a file every 10 seconds and write it to disk, hence overwriting the old file. The screenshot that follows shows the directory that was configured in the processor, with the text file that was configured for the output. It also shows the contents of the file, which will match the contents of the FlowFiles generated by the `GenerateFlowFile` processor:

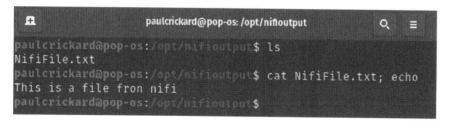

Figure 2.11 – Output of the data flow

NiFi will be the primary focus of this book and you will learn much more about building data flows starting with the next chapter. The other tool you will learn about is Apache Airflow, which we will install next.

PostgreSQL driver

Later in this chapter, you will install PostgreSQL. In order to connect to a PostgreSQL database using a NiFi ExecuteSQL processor, you need a connection pool, and that requires a **Java Database Connectivity (JDBC)** driver for the database you will be connecting to. This section shows you how to download that driver for use later. To download it, go to https://jdbc.postgresql.org/download.html and download the **PostgreSQL JDBC 4.2 driver, 42.2.10**.

Make a new folder in your NiFi installation directory named drivers. Move the postgresql-42.2.10.jar file into the folder. You will later reference this jar file in your NiFi processor.

Installing and configuring Apache Airflow

Apache Airflow performs the same role as Apache NiFi; however, it allows you to create your data flows using pure Python. If you are a strong Python developer, this is probably an ideal tool for you. It is currently one of the most popular open source data pipeline tools. What it lacks in a polished GUI – compared to NiFi – it more than makes up for in the power and freedom to create tasks.

Installing Apache Airflow can be accomplished using pip. But, before installing Apache Airflow, you can change the location of the Airflow install by exporting AIRFLOW_HOME. If you want Airflow to install to opt/airflow, export the AIRLFOW_HOME variable, as shown:

```
export AIRFLOW_HOME=/opt/airflow
```

The default location for Airflow is ~/airflow, and for this book, this is the location I will use. The next consideration before installing Airflow is to determine which sub-packages you want to install. If you do not specify any, Airflow installs only what it needs to run. If you know that you will work with PostgreSQL, then you should install the sub-package by running the following:

```
apache-airflow[postgres]
```

There is an option to install everything using `all`, or all the databases using `all_dbs`. This book will install `postgreSQL`, `slack`, and `celery`. The following table lists all the options:

Package	Command	Package	Command
All	all	kerberos	kerberos
all_dbs	all_dbs	kubernetes	kubernetes
async	async	ldap	ldap
aws	aws	mssql	mssql
azure	azure	mysql	mysql
celery	celery	oracle	oracle
cloudant	cloudant	password	password
crypto	crypto	postgres	postgres
devel	devel	presto	presto
devel_hadoop	devel_hadoop	qds	qds
druid	druid	rabbitmq	rabbitmq
gcp	gcp	redis	redis
github_enterprise	github_enterprise	samba	samba
google_auth	google_auth	slack	slack
hdfs	hdfs	ssh	ssh
hive	hive	vertica	vertica
jdbc	jdbc		

Figure 2.12 – Table of all package command options

To install Apache Airflow, with the options for `postgreSQL`, `slack`, and `celery`, use the following command:

```
pip install 'apache-airflow[postgres,slack,celery]'
```

To run Airflow, you need to initialize the database using the following:

```
airflow initdb
```

The default database for Airflow is SQLite. This is acceptable for testing and running on a single machine, but to run in production and in clusters, you will need to change the database to something else, such as PostgreSQL.

> **No Command Airflow**
>
> If the `airflow` command cannot be found, you may need to add it to your path:

```
export PATH=$PATH:/home/<username>/.local/bin
```

The Airflow web server runs on port 8080, the same port as Apache NiFi. You already changed the NiFi port to 9300 in the `nifi.properties` file, so you can start the Airflow web server using the following command:

```
airflow webserver
```

If you did not change the NiFi port, or have any other processes running on port 8080, you can specify the port for Airflow using the `-p` flag, as shown:

```
airflow webserver -p 8081
```

Next, start the Airflow scheduler so that you can run your data flows at set intervals. Run this command in a different terminal so that you do not kill the web server:

```
airflow scheduler
```

Airflow will run without the scheduler, but you will receive a warning when you launch the web server if the scheduler is not running. The warning is shown in the following screenshot:

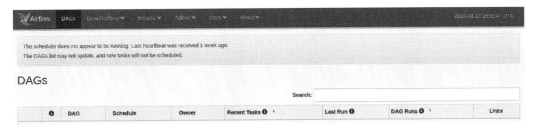

Figure 2.13 – Error message. The scheduler is not running

When the scheduler runs, you will see the warning about parallelism being set to 1 because of the use of SQLite. You can ignore this warning for now, but later, you will want to be able to run more than one task at a time. The warning is shown in the following screenshot:

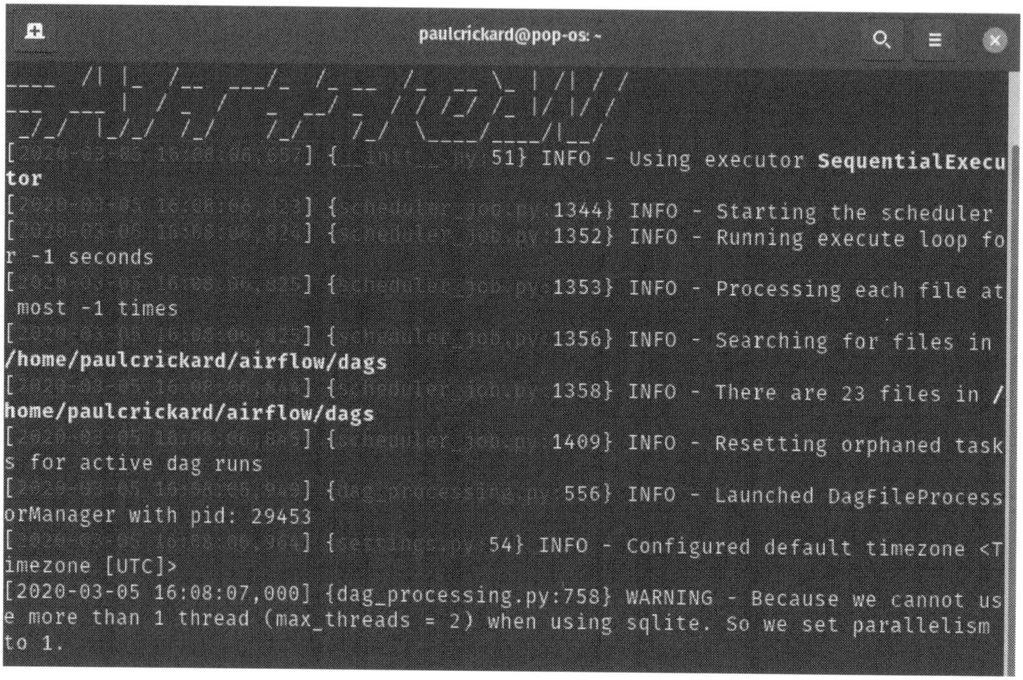

Figure 2.14 – Scheduler running but warning about SQLite

With the database initialized, the web server running, and the scheduler running, you can now browse to `http://localhost:8080` and see the Airflow GUI. Airflow installs several example data flows (**Directed Acyclic Graphs (DAGs)**) during install. You should see them on the main screen, as shown:

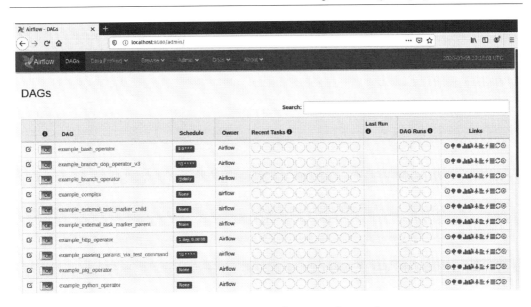

Figure 2.15 – Airflow installing several examples

Airflow DAGs are created using code, so this section will not dive deeply into the GUI, but you will explore it more as it is relevant in later chapters. Select the first DAG – example_bash_operator – and you will be taken to the tree view. Click the **Graph View** tab and you should see the DAG shown in the following screenshot:

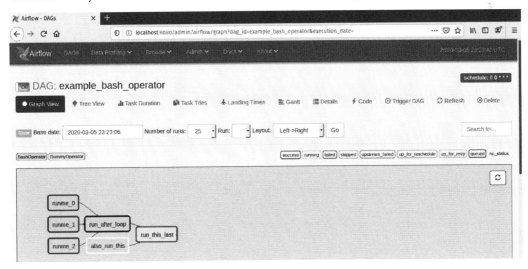

Figure 2.16 – Graph view of the execute_bash_operator DAG

The graph view clearly shows the dependencies in the DAG and the order in which tasks will run. To watch the DAG run, switch back to **Tree View**. To the left of the DAG name, switch the DAG to **On**. Select **Trigger DAG** and you will be prompted whether you want to run it now. Select **Yes** and the page will refresh. I have run the DAG several times, and you can see the status of those runs in the following screenshot:

Figure 2.17 – Multiple runs of the execute_bash_operator DAG

Notice that there are two completed, successful runs of the DAG and three runs that are still running, with four queued tasks in those runs waiting. The examples are great for learning how to use the Airflow GUI, but they will be cluttered later. While this does not necessarily create a problem, it will be easier to find the tasks you created without all the extras.

You can remove the examples by editing the `airflow.cfg` file. Using `vi` or an editor of your choice, find the following line and change `True` to `False`:

```
load_examples = True
```

The `airflow.cfg` file is shown in the following screenshot, with the cursor at the line you need to edit:

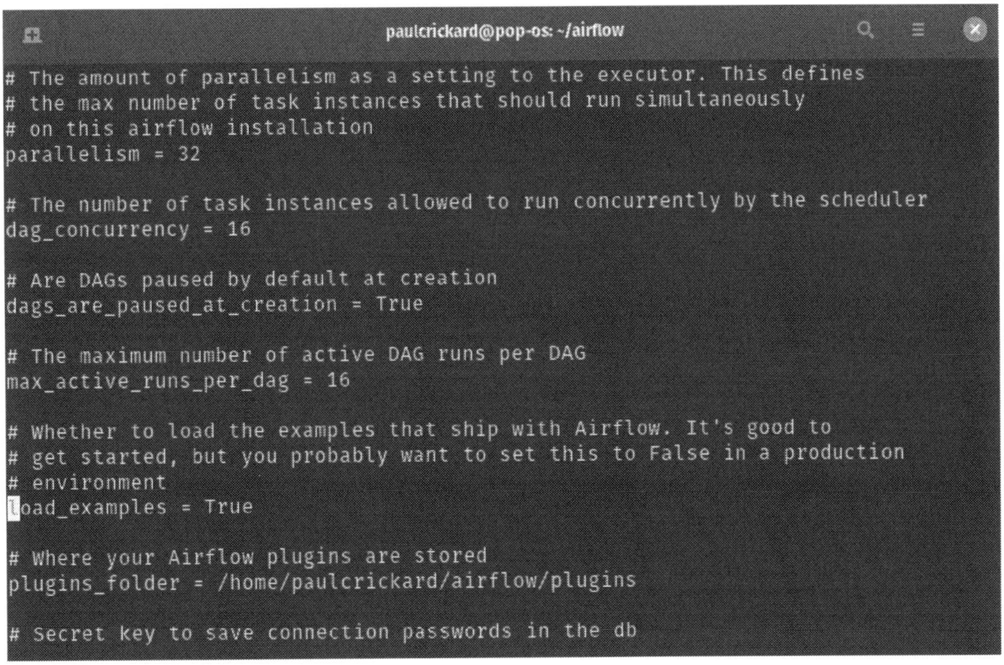

```
# The amount of parallelism as a setting to the executor. This defines
# the max number of task instances that should run simultaneously
# on this airflow installation
parallelism = 32

# The number of task instances allowed to run concurrently by the scheduler
dag_concurrency = 16

# Are DAGs paused by default at creation
dags_are_paused_at_creation = True

# The maximum number of active DAG runs per DAG
max_active_runs_per_dag = 16

# Whether to load the examples that ship with Airflow. It's good to
# get started, but you probably want to set this to False in a production
# environment
load_examples = True

# Where your Airflow plugins are stored
plugins_folder = /home/paulcrickard/airflow/plugins

# Secret key to save connection passwords in the db
```

Figure 2.18 – Setting load_examples = False

Once you have edited the `airflow.cfg` file, you must shut down the web server. Once the web server has stopped, the changes to the configuration need to be loaded into the database. Remember that you set up the database earlier as the first step after `pip`, installing Airflow using the following command:

```
airflow initdb
```

To make changes to the database, which is what you want to do after changing the `airflow.cfg` file, you need to reset it. You can do that using the following snippet:

```
airflow resetdb
```

This will load in the changes from `airflow.cfg` to the metadata database. Now, you can restart the web server. When you open the GUI at `http://localhost:8080`, it should be empty, as shown in the following screenshot:

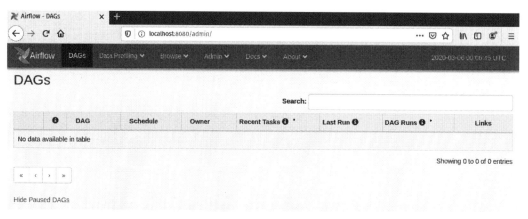

Figure 2.19 – Clean Airflow. Not a single DAG in sight

Airflow is clean and ready to load in the DAGs that you will create in the next chapter.

Installing and configuring Elasticsearch

Elasticsearch is a search engine. In this book, you will use it as a NoSQL database. You will move data both to and from Elasticsearch to other locations. To download Elasticsearch, take the following steps:

1. Use `curl` to download the files, as shown:

    ```
    curl https://artifacts.elastic.co/downloads/
    elasticsearch/elasticsearch-7.6.0-darwin-x86_64.tar.gz
    --output elasticsearch.tar.gz
    ```

2. Extract the files using the following command:

    ```
    tar xvzf elasticsearch.tar.gz
    ```

3. You can edit the `config/elasticsearch.yml` file to name your node and cluster. Later in this book, you will set up an Elasticsearch cluster with multiple nodes. For now, I have changed the following properties:

```
cluster.name: DataEngineeringWithPython
node.name: OnlyNode
```

4. Now, you can start Elasticsearch. To start Elasticsearch, run the following:

```
bin/elasticsearch
```

5. Once Elasticsearch has started, you can see the results at `http://localhost:9200`. You should see the following output:

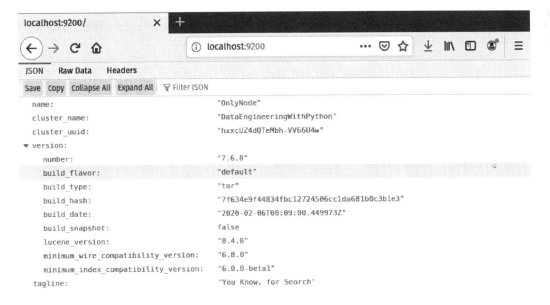

Figure 2.20 – Elasticsearch running

Now that you have a NoSQL database running, you will need a relational database as well.

Installing and configuring Kibana

Elasticsearch does not ship with a GUI, but rather an API. To add a GUI to Elasticsearch, you can use Kibana. By using Kibana, you can better manage and interact with Elasticsearch. Kibana will allow you to access the Elasticsearch API in a GUI, but more importantly, you can use it to build visualizations and dashboards of your data held in Elasticsearch. To install Kibana, take the following steps:

1. Using `wget`, add the key:

    ```
    wget -qO - https://artifacts.elastic.co/GPG-KEY-
        elasticsearch | sudo apt-key add -
    ```

2. Then, add the repository along with it:

    ```
    echo "deb https://artifacts.elastic.co/packages/7.x/
    apt stable main" | sudo tee -a /etc/apt/sources.list.d/
    elastic-7.x.list
    ```

3. Lastly, update `apt` and install Kibana:

    ```
    sudo apt-get update
    sudo apt-get install kibana
    ```

4. The configuration files for Kibana are located in `etc/kibana` and the application is in `/usr/share/kibana/bin`. To launch Kibana, run the following:

    ```
    bin/kibana
    ```

5. When Kibana is ready, browse to `http://localhost:5601`. Kibana will look for any instance of Elasticsearch running on `localhost` at port `9200`. This is where you installed Elasticsearch earlier, and also why you did not change the port in the configuration. When Kibana opens, you will be asked to choose between **Try our sample data** and **Explore on my own**, as shown:

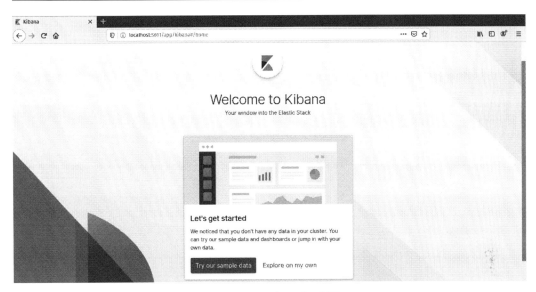

Figure 2.21 – First launch of Kibana

Explore on my own will take you to the main Kibana screen, but since you have not created an Elasticsearch index and have not loaded any data, the application will be blank.

To see the different tools available in Kibana, select **Try our sample data**, and choose the e-commerce data. The following screenshot shows the options for **Load our Sample Data**:

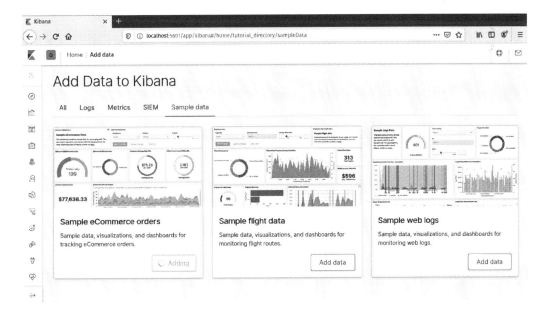

Figure 2.22 – Load sample data and visualizations

Once you have loaded the sample data, select the **Discover** icon. From the **Discover** section, you are able to look at records in the data. If there are dates, you will see a bar chart of counts on given time ranges. You can select a bar or change the date ranges from this tab. Selecting a record will show the data as a table or the JSON representation of the document. You can also run queries on the data from this tab and save them as objects to be used later in visualizations. The following screenshot shows the main **Discover** screen:

Figure 2.23 – The Discover tab

From the data available in the **Discover** tab or from a saved query, you can create visualizations. The visualizations include bar charts – horizontal and vertical, pie/donut charts, counts, markdown, heatmaps, and even a map widget to handle geospatial data. The e-commerce data contains geospatial data at the country level, but maps can also handle coordinates. The following screenshot shows a region map of the e-commerce data:

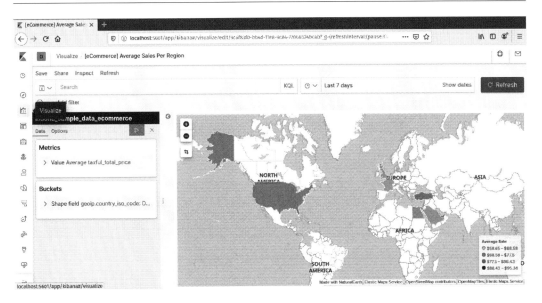

Figure 2.24 – A map visualization

When you have created several visualizations, from a single index or from multiple Elasticsearch indices, you can add them to a dashboard. Kibana allows you to load widgets using data from multiple indices. When you query or filter within the dashboard, as long as the field name exists in each of the indices, all of the widgets will update. The following screenshot shows a dashboard, made up of multiple visualizations of the e-commerce data:

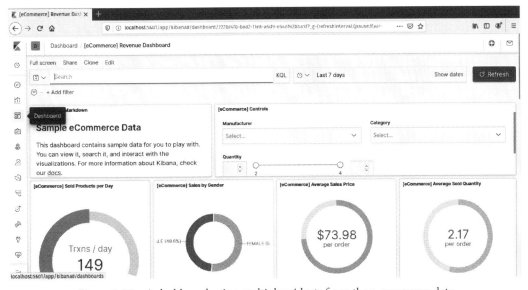

Figure 2.25 – A dashboard using multiple widgets from the e-commerce data

The **Developer Tools** tab comes in handy to quickly test Elasticsearch queries before you implement them in a data engineering pipeline. From this tab, you can create indices and data, execute queries to filter, search, or aggregate data. The results are displayed in the main window. The following screenshot shows a record being added to an index, then a search happening for a specific ID:

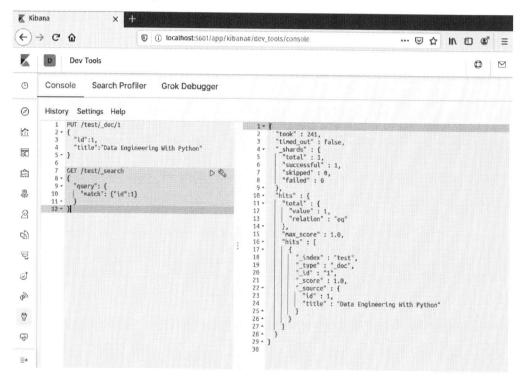

Figure 2.26 – A query on a single test record

Now that you have installed Elasticsearch and Kibana, the next two sections will walk you through installing PostgreSQL and pgAdmin 4. After that, you will have both a SQL and a NoSQL database to explore.

Installing and configuring PostgreSQL

PostgreSQL is an open source relational database. It compares to Oracle or Microsoft SQL Server. PostgreSQL also has a plugin – postGIS – which allows spatial capabilities in PostgreSQL. In this book, it will be the relational database of choice. PostgreSQL can be installed on Linux as a package:

1. For a Debian-based system, use `apt-get`, as shown:

    ```
    sudo apt-get install postgresql-11
    ```

2. Once the packages have finished installing, you can start the database with the following:

    ```
    sudo pg_ctlcluster 11 main start
    ```

3. The default user, `postgres`, does not have a password. To add one, connect to the default database:

    ```
    sudo -u postgres psql
    ```

4. Once connected, you can alter the user and assign a password:

    ```
    ALTER USER postgres PASSWORD ,postgres';
    ```

5. To create a database, you can enter the following command:

    ```
    sudo -u postgres createdb dataengineering
    ```

Using the command line is fast, but sometimes, a GUI makes life easier. PostgreSQL has an administration tool – pgAdmin 4.

Installing pgAdmin 4

pgAdmin 4 will make managing PostgreSQL much easier if you are new to relational databases. The web-based GUI will allow you to view your data and allow you to visually create tables. To install pgAdmin 4, take the following steps:

1. You need to add the repository to Ubuntu. The following commands should be added to the repository:

    ```
    wget --quiet -O - https://www.postgresql.org/media/keys/
    ACCC4CF8.asc | sudo apt-key add -
    sudo sh -c 'echo "deb http://apt.postgresql.org/pub/
    repos/apt/ `lsb_release -cs`-pgdg main" >> /etc/apt/
    ```

```
sources.list.d/pgdg.list'
sudo apt update
sudo apt install pgadmin4 pgadmin4-apache2 -y
```

2. You will be prompted to enter an email address for a username and then for a password. You should see the following screen:

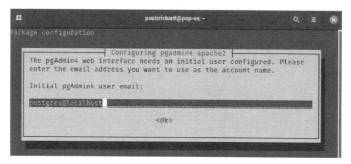

Figure 2.27 – Creating a user for pgAdmin 4

3. When the install has completed, you can browse to `http://localhost/pgadmin4` and you will be presented with the login screen, as shown in the following screenshot. Enter the credentials for the user you just created during the install:

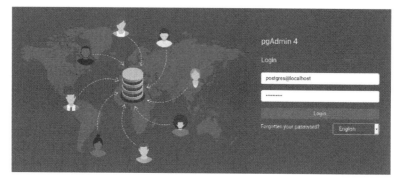

Figure 2.28 – Logging in to pgAdmin 4

Once you have logged in, you can manage your databases from the GUI. The next section will give you a brief tour of pgAdmin 4.

A tour of pgAdmin 4

After you log in to pgAdmin 4, you will see a dashboard with a server icon on the left side. There are currently no servers configured, so you will want to add the server you installed earlier in this chapter.

Click on the **Add new server** icon on the dashboard. You will see a pop-up window. Add the information for your PostgreSQL instance, as shown in the following screenshot:

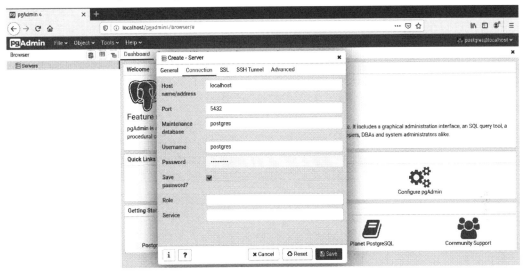

Figure 2.29 – Adding a new server

Once you add the server, you can expand the server icon and you should see the database you created earlier – `dataengineering`. Expand the `dataengineering` database, then `schemas`, then `public`. You will be able to right-click on **Tables** to add a table to the database, as shown in the following screenshot:

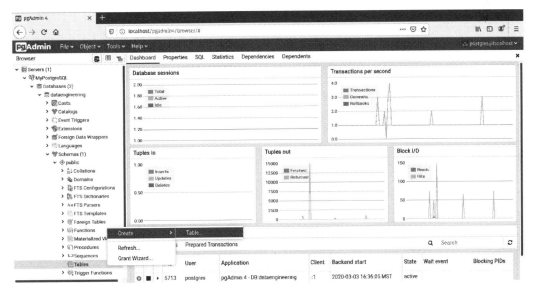

Figure 2.30 – Creating a table

To populate the table with data, name the table, then select the **Columns** tab. Create a table with some information about people. The table is shown in the following screenshot:

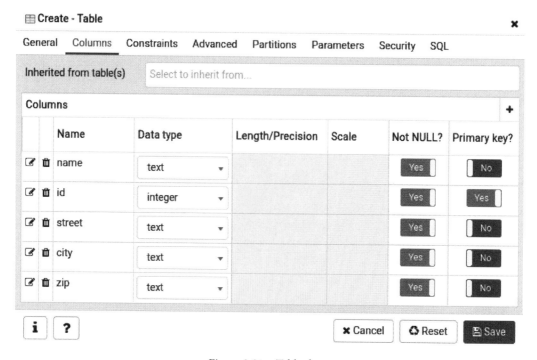

Figure 2.31 – Table data

In the next chapter, you will use Python to populate this table with data using the `faker` library.

Summary

In this chapter, you learned how to install and configure many of the tools used by data engineers. Having done so, you now have a working environment in which you can build data pipelines. In production, you would not run all these tools on a single machine, but for the next few chapters, this will help you learn and get started quickly. You now have two working databases – Elasticsearch and PostgreSQL – as well as two tools for building data pipelines – Apache NiFi and Apache Airflow.

In the next chapter, you will start to use Apache NiFi and Apache Airflow (Python) to connect to files, as well as Elasticsearch and PostgreSQL. You will build your first pipeline in NiFi and Airflow to move a CSV to a database.

3
Reading and Writing Files

In the previous chapter, we looked at how to install various tools, such as NiFi, Airflow, PostgreSQL, and Elasticsearch. In this chapter, you will be learning how to use these tools. One of the most basic tasks in data engineering is moving data from a text file to a database. In this chapter, you will read data from and write data to several different text-based formats, such as CSV and JSON.

In this chapter, we're going to cover the following main topics:

- Reading and writing files in Python
- Processing files in Airflow
- NiFi processors for handling files
- Reading and writing data to databases in Python
- Databases in Airflow
- Database processors in NiFi

Writing and reading files in Python

The title of this section may sound strange as you are probably used to seeing it written as reading and writing, but in this section, you will write data to files first, then read it. By writing it, you will understand the structure of the data and you will know what it is you are trying to read.

To write data, you will use a library named `faker`. `faker` allows you to easily create fake data for common fields. You can generate an address by simply calling `address()`, or a female name using `name_female()`. This will simplify the creation of fake data while at the same time making it more realistic.

To install `faker`, you can use `pip`:

```
pip3 install faker
```

With `faker` now installed, you are ready to start writing files. The next section will start with CSV files.

Writing and reading CSVs

The most common file type you will encounter is **Comma-Separated Values (CSV)**. A CSV is a file made up of fields separated by commas. Because commas are fairly common in text, you need to be able to handle them in CSV files. This can be accomplished by using escape characters, usually a pair of quotes around text strings that could contain a comma that is not used to signify a new field. These quotes are called escape characters. The Python standard library for handling CSVs simplifies the process of handling CSV data.

Writing CSVs using the Python CSV Library

To write a CSV with the CSV library, you need to use the following steps:

1. Open a file in writing mode. To open a file, you need to specify a filename and a mode. The mode for writing is w, but you can also open a file for reading with r, appending with a, or reading and writing with r+. Lastly, if you are handling files that are not text, you can add b, for binary mode, to any of the preceding modes to write in bytes; for example, wb will allow you to write in bytes:

    ```
    output = open('myCSV.CSV',mode='w')
    ```

2. Create `CSV_writer`. At a minimum, you must specify a file to write to, but you can also pass additional parameters, such as a dialect. A dialect can be a defined CSV type, such as Excel, or it can be options such as the delimiter to use or the level of quoting. The defaults are usually what you will need; for example, the delimiter defaults to a comma (it is a CSV writer after all) and quoting defaults to `QUOTE_MINIMAL`, which will only add quotes when there are special characters or the delimiter within a field. So, you can create the writer as shown:

```
mywriter=csv.writer(output)
```

3. Include a header. You might be able to remember what the fields are in your CSV, but it is best to include a header. Writing a header is the same as writing any other row: define the values, then you will use `writerow()`, as shown:

```
header=['name','age']
mywriter.writerow(header)
```

4. Write the data to a file. You can now write a data row by using `writerow(0)` and passing some data, as shown:

```
data=['Bob Smith',40]
mywriter.writerow(data)
output.close()
```

Now, if you look in the directory, you will have a CSV file named `myCSV.CSV` and the contents should look as in the following screenshot:

Figure 3.1 – The contents of mycsv.csv

Notice that when you used `cat` to view the file, the newlines were added. By default, `CSV_writer` uses a return and a newline (`'\r\n'`).

The preceding example was very basic. However, if you are trying to write a lot of data, you would most likely want to loop through some condition or iterate through existing data. In the following example, you will use Faker to generate 1,000 records:

```
from faker import Faker
import csv
output=open('data.CSV','w')
fake=Faker()
header=['name','age','street','city','state','zip','lng','lat']
mywriter=csv.writer(output)
mywriter.writerow(header)
for r in range(1000):
    mywriter.writerow([fake.name(),fake.random_int(min=18,
    max=80, step=1), fake.street_address(), fake.city(),fake.
    state(),fake.zipcode(),fake.longitude(),fake.latitude()])
    output.close()
```

You should now have a data.CSV file with 1,000 rows of names and ages.

Now that you have written a CSV, the next section will walk you through reading it using Python.

Reading CSVs

Reading a CSV is somewhat similar to writing one. The same steps are followed with slight modifications:

1. Open a file using with. Using with has some additional benefits, but for now, the one you will reap is not having to use close() on the file. If you do not specify a mode, open defaults to read (r). After open, you will need to specify what to refer to the file as; in this case, you will open the data.CSV file and refer to it as f:

    ```
    with open('data.csv') as f:
    ```

2. Create the reader. Instead of just using `reader()`, you will use `DictReader()`. By using the dictionary reader, you will be able to call fields in the data by name instead of position. For example, instead of calling the first item in a row as `row[0]`, you can now call it as `row['name']`. Just like the writer, the defaults are usually sufficient, and you will only need to specify a file to read. The following code opens `data.CSV` using the `f` variable name:

```
myreader=CSV.DictReader(f)
```

3. Grab the headers by reading a single line with `next()`:

```
headers=next(myreader)
```

4. Now, you can iterate through the rest of the rows using the following:

```
for row in myreader:
```

5. Lastly, you can print the names using the following:

```
print(row['name'])
```

You should only see the 1,000 names scroll by. Now you have a Python dictionary that you can manipulate any way you need. There is another way to handle CSV data in Python and that requires `pandas`.

Reading and writing CSVs using pandas DataFrames

`pandas` DataFrames are a powerful tool not only for reading and writing data but also for the querying and manipulation of data. It does require a larger overhead than the built-in CSV library, but there are times when it may be worth the trade-off. You may already have `pandas` installed, depending on your Python environment, but if you do not, you can install it with the following:

```
pip3 install pandas
```

You can think of a `pandas` DataFrame as an Excel sheet or a table. You will have rows, columns, and an index. To load CSV data into a DataFrame, the following steps must be followed:

1. Import `pandas` (usually as pd):

```
import pandas as pd
```

2. Then, read the file using `read_csv()`. The `read_csv()` method takes several optional parameters, and one required parameter – the file or file-like buffer. The two optional parameters that may be of interest are `header`, which by defaultattempts to infer the headers. If you set `header=0`, then you can use the `names` parameter with an array of column names. If you have a large file and you just want to look at a piece of it, you can use `nrows` to specify the number of rows to read, so `nrows=100` means it will only read 100 rows for the data. In the following snippet, you will load the entire file using the defaults:

```
df=pd.read_csv()('data.CSV')
```

3. Let's now look at the first 10 records by using the following:

```
df.head(10)
```

Because you used `Faker` to generate data, you will have the same schema as in the following screenshot, but will have different values:

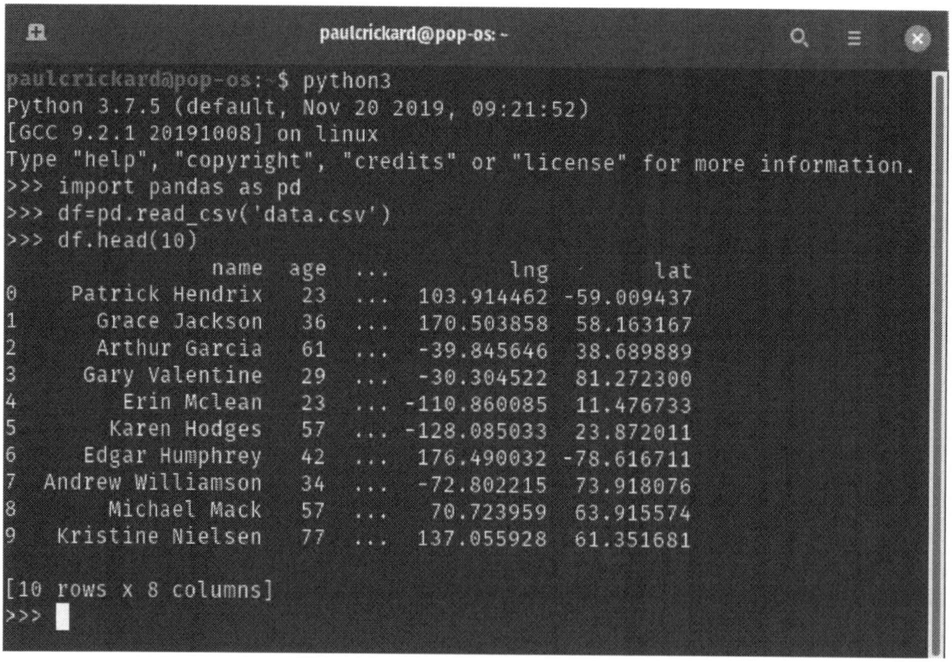

Figure 3.2 – Reading a CSV into a DataFrame and printing head()

You can create a DataFrame in Python with the following steps:

1. Create a dictionary of data. A dictionary is a data structure that stores data as a key:value pair. The value can be of any Python data type – for example, an array. Dictionaries have methods for finding `keys()`, `values()`, and `items()`. They also allow you to find the value of a key by using the key name in brackets – for example, `dictionary['key']` will return the value for that key:

    ```
    data={'Name':['Paul','Bob','Susan','Yolanda'],
     'Age':[23,45,18,21]}
    ```

2. Pass the data to the DataFrame:

    ```
    df=pd.DataFrame(data)
    ```

3. The columns are specified as the keys in the dictionary. Now that you have a DataFrame, you can write the contents to a CSV using `to_csv()` and passing a filename. In the example, we did not set an index, which means the row names will be a number from 0 to *n*, where *n* is the length of the DataFrame. When you export to CSV, these values will be written to the file, but the column name will be blank. So, in a case where you do not need the row names or index to be written to the file, pass the `index` parameter to `to_csv()`, as shown:

    ```
    df.to_csv('fromdf.CSV',index=False)
    ```

You will now have a CSV file with the contents of the DataFrame. How we can use the contents of this DataFrame for executing SQL queries will be covered in the next chapter. They will become an important tool in your toolbox and the rest of the book will lean on them heavily.

For now, let's move on to the next section, where you will learn about another common text format – **JSON**.

Writing JSON with Python

Another common data format you will probably deal with is **JavaScript Object Notation** (**JSON**). You will see JSON most often when making calls to **Application Programming Interfaces** (**APIs**); however, it can exist as a file as well. How you handle the data is very similar no matter whether you read it from a file or an API. Python, as you learned with CSV, has a standard library for handling JSON data, not surprisingly named `JSON-JSON`.

To write JSON using Python and the standard library, the following steps need to be observed:

1. Import the library and open the file you will write to. You also create the `Faker` object:

```
from faker import Faker
import json
output=open('data.JSON','w')
fake=Faker()
```

2. We will create 1,000 records, just as we did in the CSV example, so you will need to create a dictionary to hold the data. As mentioned earlier, the value of a key can be any Python data type – including an array of values. After creating the dictionary to hold the records, add a `'records'` key and initialize it with a blank array, as shown:

```
alldata={}
alldata['records']=[]
```

3. To write the records, you use `Faker` to create a dictionary, then append it to the array:

```
for x in range(1000):
       data={"name":fake.name(),"age":fake.random_int
             (min=18, max=80, step=1),
             "street":fake.street_address(),
             "city":fake.city(),"state":fake.state(),
             "zip":fake.zipcode(),
             "lng":float(fake.longitude()),
             "lat":float(fake.latitude())}
       alldata['records'].append(data)
```

4. Lastly, to write the JSON to a file, use the `JSON.dump()` method. Pass the data that you want to write and a file to write to:

```
json.dump(alldata,output)
```

You now have a data.JSON file that has an array with 1,000 records. You can read this file by taking the following steps:

1. Open the file using the following:

    ```
    with open("data.JSON","r") as f:
    ```

2. Use JSON.load() and pass the file reference to the method:

    ```
    data=json.load(f)
    ```

3. Inspect the json by looking at the first record using the following:

    ```
    data['records'][0]
    ```

    Or just use the name:

    ```
    data['records'][0]['name']
    ```

When you **load** and **dump** JSON, make sure you do not add an *s* at the end of the JSON terms. loads and dumps are different than load and dump. Both are valid methods of the JSON library. The difference is that loads and dumps are for strings – they do not serialize the JSON.

pandas DataFrames

Reading and writing JSON with DataFrames is similar to what we did with CSV. The only difference is that you change to_csv to to_json() and read_csv() to read_json().

If you have a clean, well-formatted JSON file, you can read it using the following code:

```
df=pd.read_json('data.JSON')
```

In the case of the data.JSON file, the records are nested in a records dictionary. So, loading the JSON is not as straightforward as the preceding code. You will need a few extra steps, which are as follows. To load JSON data from the file, do the following:

1. Use the pandas JSON library:

    ```
    import pandas.io.json as pd_JSON
    ```

2. Open the file and load it with the pandas version of JSON.loads():

    ```
    f=open('data.JSON','r')
    data=pd_JSON.loads(f.read())
    ```

3. To create the DataFrame, you need to normalize the JSON. Normalizing is how you can flatten the JSON to fit in a table. In this case, you want to grab the individual JSON records held in the `records` dictionary. Pass that path – `records` – to the `record_path` parameter of `json_normalize()`:

```
df=pd_JSON.json_normalize(data,record_path='records')
```

You will now have a DataFrame that contains all the records in the `data.JSON` file. You can now write them back to JSON, or CSV, using DataFrames.

When writing to JSON, you can pass the `orient` parameter, which determines the format of the JSON that is returned. The default is columns, which for the `data.JSON` file you created in the previous section would look like the following data:

```
>>> df.head(2).to_json()
'{"name":{"0":"Henry Lee","1":"Corey Combs DDS"},"
age":{"0":42,"1":43},"street":{"0":"57850 Zachary
Camp","1":"60066 Ruiz Plaza Apt. 752"},"city":{"0":"Lake
Jonathon","1":"East Kaitlin"},"state":{"0":"Rhode Island","
1":"Alabama"},"zip":{"0":"93363","1":"16297"},"lng":{"0":-
161.561209,"1":123.894456},"lat":
{"0":-72.086145,"1":-50.211986}}'
```

By changing the `orient` value to `records`, you get each row as a record in the JSON, as shown:

```
>>> df.head(2).to_JSON(orient='records')
'[{"name":"Henry Lee","age":42,"street":"57850, Zachary
Camp","city":"Lake Jonathon","state":"Rhode Island",
"zip":"93363","lng":-161.561209,"lat":72.086145},{"name":"
Corey Combs DDS","age":43,"street":"60066 Ruiz Plaza Apt.
752","city":"EastKaitlin","state":"Alabama",
"zip":"16297","lng":123.894456, "lat":-50.211986}]'
```

I find that working with JSON that is oriented around `records` makes processing it in tools such as Airflow much easier than JSON in other formats, such as split, index, columns, values, or table. Now that you know how to handle CSV and JSON files in Python, it is time to learn how to combine tasks into a data pipeline using Airflow and NiFi. In the next section, you will learn how to build pipelines in Apache Airflow.

Building data pipelines in Apache Airflow

Apache Airflow uses Python functions, as well as Bash or other operators, to create tasks that can be combined into a **Directed Acyclic Graph** (**DAG**) – meaning each task moves in one direction when completed. Airflow allows you to combine Python functions to create tasks. You can specify the order in which the tasks will run, and which tasks depend on others. This order and dependency are what make it a DAG. Then, you can schedule your DAG in Airflow to specify when, and how frequently, your DAG should run. Using the Airflow GUI, you can monitor and manage your DAG. By using what you learned in the preceding sections, you will now make a data pipeline in Airflow.

Building a CSV to a JSON data pipeline

Starting with a simple DAG will help you understand how Airflow works and will help you to add more functions to build a better data pipeline. The DAG you build will print out a message using Bash, then read the CSV and print a list of all the names. The following steps will walk you through building the data pipeline:

1. Open a new file using the Python IDE or any text editor. Import the required libraries, as shown:

```
import datetime as dt
from datetime import timedelta

from airflow import DAG
from airflow.operators.bash_operator import BashOperator
from airflow.operators.python_operator import PythonOperator

import pandas as pd
```

The first two imports bring in `datetime` and `timedelta`. These libraries are used for scheduling the DAG. The three Airflow imports bring in the required libraries for building the DAG and using the Bash and Python operators. These are the operators you will use to build tasks. Lastly, you import `pandas` so that you can easily convert between CSV and JSON.

2. Next, write a function to read a CSV file and print out the names. By combining the steps for reading CSV data and writing JSON data from the previous sections, you can create a function that reads in the data.CSV file and writes it out to JSON, as shown in the following code:

```
def CSVToJson():
    df=pd.read_CSV('/home/paulcrickard/data.CSV')
    for i,r in df.iterrows():
        print(r['name'])
    df.to_JSON('fromAirflow.JSON',orient='records')
```

This function opens the file in a DataFrame. Then, it iterates through the rows, printing only the names, and lastly, it writes the CSV to a JSON file.

3. Now, you need to implement the Airflow portion of the pipeline. Specify the arguments that will be passed to DAG(). In this book, you will use a minimal set of parameters. The arguments in this example assign an owner, a start date, the number of retries in the event of a failure, and how long to wait before retrying. They are shown in the following dictionary:

```
default_args = {
    'owner': 'paulcrickard',
    'start_date': dt.datetime(2020, 3, 18),
    'retries': 1,
    'retry_delay': dt.timedelta(minutes=5),
}
```

4. Next, pass the arguments dictionary to DAG(). Create the DAG ID, which is set to MyCSVDAG, the dictionary of arguments (the default_args variable in the preceding code), and the schedule interval (how often to run the data pipeline). The schedule interval can be set using timedelts, or you can use a crontab format with the following presets or crontab:

    a) @once

    b) @hourly – 0 * * * *

    c) @daily – 0 0 * * *

    d) @weekly – 0 0 * * 0

    e) @monthly – 0 0 1 * *

    f) @yearly – 0 0 1 1 *

crontab uses the format minute, hour, day of month, month, day of week. The value for `@yearly` is `0  0  1  1  *`, which means run yearly on January 1 (`1  1`), at 0:0 (midnight), on any day of the week (`*`).

> **Scheduling a DAG warning**
>
> The `start_date` variable of a DAG is `start_date + the schedule_interval`. This means if you schedule a DAG with a `start_date` value of today, and a `schedule_interval` value of daily, the DAG will not run until tomorrow.

The DAG is created with the following code:

```
with DAG('MyCSVDAG',
        default_args=default_args,
        schedule_interval=timedelta(minutes=5),
        # '0 * * * *',
        ) as dag:
```

5. You can now create your tasks using operators. Airflow has several prebuilt operators. You can view them all in the documentation at `https://airflow. apache.org/docs/stable/_api/airflow/operators/index.html`. In this book, you will mostly use the Bash, Python, and Postgres operators. The operators allow you to remove most of the boilerplate code that is required to perform common tasks. In the following snippet, you will create two tasks using the Bash and Python operators:

```
print_starting = BashOperator(task_id='starting',
                    bash_command='echo "I am reading the
                    CSV now....."')


CSVJson = PythonOperator(task_id='convertCSVtoJson',
                    python_callable=CSVToJson)
```

The preceding snippet creates a task using the `BashOperator` operator, which prints out a statement to let you know it is running. This task serves no purpose other than to allow you to see how to connect multiple tasks together. The next task, `CSVJson`, uses the `PythonOperator` operator to call the function you defined at the beginning of the file (`CSVToJson()`). The function reads the `data.CSV` file and prints the `name` field in every row.

6. With the tasks defined, you now need to make the connections between the tasks. You can do this using the `set_upstream()` and `set_downstream()` methods or with the bit shift operator. By using upstream and downstream, you can make the graph go from the Bash task to the Python task using either of two snippets; the following is the first snippet:

```
print_starting .set_downstream(CSVJson)
```

The following is the second snippet:

```
CSVJson.set_upstream(print_starting)
```

Using the bit shift operator, you can do the same; the following is the first option:

```
print_starting >>  CSVJson
```

The following is the second option:

```
CSVJson << print_starting
```

> **Note**
>
> Which method you choose is up to you; however, you should be consistent. In this book, you will see the bit shift operator setting the downstream.

7. To use Airflow and Scheduler in the GUI, you first need to make a directory for your DAGs. During the install and configuration of Apache Airflow, in the previous chapter, we removed the samples and so the DAG directory is missing. If you look at `airflow.cfg`, you will see the setting for `dags_folder`. It is in the format of `$AIRFLOW_HOME/dags`. On my machine, `$AIRFLOW_HOME` is home/paulcrickard/airflow. This is the directory in which you will make the `dags folder.e` configuration file showing where the folder should be.

8. Copy your DAG code to the folder, then run the following:

```
airflow webserver
airflow scheduler
```

9. Launch the GUI by opening your web browser and going to `http://localhost:8080`. You will see your DAG, as shown in the following screenshot:

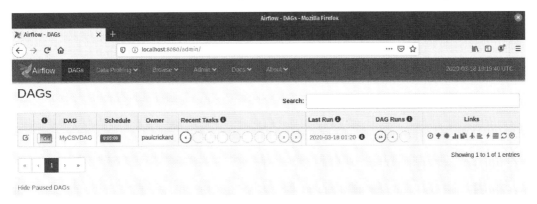

Figure 3.3 – The main screen of the Airflow GUI showing MyCSVDAG

10. Click on **DAGs** and select **Tree View**. Turn the DAG on, and then click **Go**. As the tasks start running, you will see the status of each run, as shown in the following screenshot:

Figure 3.4 – Multiple runs of the DAG and the status of each task

11. You will see that there have been successful runs – each task ran and did so successfully. But there is no output or results. To see the results, click on one of the completed squares, as shown in the following screenshot:

Figure 3.5 – Checking results by hovering over the completed task

12. You will see a popup with several options. Click the **View Log** button, as shown in the following screenshot:

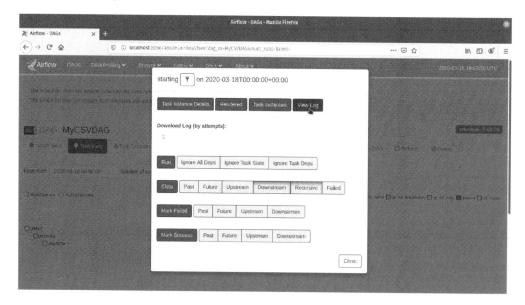

Figure 3.6 – Selecting View Log to see what happened in your task

13. You will be redirected to the log screen for the task. Looking at a successful run of the CSV task, you should see a log file similar to the one in the following screenshot:

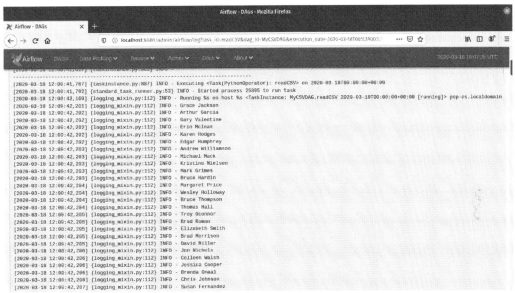

Figure 3.7 – Log of the Python task showing the names being printed

Congratulations! You have built a data pipeline with Python and ran it in Airflow. The result of your pipeline is a JSON file in your `dags` directory that was created from your `data.CSV` file. You can leave it running and it will continue to run at the specified `schedule_interval` time. Building more advanced pipelines will only require you to write more functions and connect them with the same process. But before you move on to more advanced techniques, you will need to learn how to use Apache NiFi to build data pipelines.

Handling files using NiFi processors

In the previous sections, you learned how to read and write CSV and JSON files using Python. Reading files is such a common task that tools such as NiFi have prebuilt processors to handle it. In this section, you will learn how to handle files using NiFi processors.

Working with CSV in NiFi

Working with files in NiFi requires many more steps than you had to use when doing the same tasks in Python. There are benefits to using more steps and using Nifi, including that someone who does not know code can look at your data pipeline and understand what it is you are doing. You may even find it easier to remember what it is you were trying to do when you come back to your pipeline in the future. Also, changes to the data pipeline do not require refactoring a lot of code; rather, you can reorder processors via drag and drop.

In this section, you will create a data pipeline that reads in the `data.CSV` file you created in Python. It will run a query for people over the age of 40, then write out that record to a file.

The result of this section is shown in the following screenshot:

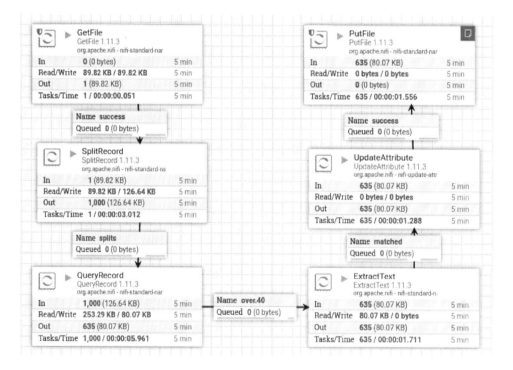

Figure 3.8 – The data pipeline you will build in this section

The following sections will walk you through building a data pipeline.

Reading a file with GetFile

The first step in your data pipeline is to read in the data.csv file. To do that, take the following steps:

1. Drag the **Processor** icon from the NiFi toolbar to the canvas. Search for **GetFile** and then select it.

2. To configure the GetFile processor, you must specify the input directory. In the Python examples earlier in this chapter, I wrote the data.CSV file to my home directory, which is home/paulcrickard, so this is what I will use for the input directory.

3. Next, you will need to specify a file filter. This field allows the NiFi expression language, so you could use **regular expressions** (**regex**) and specify any file ending with CSV – [^\.].*\.CSV – but for this example, you can just set the value to data.csv.

4. Lastly, the **Keep Source File** property should be set to **true**. If you leave it as **false**, NiFi will delete the file once it has processed it. The complete configuration is shown in the following screenshot:

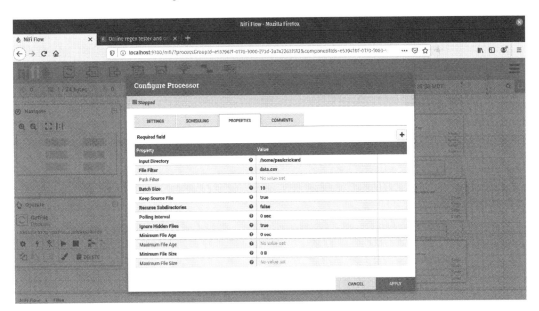

Figure 3.9 – GetFile processor configuration

Splitting records into distinct flowfiles

Now you can pass the success relationship from the GetFile processor to the SplitRecord processor:

1. The SplitRecord processor will allow you to separate each row into a separate flowfile. Drag and drop it on the canvas. You need to create a record reader and a record writer – NiFi already has several that you can configure. Click on the box next to **Record Reader** and select **Create new service**, as shown in the following screenshot:

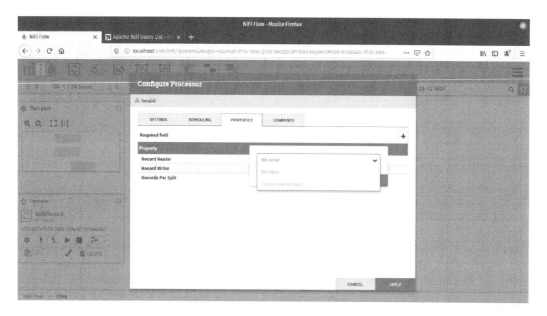

Figure 3.10 – A list of available readers

2. You will need to choose the type of reader. Select **CSVReader** from the dropdown. Select the dropdown for **Record Writer** and choose **CSVRecordSetWriter**:

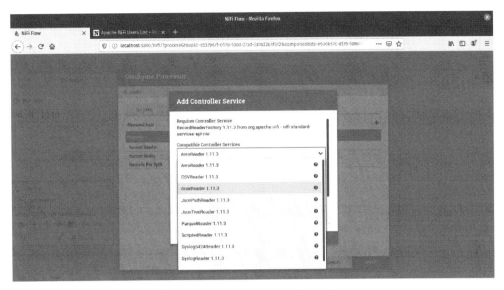

Figure 3.11 – A list of available readers

3. To configure **CSVReader** and **CSVRecordSetWriter**, click the arrow to the right of either one. This will open the **Files Configuration** window on the **CONTROLLER SERVICES** tab. You will see the screen shown in the following screenshot:

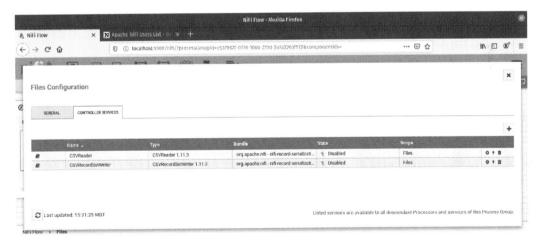

Figure 3.12 – Configuring the reader and writer

The three icons to the right are as follows:

- A gear for settings
- A lightning bolt for enabling and disabling the service (it is currently disabled)
- A trash can to delete it

Select the gear for **CSV Reader**. The default configuration will work, except for the **Treat First Line as Header** property, which should be set to **true**. Click the gear for **CSV RecordSetWriter** and you can see the available properties. The defaults are sufficient in this example. Now, click the lightning bolt to enable the services.

Filtering records with the QueryRecord processor

You now have a pipeline that will read a CSV and split the rows into individual flowfiles. Now you can process each row with the QueryRecord processor. This processor will allow you to execute a SQL command against the flowfile. The contents of the new flowfile will be the results of the SQL query. In this example, you will select all records where the age of the person is over 40:

1. Drag and drop the QueryRecord processor to the canvas. To query the flowfile, you need to specify a record reader and writer. You have already created one of each of these and they are available in the dropdown now. The **Include Zero Record FlowFiles** property should be set to **false**. This property will route records that do not meet the criteria to the same relationship (which you do not want).

2. Lastly, click the plus sign in the right-hand corner and specify a property name in the popup. The name of the property will become a relationship when you create a connection from this processor. Name the property over.40. Then, the value popup will appear. This is where you will enter the SQL query. The results of the query will become the contents of the flowfile. Since you want the records of people over 40 years of age, the query is as follows:

```
Select * from FlowFile where age > 40
```

The Select * query is what returns the entire flowfile. If you only wanted the name of the person and for the field to be full_name, you could run the following SQL:

```
Select name as full_name from FlowFile where age > 40
```

The point I am attempting to drive home here is that you can execute SQL and modify the flowfile to something other than the contents of the row – for example, running and aggregation and a group by.

Extracting data from a flowfile

The next processor will extract a value from the flowfile. That processer is ExtractText. The processor can be used on any flowfile containing text and uses regex to pull any data from the flowfile and assign it to an attribute.

To configure the processor, click the plus sign and name the property. You will extract the person name from the flowfile, so you can name the property name. The value will be regex and should be as follows:

```
\n([^,]*),
```

Without a full tutorial on regex, the preceding regex statement looks for a newline and a comma – \n and the comma at the end – and grabs the text inside. The parentheses say to take the text and return any characters that are not ^ or a comma. This regex returns the person's name. The flowfile contains a header of field names in CSV, a new line, followed by values in CSV. The name field is the first field on the second line – after the newline and before the first comma that specifies the end of the name field. This is why the regex looks for the text between the newline and the comma.

Modifying flowfile attributes

Now that you have pulled out the person name as an attribute, you can use the UpdateAttribute processor to change the value of existing attributes. By using this processor, you will modify the default filename attribute that NiFi has provided the flowfile all the way at the beginning in the GetFile processor. Every flowfile will have the filename data.CSV. If you try to write the flowfiles out to CSV, they will all have the same name and will either overwrite or fail.

Click the plus sign in the configuration for the UpdateAttribute processor and name the new property filename. The value will use the NiFi Expression Language. In the Expression Language, you can grab the value of an attribute using the format ${attribute name}. So, to use the name attribute, set the value to ${name}.

Saving a flowfile to disk

Using the PutFile processor, you can write the contents of a flowfile to disk. To configure the processor, you need to specify a directory in which to write the files. I will again use my home directory.

Next, you can specify a conflict resolution strategy. By default, it will be set to fail, but it allows you to overwrite an existing file. If you were running this data pipeline, aggregating data every hour and writing the results to files, maybe you would set the property to overwrite so that the file always holds the most current data. By default, the flowfile will write to a file on disk with the property filename as the filename.

Creating relationships between the processors

The last step is to make connections for specified relationships between the processors:

1. Grab the `GetFile` processor, drag the arrow to the `SplitRecord` processor, and check the relationship success in the popup.

2. From the `SplitRecord` processor, make a connection to the `QueryRecord` processor and select the relationship splits. This means that any record that was split will be sent to the next processor.

3. From `QueryRecord`, connect to the `ExtractText` processor. Notice the relationship you created is named `over.40`. If you added more SQL queries, you would get additional relationships. For this example, use the `over.40` relationship.

4. Connect `ExtractText` to the `UpdateAttribute` processor for the relationship matched.

5. Lastly, connect `UpdateAttribute` to the `PutFile` processor for the relationship success.

The data pipeline is now complete. You can click on each processor and select **Run** to start it – or click the run icon in the operate window to start them all at once.

When the pipeline is completed, you will have a directory with all the rows where the person was over 40. Of the 1,000 records, I have 635 CSVs named for each person. You will have different results based on what `Faker` used as the age value.

This section showed you how to read in a CSV file. You also learned how you can split the file into rows and then run queries against them, as well as how to modify attributes of a flowfile and use it in another processor. In the next section, you will build another data pipeline using JSON.

Working with JSON in NiFi

While having a different structure, working with JSON in NiFi is very similar to working with CSV. There are, however, a few processors for dealing exclusively with JSON. In this section, you will build a flow similar to the CSV example – read a file, split it into rows, and write each row to a file – but you will perform some more modifications of the data within the pipeline so that the rows you write to disk are different than what was in the original file. The following diagram shows the completed data pipeline:

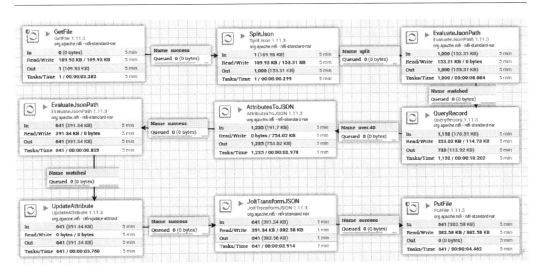

Figure 3.13 – The completed JSON data pipeline

To build the data pipeline, take the following steps:

1. Place the GetFile processor on to the canvas. To configure the processor, specify the **Input Directory** values as home/paulcrickard – and the **File Filter** value as data.JSON.

2. In the CSV example, you used the SplitRecord processor. Here, for JSON, you can use the SplitJson processor. You will need to configure the **JsonPath Expression** property. This property is looking for an array that contains JSON elements. The JSON file is in the following format:

```
{"records":[ { } ] }
```

Because each record is in an array, you can pass the following value to the **JsonPath Expression** property:

```
$.records
```

This will split records inside of the array, which is the result you want.

3. The records will now become individual flowfiles. You will pass the files to the
    `EvaluateJsonPath` processor. This processor allows you to extract values from
    the flowfile. You can either pass the results to the flowfile content or to an attribute.
    Set the value of the **Destination** property to `flowfile-attribute`. You can
    then select attributes to create using the plus sign. You will name the attribute, then
    specify the value. The value is the JSON path, and you use the format $.key. The
    configured processor is shown in the following screenshot:

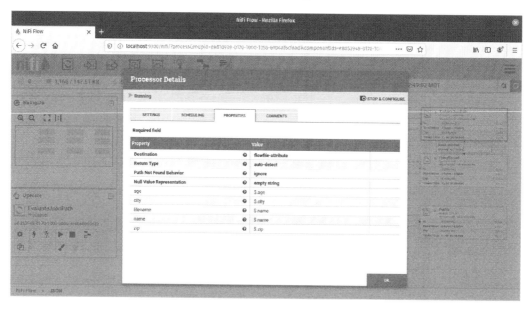

Figure 3.14 – Configuration for extracting values from the flowfile

These attributes will not be passed down the data pipeline with the flowfile.

4. Now, you can use the `QueryRecord` processor, just like you did with the CSV
    example. The difference with JSON is that you need to create a new record
    reader and recordset writer. Select the option to create a new service. Select
    JsonTreeReader and **JsonRecordsetWriter**. Click the arrow to go to the **Controller
    services** tab and click the lightning bolt to activate the services. The default
    configurations will work in this example. In the processor, add a new property using
    the plus sign. Name it `over.40` and set the value to the following:

```
Select * from FlowFile where age > 40
```

5. The next processor is the `AttributesToJSON` processor. This processor allows you to replace the flowfile content with the attributes you extracted in the `EvaluateJsonPath` processor shown in *step 3*. Set the **Destination** property to `flowfile-content`. This processor also allows you to specify a comma-separated list of attributes in the **Attributes List** property. This can come in handy if you only want certain attributes. In this example, you leave it blank and several attributes you do not extract will be added to the flowfile content. All of the metadata attributes that NiFi writes will now be a part of the flowfile. The flowfile will now look as in the following snippet:

```
### Run it at night ###
```

6. Using the `EvalueJsonPath` processor again, you will create an attribute named `uuid`. Now that the metadata from NiFi is in the flowfile, you have the unique ID of the flowfile. Make sure to set **Destination** to `flowfile-attribute`. You will extract it now so that you can pass it to the next processor – `UpdateAttribute`.

7. In the CSV example, you updated the filename using the `UpdateAttribute` processor. You will do the same here. Click on the plus sign and add an attribute named `filename`. Set the value to `${uuid}`.

8. One way to modify JSON using NiFi is through **Jolt transformations**. The **JSON Language for Transform** library allows you to modify JSON. A full tutorial on Jolt is beyond the scope of this book, but the processor allows you to select from several Jolt transformation DSLs. In this example, you will use a simple remove, which will delete a field. NiFi abbreviates the Jolt JSON because you have already specified what you are doing in the configuration. In the **Jolt Specification** property, enter the JSON, as shown in the following snippet:

```
{
    "zip": ""
}
```

The preceding snippet will remove the `zip` field from the flowfile.

9. Lastly, use the `PutFile` processor to write each row to disk. Configure the **Directory** and **Conflict Resolution Strategy** properties. By setting the **Conflict Resolution Strategy** property to **ignore**, the processor will not warn you if it has already processed a file with the same name.

Create the connections and relationships between the processors:

- Connect `GetFile` to `SplitJson` for relationship success.
- Connect `SplitJson` to `EvaluateJsonPath` for relationship splits.
- Connect `EvaluateJsonPath` to `QueryRecord` for relationship matched.
- Connect `QueryRecord` to `AttributesToJSON` for relationship `over.40`.
- Connect `AttributesToJSON` to `UpdateAttribute` for relationship success.
- Connect `UpdateAttributes` to `JoltTransformJSON` for relationship success.
- Connect `JoltTransformJSON` to `PutFile` for relationship success.

Run the data pipeline by starting each processor or clicking **Run** in the operate box. When complete, you will have a subset of 1,000 files – all people over 40 – on disk and named by their unique ID.

Summary

In this chapter, you learned how to process CSV and JSON files using Python. Using this new skill, you have created a data pipeline in Apache Airflow by creating a Python function to process a CSV and transform it into JSON. You should now have a basic understanding of the Airflow GUI and how to run DAGs. You also learned how to build data pipelines in Apache NiFi using processors. The process for building more advanced data pipelines is the same, and you will learn the skills needed to accomplish this throughout the rest of this book.

In the next chapter, you will learn how to use Python, Airflow, and NiFi to read and write data to databases. You will learn how to use PostgreSQL and Elasticsearch. Using both will expose you to standard relational databases that can be queried using SQL and NoSQL databases that allow you to store documents and use their own query languages.

4
Working with Databases

In the previous chapter, you learned how to read and write text files. Reading log files or other text files from a data lake and moving them into a database or data warehouse is a common task for data engineers. In this chapter, you will use the skills you gained working with text files and learn how to move that data into a database. This chapter will also teach you how to extract data from relational and NoSQL databases. By the end of this chapter, you will have the skills needed to work with databases using Python, NiFi, and Airflow. It is more than likely that most of your data pipelines will end with a database and very likely that they will start with one as well. With these skills, you will be able to build data pipelines that can extract and load, as well as start and finish, with both relational and NoSQL databases.

In this chapter, we're going to cover the following main topics:

- Inserting and extracting relational data in Python
- Inserting and extracting NoSQL database data in Python
- Building database pipelines in Airflow
- Building database pipelines in NiFi

Inserting and extracting relational data in Python

When you hear the word **database**, you probably picture a relational database – that is, a database made up of tables containing columns and rows with relationships between the tables; for example, a purchase order system that has inventory, purchases, and customer information. Relational databases have been around for over 40 years and come from the relational data model developed by E. F. Codd in the late 1970s. There are several vendors of relational databases – including IBM, Oracle, and Microsoft – but all of these databases use a similar dialect of **SQL**, which stands for **Structured Query Language**. In this book, you will work with a popular open source database – **PostgreSQL**. In the next section, you will learn how to create a database and tables.

Creating a PostgreSQL database and tables

In *Chapter 2, Building Our Data Engineering Infrastructure*, you created a database in PostgreSQL using pgAdmin 4. The database was named `dataengineering` and you created a table named `users` with columns for name, street, city, ZIP, and ID. The database is shown in the following screenshot:

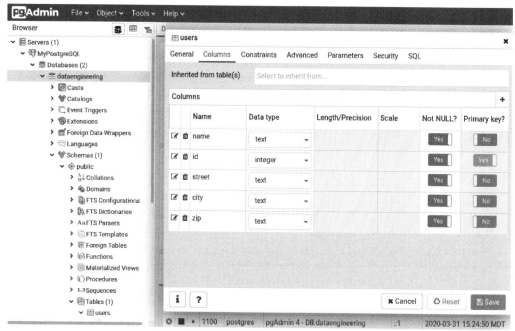

Figure 4.1 – The dataengineering database

If you have the database created, you can skip this section, but if you do not, this section will quickly walk you through creating one.

To create a database in PostgreSQL with pgAdmin 4, take the following steps:

1. Browse to `http://localhost/pgadmin4` and log in using the account you created during the installation of `pgAdmin` in *Chapter 2, Building Our Data Engineering Infrastructure.*

2. Expand the server icon in the **Browser** pane. Right-click on the **MyPostgreSQL** icon and select **Create | Database**.

3. Name the database `dataengineering`. You can leave the user as `postgres`.

4. Expand the `dataengineering` icon, then expand **Schemas**, then **public**, then **Tables**. Right-click on **Tables**, then click **Create | Table**.

5. Name the table `users`. Click the **Columns** tab and then, using the plus sign on the right, create columns to match the preceding screenshot of the database. The columns' names and types will be as follows:

   a) name: `text`

   b) id: `integer`

   c) street: `text`

   d) city: `text`

   e) zip: `text`

Now you have a database and a table created in PostgreSQL and can load data using Python. You will populate the table in the next section.

Inserting data into PostgreSQL

There are several libraries and ways to connect to a database in Python – `pyodbc`, `sqlalchemy`, `psycopg2`, and using an API and requests. In this book, we will use the `psycopg2` library to connect to PostgreSQL because it is built specifically to connect to PostgreSQL. As your skills progress, you may want to look into tools such as **SQLAlchemy**. SQLAlchemy is a toolkit and an object-relational mapper for Python. It allows you to perform queries in a more Pythonic way – without SQL – and to map Python classes to database tables.

Installing psycopg2

You can check whether you have `psycopg2` installed by running the following command:

```
python3 -c "import psycopg2; print(psycopg2.__version__)"
```

The preceding command runs `python3` with the command flag. The flag tells Python to run the commands as a Python program. The quoted text imports `psycopg2` and then prints the version. If you receive an error, it is not installed. You should see a version such as 2.8.4 followed by some text in parentheses. The library should have been installed during the installation of Apache Airflow because you used all the additional libraries in *Chapter 2, Building Our Data Engineering Infrastructure*.

If it is not installed, you can add it with the following command:

```
pip3 install psycopg2
```

Using `pip` requires that there are additional dependencies present for it to work. If you run into problems, you can also install a precompiled binary version using the following command:

```
pip3 install psycopg2-binary
```

One of these two methods will get the library installed and ready for us to start the next section.

Connecting to PostgreSQL with Python

To connect to your database using `psycopg2`, you will need to create a connection, create a cursor, execute a command, and get the results. You will take these same steps whether you are querying or inserting data. Let's walk through the steps as follows:

1. Import the library and reference it as `db`:

    ```
    import psycopg2 as db
    ```

2. Create a connection string that contains the host, database, username, and password:

    ```
    conn_string="dbname='dataengineering' host='localhost'
    user='postgres' password='postgres'"
    ```

3. Create the connection object by passing the connection string to the `connect()` method:

```
conn=db.connect(conn_string)
```

4. Next, create the cursor from the connection:

```
cur=conn.cursor()
```

You are now connected to the database. From here, you can issue any SQL commands. In the next section, you will learn how to insert data into PostgreSQL

Inserting data

Now that you have a connection open, you can insert data using SQL. To insert a single person, you need to format a SQL `insert` statement, as shown:

```
query = "insert into users (id,name,street,city,zip)
values({},'{}','{}','{}','{}')".format(1,'Big Bird','Sesame
Street','Fakeville','12345')
```

To see what this query will look like, you can use the `mogrify()` method.

> **What is mogrify?**
>
> According to the `psycopg2` docs, the `mogrify` method will return a query string after arguments binding. The string returned is exactly the one that would be sent to the database running the `execute()` method or similar. In short, it returns the formatted query. This is helpful as you can see what you are sending to the database, because your SQL query can often be a source of errors.

Pass your query to the `mogrify` method:

```
cur.mogrify(query)
```

The preceding code will create a proper SQL `insert` statement; however, as you progress, you will add multiple records in a single statement. To do so, you will create a tuple of tuples. To create the same SQL statement, you can use the following code:

```
query2 = "insert into users (id,name,street,city,zip)
values(%s,%s,%s,%s,%s)"
data=(1,'Big Bird','Sesame Street','Fakeville','12345')
```

Notice that in `query2`, you did not need to add quotes around strings that would be passed in as you did in `query` when you used { }. Using the preceding formatting, `psycopg2` will handle the mapping of types in the query string. To see what the query will look like when you execute it, you can use `mogrify` and pass the data along with the query:

```
cur.mogrify(query2,data)
```

The results of `mogrify` on `query` and `query2` should be identical. Now, you can execute the query to add it to the database:

```
cur.execute(query2,data)
```

If you go back to pgAdmin 4, right-click on the **users** table, then select **View/Edit Data | All Rows**, you can see that no data has been added to the table. Why is that? Did the code fail? It did not. When you execute any statement that modifies the database, such as an `insert` statement, you need to make it permanent by committing the transaction using the following code:

```
conn.commit()
```

Now, in pgAdmin 4, you should be able to see the record, as shown in the following screenshot:

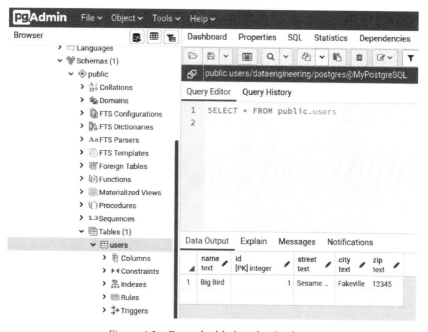

Figure 4.2 – Record added to the database

The record is now added to the database and visible in pgAdmin 4. Now that you have entered a single record, the next section will show you how to enter multiple records.

Inserting multiple records

To insert multiple records, you could loop through data and use the same code shown in the preceding section, but this would require a transaction per record in the database. A better way would be to use a single transaction and send all the data, letting `psycopg2` handle the bulk insert. You can accomplish this by using the `executemany` method. The following code will use `Faker` to create the records and then `executemany()` to insert them:

1. Import the needed libraries:

```
import psycopg2 as db
from faker import Faker
```

2. Create the `faker` object and an array to hold all the data. You will initialize a variable, `i`, to hold an ID:

```
fake=Faker()
data=[]
i=2
```

3. Now, you can look, iterate, and append a fake tuple to the array you created in the previous step. Increment `i` for the next record. Remember that in the previous section, you created a record for `Big Bird` with an ID of `1`. That is why you will start with 2 in this example. We cannot have the same primary key in the database table:

```
for r in range(1000):
    data.append((i,fake.name(),fake.street_address(),
                fake.city(),fake.zipcode()))
    i+=1
```

4. Convert the array into a tuple of tuples:

```
data_for_db=tuple(data)
```

5. Now, you are back to the `psycopg` code, which will be similar to the example from the previous section:

```
conn_string="dbname='dataengineering' host='localhost'
user='postgres' password='postgres'"
conn=db.connect(conn_string)
cur=conn.cursor()
query = "insert into users (id,name,street,city,zip)
values(%s,%s,%s,%s,%s)"
```

6. You can print out what the code will send to the database using a single record from the `data_for_db` variable:

```
print(cur.mogrify(query,data_for_db[1]))
```

7. Lastly, use `executemany()` instead of `execute()` to let the library handle the multiple inserts. Then, commit the transaction:

```
cur.executemany(query,data_for_db)
conn.commit()
```

Now, you can look at pgAdmin 4 and see the 1,000 records. You will have data similar to what is shown in the following screenshot:

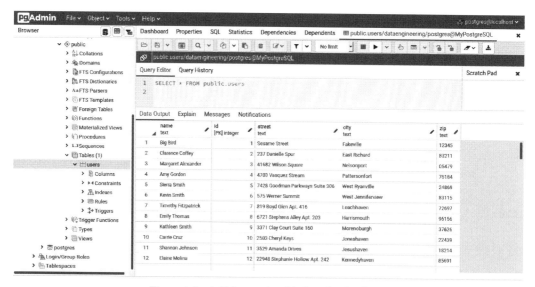

Figure 4.3 – 1,000 records added to the database

Your table should now have 1,001 records. Now that you can insert data into PostgreSQL, the next section will show you how to query it in Python.

Extracting data from PostgreSQL

Extracting data using `psycopgs` follows the exact same procedure as inserting, the only difference being that you will use a `select` statement instead of `insert`. The following steps show you how to extract data:

1. Import the library, then set up your connection and cursor:

```
import psycopg2 as db
conn_string="dbname='dataengineering' host='localhost'
user='postgres' password='postgres'"
conn=db.connect(conn_string)
cur=conn.cursor()
```

2. Now, you can execute a query. In this example, you will select all records from the `users` table:

```
query = "select * from users"
cur.execute(query)
```

3. Now, you have an iterable object with the results. You can iterate over the cursor, as shown:

```
for record in cur:
    print(record)
```

4. Alternatively, you could use one of the `fetch` methods:

```
cur.fetchall()
cur.fetchmany(howmany)   # where howmany equals the number
of records you want returned
cur.fetchone()
```

5. To grab a single record, you can assign it to a variable and look at it. Note that even when you select one record, the cursor returns an array:

```
data=cur.fetchone()
print(data[0])
```

6. Regardless of whether you are fetching one or many, you need to know where you are and how many records there are. You can get the row count of the query using the following code:

```
cur.rowcount
# 1001
```

7. You can get the current row number using rownumber. If you use fetchone() and then call rownumber again, it should increment with your new position:

```
cur.rownumber
```

The last thing to mention is that you can also query a table and write it out to a CSV file using the copy_to() method.

8. Create the connection and the cursor:

```
conn=db.connect(conn_string)
cur=conn.cursor()
```

9. Open a file to write the table to:

```
f=open('fromdb.csv','w')
```

10. Then, call copy_to and pass the file, the table name, and the separator (which will default to tabs if you do not include it). Close the file, and you will have all the rows as a CSV:

```
cur.copy_to(f,'users',sep=',')
f.close()
```

11. You can verify the results by opening the file and printing the contents:

```
f=open('fromdb.csv','r')
f.read()
```

Now that you know how to read and write to a database using the psycopg2 library, you can also read and write data using DataFrames, which you will learn about in the next section.

Extracting data with DataFrames

You can also query data using `pandas` DataFrames. To do so, you need to establish a connection using `psycopg2`, and then you can skip the cursor and go straight to the query. DataFrames give you a lot of power in filtering, analyzing, and transforming data. The following steps will walk you through using DataFrames:

1. Set up the connection:

```
import psycopg2 as db
import pandas as pd
conn_string="dbname='dataengineering' host='localhost'
user='postgres' password='postgres'"
conn=db.connect(conn_string)
```

2. Now, you can execute the query in a DataFrame using the `pandas read_sql()` method. The method takes a query and a connection:

```
df=pd.read_sql("select * from users", conn)
```

3. The result is a DataFrame, `df`, with the full table users. You now have full access to all the DataFrame tools for working with the data – for example, you can export it to JSON using the following code:

```
df.to_json(orient='records')
```

Now that you know how to work with data in a relational database, it is time to learn about NoSQL databases. The next section will show you how to use Python with Elasticsearch.

Inserting and extracting NoSQL database data in Python

Relational databases may be what you think of when you hear the term database, but there are several other types of databases, such as columnar, key-value, and time-series. In this section, you will learn how to work with Elasticsearch, which is a NoSQL database. NoSQL is a generic term referring to databases that do not store data in rows and columns. NoSQL databases often store their data as JSON documents and use a query language other than SQL. The next section will teach you how to load data into Elasticsearch.

Installing Elasticsearch

To install the `elasticsearch` library, you can use `pip3`, as shown:

```
pip3 install elasticsearch
```

Using `pip` will install the newest version, which, if you installed Elasticsearch according to the instructions in *Chapter 2, Building Our Data Engineering Infrastructure*, is what you will need. You can get the library for Elasticsearch versions 2, 5, 6, and 7. To verify the installation and check the version, you can use the following code:

```
import elasticsearch
elasticsearch.__version__
```

The preceding code should print something like the following:

```
(7.6.0)
```

If you have the right version for your Elasticsearch version, you are ready to start importing data.

Inserting data into Elasticsearch

Before you can query Elasticsearch, you will need to load some data into an index. In the previous section, you used a library, `psycopg2`, to access PostgreSQL. To access Elasticsearch, you will use the `elasticsearch` library. To load data, you need to create the connection, then you can issue commands to Elasticsearch. Follow the given steps to add a record to Elasticsearch:

1. Import the libraries. You can also create the `Faker` object to generate random data:

   ```
   from elasticsearch import Elasticsearch
   from faker import Faker
   fake=Faker()
   ```

2. Create a connection to Elasticsearch:

   ```
   es = Elasticsearch()
   ```

3. The preceding code assumes that your `Elasticsearch` instance is running on `localhost`. If it is not, you can specify the IP address, as shown:

   ```
   es=Elasticsearch({'127.0.0.1'})
   ```

Now, you can issue commands to your `Elasticsearch` instance. The `index` method will allow you to add data. The method takes an index name, the document type, and a body. The body is what is sent to Elasticsearch and is a JSON object. The following code creates a JSON object to add to the database, then uses `index` to send it to the `users` index (which will be created automatically during the index operation):

```
doc={"name": fake.name(),"street": fake.street_address(),
"city": fake.city(),"zip":fake.zipcode()}
res=es.index(index="users",doc_type="doc",body=doc)
print(res['result']) #created
```

The preceding code should print the word `created` to the console, meaning the document has been added. Elasticsearch returns an object with a result key that will let you know whether the operation failed or succeeded. `created`, in this case, means the index operation succeeded and created the document in the index. Just as with the PostgreSQL example earlier in this chapter, you could iterate and run the `index` command, or you can use a bulk operation to let the library handle all the inserts for you.

Inserting data using helpers

Using the `bulk` method, you can insert many documents at a time. The process is similar to inserting a single record, except that you will generate all the data, then insert it. The steps are as follows:

1. You need to import the `helpers` library to access the `bulk` method:

   ```
   from elasticsearch import helpers
   ```

2. The data needs to be an array of JSON objects. In the previous example, you created a JSON object with attributes. In this example, the object needs to have some additional information. You must specify the index and the type. Underscores in the names are used for Elasticsearch fields. The `_source` field is where you would put the JSON document you want to insert in the database. Outside the JSON is a `for` loop. This loop creates the 999 (you already added one and you index from 0 – to 998) documents:

   ```
   actions = [
     {
         "_index": "users",
         "_type": "doc",
         "_source": {
           "name": fake.name(),
   ```

```
        "street": fake.street_address(),
        "city": fake.city(),
        "zip":fake.zipcode()}
    }
    for x in range(998) # or for i,r in df.iterrows()
]
```

3. Now, you can call the `bulk` method and pass it the `elasticsearch` instance and the array of data. You can print the results to check that it worked:

```
res = helpers.bulk(es, actions)
print(res['result'])
```

You should now have 1,000 records in an Elasticsearch index named `users`. We can verify this in Kibana. To add the new index to Kibana, browse to your Kibana dashboard at `http://localhost:5601`. Selecting **Management** at the bottom left of the toolbar, you can then create an index pattern by clicking the blue **+ Create index pattern** button, as shown in the following screenshot:

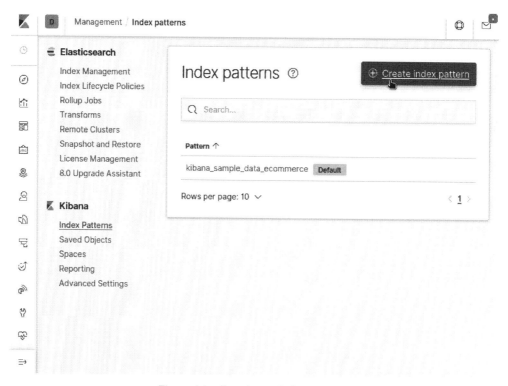

Figure 4.4 – Creating an index pattern

Add an Elasticsearch index pattern to Kibana. On the next screen, enter the name of the index – users. Kibana will start pattern matching to find the index. Select the users index from the dropdown and click the **Create Index Pattern** button. You will be presented with the mappings and details of the new index. On the Kibana toolbar, select **Discover**, which is the topmost icon. From the dropdown, select your new index (users), as shown in the following screenshot; you should see your documents:

Figure 4.5 – All of your documents in the Discover tab

Now that you can create a record individually or using the bulk method, the next section will teach you how you can query your data.

Querying Elasticsearch

Querying Elasticsearch follows the exact same steps as inserting data. The only difference is you use a different method – search – to send a different body object. Let's walk through a simple query on all the data:

1. Import the library and create your elasticsearch instance:

```
from elasticsearch import Elasticsearch
es = Elasticsearch()
```

2. Create the JSON object to send to Elasticsearch. The object is a query, using the match_all search:

```
doc={"query":{"match_all":{}}}
```

3. Pass the object to Elasticsearch using the `search` method. Pass the index and the return size. In this case, you will only return 10 records. The maximum return size is 10,000 documents:

```
res=es.search(index="users",body=doc,size=10)
```

4. Lastly, you can print the documents:

```
print(res['hits']['hits'])
```

Or you can iterate through grabbing `_source` only:

```
for doc in res['hits']['hits']:
    print(doc['_source'])
```

You can load the results of the query into a `pandas` DataFrame – it is JSON, and you learned how to read JSON in *Chapter 3*, *Reading and Writing Files*. To load the results into a DataFrame, import `json_normalize` from the `pandas json` library, and use it (`json_normalize`) on the JSON results, as shown in the following code:

```
from pandas.io.json import json_normalize
df=json_normalize(res['hits']['hits'])
```

Now you will have the results of the search in a DataFrame. In this example, you just grabbed all the records, but there are other queries available besides `match_all`.

Using the `match_all` query, I know I have a document with the name `Ronald Goodman`. You can query on a field using the `match` query:

```
doc={"query":{"match":{"name":"Ronald Goodman"}}}
res=es.search(index="users",body=doc,size=10)
print(res['hits']['hits'][0]['_source'])
```

You can also use a Lucene syntax for queries. In Lucene, you can specify `field:value`. When performing this kind of search, you do not need a document to send. You can pass the q parameter to the `search` method:

```
res=es.search(index="users",q="name:Ronald Goodman",size=10)
print(res['hits']['hits'][0]['_source'])
```

Using the `City` field, you can search for `Jamesberg`. It will return two records: one for `Jamesberg` and one for `Lake Jamesberg`. Elasticsearch will tokenize strings with spaces in them, splitting them into multiple strings to search:

```
# Get City Jamesberg - Returns Jamesberg and Lake Jamesberg
doc={"query":{"match":{"city":"Jamesberg"}}}
res=es.search(index="users",body=doc,size=10)
print(res['hits']['hits'])
```

The results are the two records in the following code block:

```
[{'_index': 'users', '_type': 'doc', '_id': 'qDYoOHEBxMEH3Xr-
PgMT', '_score': 6.929674, '_source': {'name': 'Tricia
Mcmillan', 'street': '8077 Nancy #Mills Apt. 810', 'city':
'Jamesberg', 'zip': '63792'}}, {'_index': 'users', '_type':
'doc', '_id': 'pTYoOHEBxMEH3Xr-PgMT', '_score': 5.261652, '_
source': {'name': 'Ryan Lowe', 'street': '740 Smith Pine Suite
065', 'city': 'Lake Jamesberg', 'zip': '38837'}}]
```

You can use Boolean queries to specify multiple search criteria. For example, you can use `must`, `must not`, and `should` before your queries. Using a Boolean query, you can filter out `Lake Jamesberg`. Using a `must` match on `Jamesberg` as the city (which will return two records), and adding a filter on the ZIP, you can make sure only `Jamesberg` with the ZIP `63792` is returned. You could also use a `must not` query on the `Lake Jameson` ZIP:

```
# Get Jamesberg and filter on zip so Lake Jamesberg is removed
doc={"query":{"bool":{"must":{"match":{"city":"Jamesberg"}},
"filter":{"term":{"zip":"63792"}}}}}
res=es.search(index="users",body=doc,size=10)
print(res['hits']['hits'])
```

Now, you only get the single record that you wanted:

```
[{'_index': 'users', '_type': 'doc', '_id': 'qDYoOHEBxMEH3Xr-
PgMT', '_score': 6.929674, '_source': {'name': 'Tricia
Mcmillan', 'street': '8077 Nancy #Mills Apt. 810', 'city':
'Jamesberg', 'zip': '63792'}}]
```

Your queries only returned a few documents, but in production, you will probably have large queries with tens of thousands of documents being returned. The next section will show you how to handle all that data.

Using scroll to handle larger results

In the first example, you used a size of 10 for your search. You could have grabbed all 1,000 records, but what do you do when you have more than 10,000 and you need all of them? Elasticsearch has a scroll method that will allow you to iterate over the results until you get them all. To scroll through the data, follow the given steps:

1. Import the library and create your `Elasticsearch` instance:

```
from elasticsearch import Elasticsearch
es = Elasticsearch()
```

2. Search your data. Since you do not have over 10,000 records, you will set the size to `500`. This means you will be missing 500 records from your initial search. You will pass a new parameter to the search method – `scroll`. This parameter specifies how long you want to make the results available for. I am using 20 milliseconds. Adjust this number to make sure you have enough time to get the data – it will depend on the document size and network speed:

```
res = es.search(
    index = 'users',
    doc_type = 'doc',
    scroll = '20m',
    size = 500,
    body = {"query":{"match_all":{}}}
)
```

3. The results will include `_scroll_id`, which you will need to pass to the `scroll` method later. Save the scroll ID and the size of the result set:

```
sid = res['_scroll_id']
size = res['hits']['total']['value']
```

4. To start scrolling, use a `while` loop to get records until the size is 0, meaning there is no more data. Inside the loop, you will call the `scroll` method and pass `_scroll_id` and how long to scroll. This will grab more of the results from the original query:

```
while (size > 0):
    res = es.scroll(scroll_id = sid, scroll = '20m')
```

5. Next, get the new scroll ID and the size so that you can loop through again if the data still exists:

```
sid = res['_scroll_id']
size = len(res['hits']['hits'])
```

6. Lastly, you can do something with the results of the scrolls. In the following code, you will print the source for every record:

```
for doc in res['hits']['hits']:
    print(doc['_source'])
```

Now you know how to create documents in Elasticsearch and how to query them, even when there is more than the maximum return value of 10,000. You can do the same using relational databases. It is now time to start putting these skills to use in building data pipelines. The next two sections will teach you how to use databases in your data pipelines using Apache Airflow and NiFi.

Building data pipelines in Apache Airflow

In the previous chapter, you built your first Airflow data pipeline using a Bash and Python operator. This time, you will combine two Python operators to extract data from PostgreSQL, save it as a CSV file, then read it in and write it to an Elasticsearch index. The complete pipeline is shown in the following screenshot:

Figure 4.6 – Airflow DAG

The preceding **Directed Acyclic Graph** (**DAG**) looks very simple; it is only two tasks, and you could combine the tasks into a single function. This is not a good idea. In *Section 2, Deploying Pipelines into Production*, you will learn about modifying your data pipelines for production. A key tenant of production pipelines is that each task should be atomic; that is, each task should be able to stand on its own. If you had a single function that read a database and inserted the results, when it fails, you have to track down whether the query failed or the insert failed. As your tasks get more complicated, it will take much more work to debug. The next section will walk you through building the data pipeline.

Setting up the Airflow boilerplate

Every DAG is going to have some standard, boilerplate code to make it run in Airflow. You will always import the needed libraries, and then any other libraries you need for your tasks. In the following code block, you import the operator, DAG, and the time libraries for Airflow. For your tasks, you import the pandas, psycopg2, and elasticsearch libraries:

```
import datetime as dt
from datetime import timedelta

from airflow import DAG
from airflow.operators.bash_operator import BashOperator
from airflow.operators.python_operator import PythonOperator

import pandas as pd
import psycopg2 as db
from elasticsearch import Elasticsearch
```

Next, you will specify the arguments for your DAG. Remember that the start time should be a day behind if you schedule the task to run daily:

```
default_args = {
    'owner': 'paulcrickard',
    'start_date': dt.datetime(2020, 4, 2),
    'retries': 1,
    'retry_delay': dt.timedelta(minutes=5),
}
```

Now, you can pass the arguments to the DAG, name it, and set the run interval. You will define your operators here as well. In this example, you will create two Python operators – one to get data from PostgreSQL and one to insert data in to Elasticsearch. The `getData` task will be upstream and the `insertData` task downstream, so you will use the `>>` bit shift operator to specify this:

```
with DAG('MyDBdag',
         default_args=default_args,
         schedule_interval=timedelta(minutes=5),
                        # '0 * * * *',
         ) as dag:

    getData = PythonOperator(task_id='QueryPostgreSQL',
            python_callable=queryPostgresql)

    insertData = PythonOperator
    (task_id='InsertDataElasticsearch',
            python_callable=insertElasticsearch)

getData >> insertData
```

Lastly, you will define the tasks. In the preceding operators, you named them `queryPostgresql` and `insertElasticsearch`. The code in these tasks should look very familiar; it is almost identical to the code from the previous sections in this chapter.

To query PostgreSQL, you create the connection, execute the `sql` query using the pandas `read_sql()` method, and then use the pandas `to_csv()` method to write the data to disk:

```
def queryPostgresql():
    conn_string="dbname='dataengineering' host='localhost'
    user='postgres' password='postgres'"
    conn=db.connect(conn_string)
    df=pd.read_sql("select name,city from users",conn)
    df.to_csv('postgresqldata.csv')
    print("-------Data Saved------")
```

To insert the data into Elasticsearch, you create the Elasticsearch object connecting to `localhost`. Then, read the CSV from the previous task into a DataFrame, iterate through the DataFrame, converting each row into JSON, and insert the data using the `index` method:

```
def insertElasticsearch():
    es = Elasticsearch()
    df=pd.read_csv('postgresqldata.csv')
    for i,r in df.iterrows():
        doc=r.to_json()
        res=es.index(index="frompostgresql",
                  doc_type="doc",body=doc)
        print(res)
```

Now you have a complete data pipeline in Airflow. In the next section, you will run it and view the results.

Running the DAG

To run the DAG, you need to copy your code to your $AIRFLOW_HOME/dags folder. After moving the file, you can run the following commands:

```
airflow webserver
airflow scheduler
```

When these commands complete, browse to http://localhost:8080 to see the Airflow GUI. Select **MyDBdag**, and then select **Tree View**. You can schedule five runs of the DAG and click **Go**. As it runs, you should see the results underneath, as shown in the following screenshot:

Figure 4.7 – Task showing successful runs and queued runs

To verify that the data pipeline was successful, you can view the data in Elasticsearch using Kibana. To see the results, browse to Kibana at `http://localhost:5601`. You will need to create a new index in Kibana. You performed this task in the *Inserting data using helpers* section of this chapter. But to recap, you will select **Management** in Kibana from the bottom of the left-hand toolbar in Kibana, then create the index pattern by clicking the **Create index pattern** button. Start typing the name of the index and Kibana will find it, then click **Create**. Then, you can go to the **Discover** tab on the toolbar and view the data. You should see records as shown in the following screenshot:

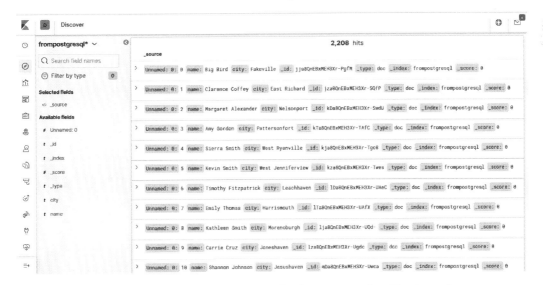

Figure 4.8 – Airflow data pipeline results showing records in Elasticsearch

You will see that there are documents containing only names and cities, as specified in your data pipeline task. One thing to note is that we now have over 2,000 records. There were only 1,000 records in the PostgreSQL database, so what happened? The data pipeline ran multiple times, and each time, it inserted the records from PostgreSQL. A second tenant of data pipelines is that they should be idempotent. That means that no matter how many times you run it, the results are the same. In this case, they are not. You will learn how to fix this in *Section 2*, *Deploying Pipelines into Production*, in *Chapter 7*, *Features of a Production Pipeline*. For now, the next section of this chapter will teach you how to build the same data pipeline in Apache NiFi.

Handling databases with NiFi processors

In the previous sections, you learned how to read and write CSV and JSON files using Python. Reading files is such a common task that tools such as NiFi have prebuilt processors to handle it. In this section, you will build the same data pipeline as in the previous section. In NiFi, the data pipeline will look as shown in the following screenshot:

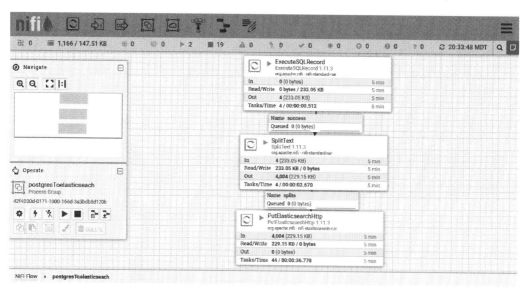

Figure 4.9 – A NiFi data pipeline to move data from PostgreSQL to Elasticsearch

The data pipeline contains one more task than the Airflow version, but otherwise, it should look straightforward. The following sections will walk you through building the data pipeline.

Extracting data from PostgreSQL

The processor most used for handling relational databases in NiFi is the
ExecuteSQLRecord processor. Drag the **Processor** icon to the canvas, and search for
the ExecuteSQLRecord processor. Once it has been added to the canvas, you need to
configure it.

Configuring the ExecuteSQLCommand processor

To configure the processor, you need to create a database connection pool, as shown in the
following screenshot:

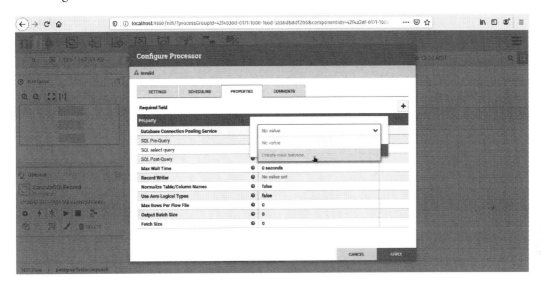

Figure 4.10 – Creating a database connection pooling service

After selecting **Create new service...**, you will see a popup for adding the controller
service. Select the default option, **DBCPConnectionPool**, and to make it easy to
remember which database this service is for, you can name it after the database –
dataengineering. Notice how I did not name it PostgreSQL. As you add more
services, you will add more PostgreSQL connections for different databases. It would
then be hard to remember which PostgreSQL database the service was for.

To configure the service, select the arrow in the processor configuration. The configuration for the service should look as in the following screenshot:

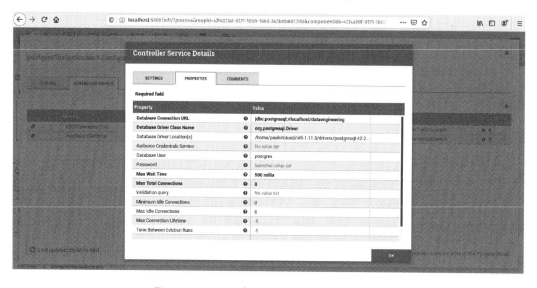

Figure 4.11 – Configuring the database service

The configuration requires you to specify the connection URL, which is a Java database connection string. The string specifies **Java Database Connectivity (JDBC)** and the database type – PostgreSQL. It then names the host, localhost, and the database name, dataengineering. The driver class specifies the postgresql driver. The location of the driver is where you downloaded it in *Chapter 2, Building Our Data Engineering Infrastructure*. It should be in your home directory in the nifi folder, in a subdirectory named drivers. Lastly, you need to enter the username and password for the database.

Next, you need to create a record writer service. Select **Create new service...**, choose **JSONRecordSetWriter**, and click the arrow to configure it. There is one important configuration setting that you cannot skip – **Output Grouping**. You must set this property to **One Line Per Object**. The finished configuration will look as in the following screenshot:

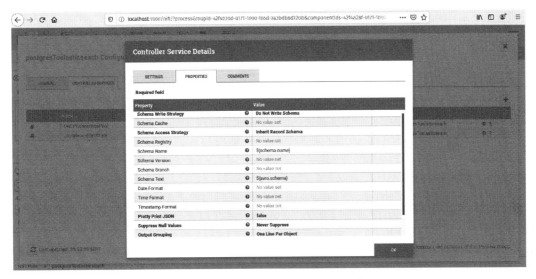

Figure 4.13 – The JSONRecordSetWriter configuration

Now that you have set up the services for the processor, you need to finish configuring the process. The last parameter you need to configure is **SQL Select Query**. This is where you can specify the SQL command to run against the database. For example, you can enter the following:

```
select name, city from users
```

This will grab all the records in the PostgreSQL database, but only the name and city fields. You can now move on to the next processor in the pipeline.

Configuring the SplitText processor

Now that you have configured the **ExecuteSQLRecord** processor, you will receive an array of records. To process this data, you need to have a flowfile per record. To do that, you can use the **SplitText** processor. Drag it to the canvas and open the **Properties** tab by double-clicking on the processor – or right-click and select **Properties**. The processor defaults work, but make sure that **Line Split Count** is set to **1**, **Header Line Count** is **0** – your data does not have a header when it comes from the **ExecuteSQLRecord** processor – and **Remove Trailing Newlines** is **true**.

These settings will allow the processor to take each line of the flowfile and split it into a new flowfile. So, your one incoming flowfile will come out of this processor as 1,000 flow files.

Configuring the PutElasticsearchHttp processor

The last step in the data pipeline is to insert the flowfiles into Elasticsearch. You can do that using the **PutElasticsearchHttp** processor. There are four different **PutElasticsearch** processors. Only two will be relevant in this book – **PutElasticsearchHttp** and **PutelasticsearchHttpRecord**. These are the processors to insert a single record or to use the bulk API. The other two processors – **Putelasticsearch** and **Putelasticsearch5** – are for older versions of Elasticsearch (2 and 5).

To configure the processor, you must specify the URL and the port. In this example, you will use `http://localhost:9200`. The index will be `fromnifi`, but you can name it anything you would like. The type is `doc` and the index operation will be `index`. In *Section 2*, *Deploying Pipelines into Production*, you will use other index operations and you will specify the ID of the records that you insert.

Running the data pipeline

Now that you have configured all of the processors, you can connect them by dragging the arrow from **ExecuteSQLRecord** to the **SplitRecord** processor for success. Then, connect the **SplitRecord** processor to the **PutElasticsearchHttp** processor for splits. Lastly, terminate the **PutElasticsearchHttp** processor for all relationships.

Run each of the processors, or in the **Operations** pane, select **Run** to start them all. You will see one flowfile in the first queue, then it will split into 1,000 flowfiles in the second queue. The queue will empty in batches of 100 as they are inserted into Elasticsearch.

To verify the results, you can use the `elasticsearch` API, and not Kibana. In your browser, go to `http://localhost:9200/_cat/indices`. This is the REST endpoint to view the indices in your Elasticsearch database. You should see your new index, `fromnifi`, and the total number of documents, as shown in the following screenshot:

```
yellow open frompostgresql                u3EVJEFJR-eDPtrufvSNkA 1 1 2208 0 250.4kb 250.4kb
yellow open fromnifi                       NBAL_aLdQly4iK90kDFauw 1 1 1001 0 233.8kb 233.8kb
yellow open test                           VWacjWq_S9a0fW6l-YbcIA 1 1    1 0   3.9kb   3.9kb
green  open kibana_sample_data_ecommerce  -6sdGU13T12GIjE2rU_ZlQ 1 0 4675 0   4.9mb   4.9mb
green  open .kibana_task_manager_1         1nLCVInfTa6XmmifoGntXA 1 0    2 0    13kb    13kb
green  open .apm-agent-configuration       51toZCyRS2yWlnLJZWF5-A 1 0    0 0    283b    283b
green  open .kibana_1                      g5gxKq0xR0y71FCG0rKiMw 1 0   66 5 993.3kb 993.3kb
yellow open users                          8K7wOmQ4S9Ogxh2TqBybKw 1 1 1003 0 286.6kb 286.6kb
```

Figure 4.13 – The index contains all the records from PostgreSQL

The number of documents in the index will vary depending on whether you left the pipeline running or not. Just as in the Airflow example, this pipeline is not idempotent. As it runs, it will keep adding the same records with a different ID into Elasticsearch. This is not the behavior you will want in production and we will fix this in *Section 2, Deploying Pipelines into Production*.

Summary

In this chapter, you learned how to use Python to query and insert data into both relational and NoSQL databases. You also learned how to use both Airflow and NiFi to create data pipelines. Database skills are some of the most important for a data engineer. There will be very few data pipelines that do not touch on them in some way. The skills you learned in this chapter provide the foundation for the other skills you will need to learn – primarily SQL. Combining strong SQL skills with the data pipeline skills you learned in this chapter will allow you to accomplish most of the data engineering tasks you will encounter.

In the examples, the data pipelines were not idempotent. Every time they ran, you got new results, and results you did not want. We will fix that in *Section 2, Deploying Pipelines into Production*. But before you get to that, you will need to learn how to handle common data issues, and how to enrich and transform your data.

The next chapter will teach you how to use Python to work with your data in between the extract and load phases of your data pipelines.

5
Cleaning, Transforming, and Enriching Data

In the previous two chapters, you learned how to build data pipelines that could read and write from files and databases. In many instances, these skills alone will enable you to build production data pipelines. For example, you will read files from a data lake and insert them into a database. You now have the skills to accomplish this. Sometimes, however, you will need to do something with the data after extraction but prior to loading. What you will need to do is clean the data. Cleaning is a vague term. More specifically, you will need to check the validity of the data and answer questions such as the following: Is it complete? Are the values within the proper ranges? Are the columns the proper type? Are all the columns useful?

In this chapter, you will learn the basic skills needed to perform exploratory data analysis. Once you have an understanding of the data, you will use that knowledge to fix common data problems that you have discovered – such as dropping columns and replacing nulls. You will learn many useful methods available in the `pandas` library for Python. These skills will allow you to quickly perform exploratory data analysis and allow you to clean the data, all within Python. These skills will become the tools for the transform stage of the ETL data engineering process.

In this chapter, we're going to cover the following main topics:

- Performing exploratory data analysis in Python
- Handling common data issues using pandas
- Cleaning data using Airflow

Performing exploratory data analysis in Python

Before you can clean your data, you need to know what your data looks like. As a data engineer, you are not the domain expert and are not the end user of the data, but you should know what the data will be used for and what valid data would look like. For example, you do not need to be a demographer to know that an `age` field should not be negative, and the frequency of values over 100 should be low.

Downloading the data

In this chapter, you will use real e-scooter data from the City of Albuquerque. The data contains trips taken using e-scooters from May to July 22, 2019. You will need to download the e-scooter data from `https://github.com/PaulCrickard/escooter/blob/master/scooter.csv`. The repository also contains the original Excel file as well as some other summary files provided by the City of Albuquerque.

Basic data exploration

Before you can clean your data, you have to know what your data looks like. The process of understanding your data is called **exploratory data analysis** (**EDA**). You will look at the shape of your data, the number of rows and columns, as well as the data types in the columns, and the ranges of values. You can perform a much more in-depth analysis, such as the distribution of the data, or the skewness, but for this section, you will learn how to quickly understand your data so that in the next section, you can clean it.

In the two previous chapters, you learned how to import files and databases into pandas DataFrames. That knowledge will be expanded in this section, as DataFrames will be the tool used for the EDA.

To begin with, you will need to import `pandas` and read the `.csv` file:

```
import pandas as pd
df=pd.read_csv('scooter.csv')
```

With the data in a DataFrame, you can now explore it, and then analyze it.

Exploring the data

Now you can start to look at the data. The first thing you will probably want to do is print it out. But before you get to that, take a look at the columns and the data types using `columns` and `dtypes`:

```
df.columns
Index(['month', 'trip_id', 'region_id', 'vehicle_id',
       'started_at', 'ended_at', 'DURATION',
       'start_location_name', 'end_location_name',
       'user_id', 'trip_ledger_id'],
      dtype='object')
df.dtypes
month                   object
trip_id                  int64
region_id                int64
vehicle_id               int64
started_at              object
ended_at                object
DURATION                object
start_location_name     object
end_location_name       object
user_id                  int64
trip_ledger_id           int64
```

You will see that you have eleven columns, five of which are integers (all of the columns with ID in their name) and the rest are objects. Objects are what a DataFrame uses as `dtype` when there are mixed types. Also, `DURATION` should stand out because it is the only column name in all capitals. In the next section, you will fix common errors, such as the column cases are not uniform (all lowercase or uppercase) and make the `dtypes` object proper types, such as `strings` for text data and `datetimes` for dates and times.

Now you know what you have for columns and types, let's look at the data. You can print out the first five records using `head()`:

```
df.head()
   month  trip_id  ...    user_id  trip_ledger_id
0    May  1613335  ...    8417864         1488546
```

1	May	1613639	...	8417864	1488838
2	May	1613708	...	8417864	1488851
3	May	1613867	...	8417864	1489064
4	May	1636714	...	35436274	1511212
[5 rows x 11 columns]					

The opposite of `head()` is `tail()`. Both of these methods default to showing 5 rows. However, you can pass an integer as a parameter that specifies how many rows to show. For example, you could pass `head(10)` to see the first 10 rows.

Notice in both the `head()` and `tail()` output that the third column is . . ., and then there are two more columns after this. The display is cropping out the columns in the middle. If you were to print the entire DataFrame, the same thing would happen with the rows as well. To display all the columns, you can change the number of columns to show using the `set_options` method:

```
pd.set_option('display.max_columns', 500)
```

Now, when you use `head()`, you will see all the column. However, depending on the width of your display, the output may be wrapped to fit.

The `head` and `tail` methods display all the columns, but if you are only interested in a single column, you can specify it like you would in a Python dictionary. The following code prints the `DURATION` column:

```
df['DURATION']
```

0	0:07:03
1	0:04:57
2	0:01:14
3	0:06:58
4	0:03:06
	...
34221	0:14:00
34222	0:08:00
34223	1:53:00
34224	0:12:00
34225	1:51:00

Again, notice that the output is cropped with . . ., but this time for the rows. The result is the combination of `head()` and `tail()`. You could change this using the `display_max_rows` option as you did earlier with columns, but for this exploration, it is unnecessary.

Just like you can display a single column, you can display a list of columns using double `[]`, as shown in the following code block:

```
df[['trip_id','DURATION','start_location_name']]
```

	trip_id	DURATION	start_location_name
0	1613335	0:07:03	1901 Roma Ave NE, Albuquerque, NM 87106, USA
1	1613639	0:04:57	1 Domenici Center en Domenici Center, Albuquer...
2	1613708	0:01:14	1 Domenici Center en Domenici Center, Albuquer...
3	1613867	0:06:58	Rotunda at Science & Technology Park, 801 Univ...
4	1636714	0:03:06	401 2nd St NW, Albuquerque, NM 87102, USA
...	...	...	...
34221	2482235	0:14:00	Central @ Broadway, Albuquerque, NM 87102, USA
34222	2482254	0:08:00	224 Central Ave SW, Albuquerque, NM 87102, USA
34223	2482257	1:53:00	105 Stanford Dr SE, Albuquerque, NM 87106, USA
34224	2482275	0:12:00	100 Broadway Blvd SE, Albuquerque, NM 87102, USA
34225	2482335	1:51:00	105 Stanford Dr SE, Albuquerque, NM 87106, USA

You can also pull a sample from your data using `sample()`. The sample methods allow you to specify how many rows you would like to pull. The results are shown in the following code block:

```
df.sample(5)
```

	month	trip_id	...	user_id	trip_ledger_id
4974	June	1753394	...	35569540	1624088

18390	June	1992655	...	42142022	1857395
3132	May	1717574	...	37145791	1589327
1144	May	1680066	...	36146147	1553169
21761	June	2066449	...	42297442	1929987

Notice that the index of the rows is not incremental, but rather it jumps around. It should, as it is a sample.

You can also slice the data. Slicing takes the format of [start:end], where a blank is the first or last row depending on which position is blank. To slice the first 10 rows, you can use the following notation:

```
df[:10]
```

	month	trip_id	...	user_id	trip_ledger_id
0	May	1613335	...	8417864	1488546
1	May	1613639	...	8417864	1488838
2	May	1613708	...	8417864	1488851
3	May	1613867	...	8417864	1489064
4	May	1636714	...	35436274	1511212
5	May	1636780	...	34352757	1511371
6	May	1636856	...	35466666	1511483
7	May	1636912	...	34352757	1511390
8	May	1637035	...	35466666	1511516
9	May	1637036	...	34352757	1511666

Likewise, to grab the rows from 10 to the end (34,225), you can use the following notation:

```
df[10:]
```

You can also slice the frame starting on the third row and ending before nine, as shown in the following code block:

```
df[3:9]
```

	month	trip_id	...	user_id	trip_ledger_id
3	May	1613867	...	8417864	1489064
4	May	1636714	...	35436274	1511212
5	May	1636780	...	34352757	1511371
6	May	1636856	...	35466666	1511483
7	May	1636912	...	34352757	1511390
8	May	1637035	...	35466666	1511516

Sometimes, you know the exact row you want, and instead of slicing it, you can select it using `loc()`. The `loc` method takes the index name, which, in this example, is an integer. The following code and output show a single row selected with `loc()`:

```
df.loc[34221]
month                                                          July
trip_id                                                     2482235
region_id                                                       202
vehicle_id                                                  2893981
started_at                                         7/21/2019 23:51
ended_at                                            7/22/2019 0:05
DURATION                                                   0:14:00
start_location_name   Central @ Broadway, Albuquerque, NM 87102,
                                                              USA
end_location_name     1418 4th St NW, Albuquerque, NM 87102, USA
user_id                                                    42559731
trip_ledger_id                                              2340035
```

Using `at()`, with the position, as you did in the slicing examples, and a column name, you can select a single value. For example, this can be done to know the duration of the trip in the second row:

```
df.at[2, 'DURATION']
'0:01:14'
```

Slicing and using `loc()` and `at()` pull data based on position, but you can also use DataFrames to select rows based on some condition. Using the `where` method, you can pass a condition, as shown in the following code block:

```
user=df.where(df['user_id']==8417864)
user
```

	month	trip_id	...	user_id	trip_ledger_id
0	May	1613335.0	...	8417864.0	1488546.0
1	May	1613639.0	...	8417864.0	1488838.0
2	May	1613708.0	...	8417864.0	1488851.0
3	May	1613867.0	...	8417864.0	1489064.0
4	NaN	NaN	...	NaN	NaN
...	...	...	...	...	...
34221	NaN	NaN	...	NaN	NaN

34222	NaN	NaN	...	NaN	NaN
34223	NaN	NaN	...	NaN	NaN
34224	NaN	NaN	...	NaN	NaN
34225	NaN	NaN	...	NaN	NaN

The preceding code and results show the results of `where` with the condition of the user ID being equal to `8417864`. The results replace values that do not meet the criteria as NaN. This will be covered in the next section.

You can get the same results similar to the preceding example with the exception of using a different notation, and this method will not include the NaN rows. You can pass the condition into the DataFrame as you did with column names. The following example shows you how:

```
df[(df['user_id']==8417864)]
```

The results of the preceding code is the same as the `where()` example, but without the NaN rows, so the DataFrame will only have four rows.

Using both notations, you can combine conditional statements. By using the same user ID condition, you can add a trip ID condition. The following example shows you how:

```
one=df['user_id']==8417864
two=df['trip_ledger_id']==1488838
df.where(one & two)
```

	month	trip_id	...	user_id	trip_ledger_id
0	NaN	NaN	...	NaN	NaN
1	May	1613639.0	...	8417864.0	1488838.0
2	NaN	NaN	...	NaN	NaN
3	NaN	NaN	...	NaN	NaN
4	NaN	NaN	...	NaN	NaN

Using the second notation, the output is as follows:

```
df[(one)&(two)]
    month   trip_id  ...    user_id  trip_ledger_id
1     May   1613639  ...    8417864         1488838
```

In the preceding examples, the conditions were assigned to a variable and combined in both the `where` and secondary notation, generating the expected results.

Analyzing the data

Now that you have seen the data, you can start to analyze it. By using the `describe` method, you can see a series of statistics pertaining to your data. In statistics, there is a set of statistics referred to as the five-number summary, and `describe()` is a variant of that:

```
df.describe()
                trip_id   region_id     vehicle_id         user_id
trip_ledger_id
count    3.422600e+04     34226.0    3.422600e+04    3.422600e+04
3.422600e+04
mean     2.004438e+06       202.0    5.589507e+06    3.875420e+07
1.869549e+06
std      2.300476e+05         0.0    2.627164e+06    4.275441e+06
2.252639e+05
min      1.613335e+06       202.0    1.034847e+06    1.080200e+04
1.488546e+06
25%      1.813521e+06       202.0    3.260435e+06    3.665710e+07
1.683023e+06
50%      1.962520e+06       202.0    5.617097e+06    3.880750e+07
1.827796e+06
75%      2.182324e+06       202.0    8.012871e+06    4.222774e+07
2.042524e+06
max      2.482335e+06       202.0    9.984848e+06    4.258732e+07
2.342161e+06
```

The `describe` method is not very useful unless you have numeric data. If you were looking at ages for example, it would quickly show you the distribution of ages, and you would be able to quickly see errors such as negative ages or too many ages over 100.

Using `describe()` on a single column is sometimes more helpful. Let's try looking at the `start_location_name` column. The code and results are shown in the following code block:

```
df['start_location_name'].describe()
count                                                      34220
unique                                                      2972
top        1898 Mountain Rd NW, Albuquerque, NM 87104, USA
freq                                                        1210
```

The data is not numeric, so we get a different set of statistics, but these provide some insight. Of the 34220 starting locations, there are actually 2972 unique locations. The top location (1898 Mountain Rd NW) accounts for 1210 trip starting locations. Later, you will geocode this data — add coordinates to the address — and knowing the unique values means you only have to geocode those 2,972 and not the full 34,220.

Another method that allows you to see details about your data is `value_counts`. The `value_counts` method will give you the value and count for all unique values. We need to call it to a single column, which is done in the following snippet:

```
df['DURATION'].value_counts()
0:04:00        825
0:03:00        807
0:05:00        728
0:06:00        649
0:07:00        627
```

From this method, you can see that `0:04:00` is at the top with a frequency of 825 — which you could have found out with `describe()` — but you can also see the frequency of all the other values. To see the frequency as a percentage, you can pass the normalize parameter (which is `False` by default):

```
df['DURATION'].value_counts(normalize=True)
0:04:00        0.025847
0:03:00        0.025284
0:05:00        0.022808
0:06:00        0.020333
0:07:00        0.019644
```

You will notice that no single value makes up a significant percentage of the duration.

You can also pass the `dropna` parameter. By default, `value_counts()` sets it to `True` and you will not see them. Setting it to `False`, you can see that `end_location_name` is missing `2070` entries:

```
df['end_location_name'].value_counts(dropna=False)
```

NaN	2070
1898 Mountain Rd NW, Albuquerque, NM 87104, USA	802
Central @ Tingley, Albuquerque, NM 87104, USA	622
330 Tijeras Ave NW, Albuquerque, NM 87102, USA	529
2550 Central Ave NE, Albuquerque, NM 87106, USA	478
	...
507 Bridge Blvd SW, Albuquerque, NM 87102, USA	1
820 2nd St NW, Albuquerque, NM 87102, USA	1
909 Alcalde Pl SW, Albuquerque, NM 87104, USA	1
817 Slate Ave NW, Albuquerque, NM 87102, USA	1

The best way to find out how many missing values you have in your columns is to use the `isnull()` method. The following code combines `isnull()` with `sum()` to get the counts:

```
df.isnull().sum()
```

month	0
trip_id	0
region_id	0
vehicle_id	0
started_at	0
ended_at	0
DURATION	2308
start_location_name	6
end_location_name	2070
user_id	0
trip_ledger_id	0

Another parameter of `value_counts()` is `bins`. The scooter dataset does not have a good column for this, but using a numeric column, you would get results like the following:

```
df['trip_id'].value_counts(bins=10)
(1787135.0, 1874035.0]      5561
(1700235.0, 1787135.0]      4900
(1874035.0, 1960935.0]      4316
(1960935.0, 2047835.0]      3922
(2047835.0, 2134735.0]      3296
(2221635.0, 2308535.0]      2876
(2308535.0, 2395435.0]      2515
(2134735.0, 2221635.0]      2490
(2395435.0, 2482335.0]      2228
(1612465.999, 1700235.0]    2122
```

These results are fairly meaningless, but if it is used on a column such as `age`, it would come in handy as you could create age groups quickly and get an idea of the distribution.

Now that you have explored and analyzed the data, you should have an understanding of what the data is and what the issues are — for example, nulls, improper `dtypes`, combined, and fields. With that knowledge, you can start to clean the data. The next section will walk you through how to fix common data problems.

Handling common data issues using pandas

Your data may feel special, it is unique, you have created the world's best systems for collecting it, and you have done everything you can to ensure it is clean and accurate. Congratulations! But your data will almost certainly have some problems, and these problems are not special, or unique, and are probably a result of your systems or data entry. The e-scooter dataset is collected using GPS with little to no human input, yet there are end locations that are missing. How is it possible that a scooter was rented, ridden, and stopped, yet the data doesn't know where it stopped? Seems strange, yet here we are. In this section, you will learn how to deal with common data problems using the e-scooter dataset.

Drop rows and columns

Before you modify any fields in your data, you should first decide whether you are going to use all the fields. Looking at the e-scooter data, there is a field named region_id. This field is a code used by the vendor to label Albuquerque. Since we are only using the Albuquerque data, we don't need this field as it adds nothing to the data.

You can drop columns using the drop method. The method will allow you to specify whether to drop a row or a column. Rows are the default, so we will specify columns, as shown in the following code block:

```
df.drop(columns=['region_id'], inplace=True)
```

Specifying the columns to drop, you also need to add inplace to make it modify the original DataFrame.

To drop a row, you only need to specify index instead of columns. To drop the row with the index of 34225, you need to use the following code:

```
df.drop(index=[34225],inplace=True)
```

The preceding code works when you want to drop an entire column or row, but what if you wanted to drop them based on conditions?

The first condition you may want to consider is where there are nulls. If you are missing data, the column and row may not be useful, or may distort the data. To handle this, you can use dropna().

By using dropna(), you can pass axis, how, thresh, subset, and inplace as parameters:

- axis specifies rows or columns with indexes or columns (0 or 1). It defaults to rows.
- how specifies whether to drop rows or columns if all the values are null or if any value is null (all or any). It defaults to any.
- thresh allows more control than allowing you to specify an integer value of how many nulls must be present.
- subset allows you to specify a list of rows or columns to search.
- inplace allows you to modify the existing DataFrame. It defaults to False.

Looking at the e-scooter data, there are six rows with no start location name:

```
df['start_location_name'][(df['start_location_name'].isnull())]
```

26042	NaN
26044	NaN
26046	NaN
26048	NaN
26051	NaN
26053	NaN

To drop these rows, you can use `dropna` on `axis=0` with `how=any`, which are the defaults. This will, however, delete rows where other nulls exist, such as `end_location_name`. So, you will need to specify the column name as a subset, as shown in the following code block:

```
df.dropna(subset=['start_location_name'],inplace=True)
```

Then, when you select nulls in the `start_location_name` field as in the preceding code block, you will get an empty series:

```
df['start_location_name'][(df['start_location_name'].isnull())]
Series([], Name: start_location_name, dtype: object)
```

Dropping an entire column based on missing values may only make sense if a certain percentage of rows are null. For example, if more than 25% of the rows are null, you may want to drop it. You could specify this in the threshold by using something like the following code for the `thresh` parameter:

```
thresh=int(len(df)*.25)
```

Before showing more advanced filters for dropping rows, you may not want to drop nulls. You may want to fill them with a value. You can use `fillna()` to fill either null columns or rows:

```
df.fillna(value='00:00:00',axis='columns')
```

9201	00:00:00
9207	00:00:00
9213	00:00:00
9219	00:00:00
9225	00:00:00

What if you want to use `fillna()` but use different values depending on the column? You would not want to have to specify a column every time and run `fillna()` multiple times. You can specify an object to map to the DataFrame and pass it as the `value` parameter.

In the following code, we will copy the rows where both the start and end location are null. Then, we will create a `value` object that assigns a street name to the `start_location_name` field and a different street address to the `end_location_name` field. Using `fillna()`, we pass the value to the `value` parameter, and then print those two columns in the DataFrame by showing the change:

```
startstop=df[(df['start_location_name'].isnull())&(df['end_
location_name'].isnull())]
value={'start_location_name':'Start St.','end_location_
name':'Stop St.'}
startstop.fillna(value=value)
startstop[['start_location_name','end_location_name']]
```

	start_location_name	end_location_name
26042	Start St.	Stop St.
26044	Start St.	Stop St.
26046	Start St.	Stop St.
26048	Start St.	Stop St.
26051	Start St.	Stop St.
26053	Start St.	Stop St.

You can drop rows based on more advanced filters; for example, what if you want to drop all the rows where the month was May? You could iterate through the DataFrame and check the month, and then drop it if it is May. Or, a much better way would be to filter out the rows, and then pass the index to the `drop` method. You can filter the DataFrame and pass it to a new one, as shown in the following code block:

```
may=df[(df['month']=='May')]
may
```

	month	trip_id	...	user_id	trip_ledger_id
0	May	1613335	...	8417864	1488546
1	May	1613639	...	8417864	1488838
2	May	1613708	...	8417864	1488851
3	May	1613867	...	8417864	1489064
4	May	1636714	...	35436274	1511212
...	...	...	...	...	...

4220	May	1737356	...	35714580	1608429
4221	May	1737376	...	37503537	1608261
4222	May	1737386	...	37485128	1608314
4223	May	1737391	...	37504521	1608337
4224	May	1737395	...	37497528	1608342

Then you can use `drop()` on the original DataFrame and pass the index for the rows in the `may` DataFrame, as shown:

```
df.drop(index=may.index,inplace=True)
```

Now, if you look at the months in the original DataFrame, you will see that May is missing:

```
df['month'].value_counts()
```

| June | 20259 |
| July | 9742 |

Now that you have removed the rows and columns that you either do not need, or that were unusable on account of missing data, it is time to format them.

Creating and modifying columns

The first thing that stood out in the preceding section was that there was a single column, duration, that was all in capital letters. Capitalization is a common problem. You will often find columns with all capitals, or with title case — where the first letter of every word is capitalized — and if a coder wrote it, you may find camel case — where the first letter is lowercase and the first letter of the next word is capital with no spaces, as in **camelCase**. The following code will make all the columns lowercase:

```
df.columns=[x.lower() for x in df.columns] print(df.columns)
Index(['month', 'trip_id', 'region_id', 'vehicle_id', 'started_
at', 'ended_at','duration', 'start_location_name', 'end_
location_name', 'user_id', 'trip_ledger_id'], dtype='object')
```

The preceding code is a condensed version of a `for` loop. What happens in the loop comes before the `for` loop. The preceding code says that for every item in `df.columns`, make it lowercase, and assign it back to `df.columns`. You can also use `capitalize()`, which is titlecase, or `upper()` as shown:

```
df.columns=[x.upper() for x in df.columns] print(df.columns)
Index(['MONTH', 'TRIP_ID', 'REGION_ID', 'VEHICLE_ID', 'STARTED_
AT', 'ENDED_AT', 'DURATION', 'START_LOCATION_NAME', 'END_
LOCATION_NAME', 'USER_ID', 'TRIP_LEDGER_ID'], dtype='object')
```

You could also make the DURATION field lowercase using the `rename` method, as shown:

```
df.rename(columns={'DURATION':'duration'},inplace=True)
```

You will notice an `inplace` parameter set to `True`. When you used psycopg2 to modify databases, you need to use `conn.commit()` to make it permanent, and you need to do the same with DataFrames. When you modify a DataFrame, the result is returned. You can store that new DataFrame (result) in a variable, and the original DataFrame is left unchanged. If you want to modify the original DataFrame and not assign it to another variable, you must use the `inplace` parameter.

The `rename` method works for fixing the case of column names but is not the best choice. It is better used for actually changing multiple column names. You can pass an object with multiple column name remapping. For example, you can remove the underscore in `region_id` using `rename`. In the following code snippet, we change the DURATION column to lowercase and remove the underscore in `region_id`:

```
df.rename(columns={'DURATION':'duration','region_
id':'region'},inplace=True)
```

It is good to know different ways to accomplish the same task, and you can decide which makes the most sense for your use case. Now that you have applied changes to the column names, you can apply these functions to the values in the columns as well. Instead of using `df.columns`, you will specify which column to modify, and then whether to make it `upper()`, `lower()`, or `capitalize()`. In the following code snippet, we have made the `month` column all capitals:

```
df['month']=df['month'].str.upper()
df['month'].head()
0    MAY
1    MAY
2    MAY
```

| 3 | MAY |
| 4 | MAY |

It may not matter what the capitalization is on your column names or the values. However, it is best to be consistent. In the case of the scooter data, having one column name in all capitals, while the rest were all lower, would become confusing. Imagine a data scientist querying data from multiple databases or your data warehouse and having to remember that all their queries needed to account for the `duration` field being in all caps, and when they forgot, their code failed.

You can add data to the DataFrame by creating columns using the `df['new column name']=value` format.

The preceding format would create a new column and assign the value to every row. You could iterate through a DataFrame and add a value based on a condition, for example:

```
for i,r in df.head().iterrows():
    if r['trip_id']==1613335:
        df.at[i,'new_column']='Yes'
    else:
        df.at[i,'new_column']='No'
df[['trip_id','new_column']].head()
    trip_id new_column
0   1613335        Yes
1   1613639         No
2   1613708         No
3   1613867         No
4   1636714         No
```

Iterating through DataFrames works but can be very slow. To accomplish the same thing as the preceding example, but more efficiently, you can use `loc()` and pass the condition, the column name, and then the value. The following example shows the code and the results:

```
df.loc[df['trip_id']==1613335,'new_column']='1613335'
df[['trip_id','new_column']].head()
    trip_id new_column
0   1613335    1613335
1   1613639         No
2   1613708         No
```

| 3 | 1613867 | No |
| 4 | 1636714 | No |

Another way to create columns is by splitting the data and then inserting it into the DataFrame. You can use `str.split()` on a series to split text on any separator, or a **pat** (short for **pattern**) as the parameter is called. You can specify how many splits you want to occur – -1 and 0 mean all splits – but any integer is allowed. For example, if you have 1,000,000 and only want two pieces, you can split (2) on the comma and get 1 and 000,000. You can also expand the splits into columns using `(expand=True)`. If you do not set `expand` to `True`, you will get a list in the column, which is the default. Furthermore, if you do not specify a separator, whitespace will be used. The defaults are shown:

```
d['started_ad=df[['trip_id','started_at']].head()
d['started_at'].str.split()
d
```

	trip_id	started_at
0	1613335	[5/21/2019, 18:33]
1	1613639	[5/21/2019, 19:07]
2	1613708	[5/21/2019, 19:13]
3	1613867	[5/21/2019, 19:29]
4	1636714	[5/24/2019, 13:38]

You can expand the data and pass it to a new variable. Then you can assign the columns to a column in the original DataFrame. For example, if you wanted to create a `date` and a `time` column, you could do the following:

```
new=d['started_at'].str.split(expand=True)
new
```

	0	1
0	5/21/2019	18:33
1	5/21/2019	19:07
2	5/21/2019	19:13
3	5/21/2019	19:29
4	5/24/2019	13:38

```
d['date']=new[0]
d['time']=new[1]
d
```

	trip_id	started_at	date	time

0	1613335	5/21/2019	18:33	5/21/2019	18:33
1	1613639	5/21/2019	19:07	5/21/2019	19:07
2	1613708	5/21/2019	19:13	5/21/2019	19:13
3	1613867	5/21/2019	19:29	5/21/2019	19:29
4	1636714	5/24/2019	13:38	5/24/2019	13:38

If you recall from the *Exploring the data* section, the data had several dtypes objects. The started_at column is an object and, looking at it, it should be clear that it is a datetime object. If you try to filter on the started_at field using a date, it will return all rows, as shown:

```
when = '2019-05-23'
x=df[(df['started_at']>when)]
len(x)
34226
```

The length of the entire DataFrame is 34226, so the filter returned all the rows. That is not what we wanted. Using to_datetime(), you can specify the column and the format. You can assign the result to the same column or specify a new one. In the following example, the started_at column is replaced with the new datetime data type:

```
d['started_at']=pd.to_datetime(df['started_
at'],format='%m/%d/%Y %H:%M')
d.dtypes
trip_id                    int64
started_at      datetime64[ns]
```

Now, the started_at column is a datetime data type and not an object. You can now run queries using dates, as we attempted earlier on the full DataFrame and failed:

```
when = '2019-05-23'
d[(d['started_at']>when)]
   trip_id          started_at
4  1636714 2019-05-24 13:38:00
```

The rest of the rows were all on 2019-05-21, so we got the results we expected.

Now that you can add and remove rows and columns, replace nulls, and create columns, in the next section, you will learn how to enrich your data with external sources.

Enriching data

The e-scooter data is geographic data — it contains locations — but it lacks coordinates. If you want to map, or perform spatial queries on this data, you will need coordinates. You can get coordinates by geocoding the location. As luck would have it, the City of Albuquerque has a public geocoder that we can use.

For this example, we will take a subset of the data. We will use the top five most frequent starting locations. We will then put them in a DataFrame using the following code:

```
new=pd.DataFrame(df['start_location_name'].value_counts().
head())
new.reset_index(inplace=True)
new.columns=['address','count']
new
```

	address	count
0	1898 Mountain Rd NW, Albuquerque, NM 87104, USA	1210
1	Central @ Tingley, Albuquerque, NM 87104, USA	920
2	2550 Central Ave NE, Albuquerque, NM 87106, USA	848
3	2901 Central Ave NE, Albuquerque, NM 87106, USA	734
4	330 Tijeras Ave NW, Albuquerque, NM 87102, USA	671

The address field has more information than we need to geocode. We only need the street address. You will also notice that the second record is an intersection – Central @ Tingley. The geocoder will want the word *and* between the streets. Let's clean the data and put it in its own column:

```
n=new['address'].str.split(pat=',',n=1,expand=True)
replaced=n[0].str.replace("@","and")
new['street']=n[0]
new['street']=replaced
new
```

	address	count	street
0	1898 Mountain Rd NW, Albuquerque, NM 87104, USA	1210	1898 Mountain Rd NW
1	Central @ Tingley, Albuquerque, NM 87104, USA	920	Central and Tingley
2	2550 Central Ave NE, Albuquerque, NM 87106, USA	848	2550 Central Ave NE
3	2901 Central Ave NE, Albuquerque, NM 87106, USA	734	2901

```
Central Ave NE
4     330 Tijeras Ave NW, Albuquerque, NM 87102, USA      671      330
Tijeras Ave NW
```

Now you can iterate through the DataFrame and geocode the street field. For this section, you will use another CSV and join it to the DataFrame.

You can enrich data by combining it with other data sources. Just like you can join data from two tables in a database, you can do the same with a pandas DataFrame. You can download the `geocodedstreet.csv` file from the book's GitHub repository. Load the data using `pd.read_csv()` and you will have a DataFrame with a `street` column, as well as a column for the `x` and `y` coordinates. The result is shown as follows:

```
geo=pd.read_csv('geocodedstreet.csv')
geo
```

	street	x	y
0	1898 Mountain Rd NW	-106.667146	35.098104
1	Central and Tingley	-106.679271	35.091205
2	2550 Central Ave NE	-106.617420	35.080646
3	2901 Central Ave NE	-106.612180	35.081120
4	330 Tijeras Ave NW	-106.390355	35.078958
5	nothing street	-106.000000	35.000000

To enrich the original DataFrame with this new data, you can either join or merge the DataFrames. Using a join, you can start with a DataFrame and then add the other as a parameter. You can pass how to join using `left`, `right`, or `inner`, just like you would in SQL. You can add a `left` and `right` suffix so the columns that overlap have a way to determine where they came from. We have joined the two DataFrames in the following example:

```
joined=new.join(other=geo,how='left',lsuffix='_new',rsuffix='_geo')
joined[['street_new','street_geo','x','y']]
```

	street_new	street_geo	x	y
0	1898 Mountain Rd NW	1898 Mountain Rd NW	-106.667146	35.098104
1	Central and Tingley	Central and Tingley	-106.679271	35.091205
2	2550 Central Ave NE	2550 Central Ave NE	-106.617420	35.080646

```
3   2901 Central Ave NE   2901 Central Ave NE -106.612180
35.081120
4     330 Tijeras Ave NW     330 Tijeras Ave NW -106.390355
35.078958
```

The `street` column is duplicated and has a `left` and `right` suffix. This works but is unnecessary, and we would end up dropping one column and renaming the remaining column, which is just extra work.

You can use merge to join the DataFrames on a column and not have the duplicates. Merge allows you to pass the DataFrames to merge as well as the field to join on, as shown:

```
merged=pd.merge(new,geo,on='street')
merged.columns
Index(['address', 'count', 'street', 'x', 'y'], dtype='object')
```

Notice how the new fields `x` and `y` came over in to the new DataFrame, but there is only a single `street` column. This is much cleaner. In either case, `joined` or `merged`, you can only use the index if you have it set on both DataFrames.

Now that you know how to clean, transform, and enrich data, it is time to put these skills together and build a data pipeline using this newfound knowledge. The next two sections will show you how to use Airflow and NiFi to build a data pipeline.

Cleaning data using Airflow

Now that you can clean your data in Python, you can create functions to perform different tasks. By combining the functions, you can create a data pipeline in Airflow. The following example will clean data, and then filter it and write it out to disk.

Starting with the same Airflow code you have used in the previous examples, set up the imports and the default arguments, as shown:

```
import datetime as dt
from datetime import timedelta
from airflow import DAG
from airflow.operators.bash_operator import BashOperator
from airflow.operators.python_operator import PythonOperator
import pandas as pd


default_args = {
    'owner': 'paulcrickard',
```

```
        'start_date': dt.datetime(2020, 4, 13),
        'retries': 1,
        'retry_delay': dt.timedelta(minutes=5),
}
```

Now you can write the functions that will perform the cleaning tasks. First, you need to read the file, then you can drop the region ID, convert the columns to lowercase, and change the `started_at` field to a `datetime` data type. Lastly, write the changes to a file. The following is the code:

```
def cleanScooter():
    df=pd.read_csv('scooter.csv')
    df.drop(columns=['region_id'], inplace=True)
    df.columns=[x.lower() for x in df.columns]
    df['started_at']=pd.to_datetime(df['started_at'],
                           format='%m/%d/%Y %H:%M')
    df.to_csv('cleanscooter.csv')
```

Next, the pipeline will read in the cleaned data and filter based on a start and end date. The code is as follows:

```
def filterData():
    df=pd.read_csv('cleanscooter.csv')
    fromd = '2019-05-23'
    tod='2019-06-03'
    tofrom = df[(df['started_at']>fromd)&
                (df['started_at']<tod)]
    tofrom.to_csv('may23-june3.csv')
```

These two functions should look familiar as the code is line for line the same as in the preceding examples, just regrouped. Next, you need to define the operators and tasks. You will use `PythonOperator` and point it to your functions. Create the DAG and the tasks as shown:

```
with DAG('CleanData',
         default_args=default_args,
         schedule_interval=timedelta(minutes=5),
         # '0 * * * *',
         ) as dag:
```

```
cleanData = PythonOperator(task_id='clean',
                           python_callable=cleanScooter)

selectData = PythonOperator(task_id='filter',
                            python_callable=filterData)
```

In this example, we will add in another task using BashOperator again. If you recall, you used it in *Chapter 3, Reading and Writing Files*, just to print a message to the terminal. This time, you will use it to move the file from the selectData task and copy it to the desktop. The code is as follows:

```
copyFile = BashOperator(task_id='copy',
                        bash_command='cp /home/
paulcrickard/may23-june3.csv /home/paulcrickard/Desktop')
```

The preceding command just uses the Linux copy command to make a copy of the file. When working with files, you need to be careful that your tasks can access them. If multiple processes attempt to touch the same file or a user tries to access it, you could break your pipeline. Lastly, specify the order of the tasks — create the direction of the DAG as shown:

```
cleanData >> selectData >> copyFile
```

Now you have a completed DAG. Copy this file to your $AIRFLOW_HOME/dags folder. Then, start Airflow with the following command:

```
airflow webserver
airflow scheduler
```

Now you can browse to `http://localhost:8080/admin` to view the GUI. Select your new DAG and click the **Tree View** tab. You will see your DAG and you can turn it on and run it. In the following screenshot, you will see the DAG and the runs of each task:

Figure 5.1 – Running the DAG

You will see that the DAG has two failed runs. This was a result of the file not being present when a task ran. I had used `move` instead of `copy` in `BashOperator`, hence the warning about being careful when handling files in Airflow.

Congratulations! You have successfully completed this chapter.

Summary

In this chapter, you learned how to perform basic EDA with an eye toward finding errors or problems within your data. You then learned how to clean your data and fix common data issues. With this set of skills, you built a data pipeline in Apache Airflow.

In the next chapter, you will walk through a project, building a 311 data pipeline and dashboard in Kibana. This project will utilize all of the skills you have acquired up to this point and will introduce a number of new skills – such as building dashboards and making API calls.

6
Building a 311 Data Pipeline

In the previous three chapters, you learned how to use Python, Airflow, and NiFi to build data pipelines. In this chapter, you will use those skills to create a pipeline that connects to **SeeClickFix** and downloads all the issues for a city, and then loads it in Elasticsearch. I am currently running this pipeline every 8 hours. I use this pipeline as a source of open source intelligence – using it to monitor quality of life issues in neighborhoods, as well as reports of abandoned vehicles, graffiti, and needles. Also, it's really interesting to see what kinds of things people complain to their city about – during the COVID-19 pandemic, my city has seen several reports of people not social distancing at clubs.

In this chapter, we're going to cover the following main topics:

- Building the data pipeline
- Building a Kibana dashboard

Building the data pipeline

This data pipeline will be slightly different from the previous pipelines in that we will need to use a trick to start it off. We will have two paths to the same database – one of which we will turn off once it has run the first time, and we will have a processor that connects to itself for the success relationship. The following screenshot shows the completed pipeline:

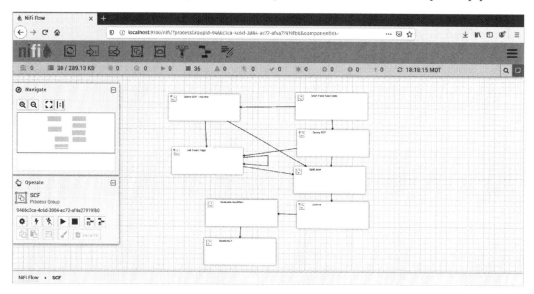

Figure 6.1 – The complete pipeline

The preceding screenshot may look complicated, but I assure you that it will make sense by the end of this chapter.

Mapping a data type

Before you can build the pipeline, you need to map a field in Elasticsearch so that you get the benefit of the coordinates by mapping them as the geopoint data type. To do that, open Kibana at `http://localhost:5601`. At the toolbar, select **Dev Tools** (the wrench icon) and enter the code shown in the left panel of the following screenshot, and then click the run arrow. If it was successful, you will see output in the right panel, as shown in the following screenshot:

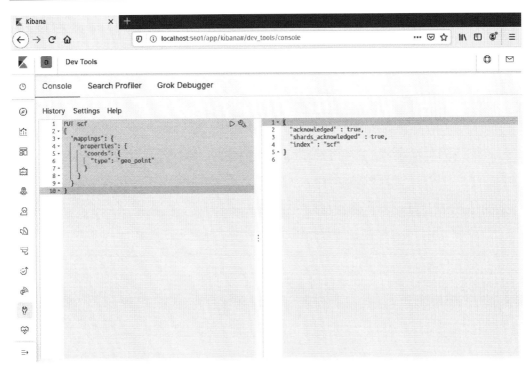

Figure 6.2 – Adding geopoint mapping

Now that you have created the `scf` index with geopoint mapping, when you run your pipeline, the `coords` field will be converted into spatial coordinates in Elasticsearch.

Let's start building.

Triggering a pipeline

In the previous section, I mentioned that you would need to trick the data pipeline into starting. Remember that this pipeline will connect to an API endpoint, and in order to do that, the NiFi processors for calling HTTP endpoints, as well as the `ExecuteScript` processer that you will use, require an incoming flowfile to start them. This processor cannot be the first processor in a data pipeline.

To start the data pipeline, you will use the `GenerateFlowFile` processor. Drag and drop the processor on the canvas. Double-click on it to change the configuration. In the **Settings** tab, name the processor. I have named it `Start Flow Fake Data`. This lets us know that this processor sends fake data just to start the flow. The configuration will use all the defaults and look like the following screenshot:

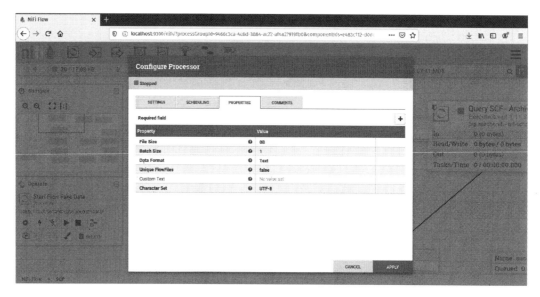

Figure 6.3 – Configuring the GenerateFlowfile processor

Lastly, in the **SCHEDULING** tab, set the processor to run at your desired interval. I use 8 because I do not want to overwhelm the API.

The processor, when running, will generate a single flowfile with 0 bytes of data. It is empty, but it does contain metadata generated by NiFi. However, this empty flowfile will do the trick and start the next processor. That is where the work begins.

Querying SeeClickFix

In the previous NiFi examples, you did not use any code, just configurations to make the processor do what you needed. We could do that in this pipeline. However, now is a good time to introduce coding using Python – Jython – into your pipelines.

Drag and drop the `ExecuteScript` processor to the canvas. Double-click on it to edit the configuration. Starting with the **Settings** tab, name it something that makes sense to you – I named it `Query SCF` so that I know it queries **SeeClickFix**. In the **Properties** tab, set **Script Engine** to **Python**. In the **Script Body** parameter, you will write the Python code that the processor will execute. The query steps are as follows:

1. You need to import the required libraries. The following code is the libraries that you will always need to include:

```
import java.io
from org.apache.commons.io import IOUtils
from java.nio.charset import StandardCharsets
from org.apache.nifi.processor.io import StreamCallback
from org.python.core.util import StringUtil
```

2. Next, you will create the class that will be called to handle the work. The `process` function will contain the code that will perform the task:

```
class ModJSON(StreamCallback):
    def __init__(self):
        pass
    def process(self, inputStream, outputStream):
        # Task Goes Here
```

3. Lastly, assume that no errors have occurred, and check whether there is a flowfile. If there is one, write the flowfile calling the class. Next, check whether an error occurred. If there was an error, you will send the flowfile to the failure relationship, otherwise, send it to the success relationship:

```
errorOccurred=False
flowFile = session.get()
if (flowFile != None):
    flowFile = session.write(flowFile, ModJSON())
    #flowFile = session.putAttribute(flowFile)
    if(errorOccurred):
        session.transfer(flowFile, REL_FAILURE)
    else:
        session.transfer(flowFile, REL_SUCCESS)
```

The preceding code is the boiler plate for any Python `ExecuteScript` processor. The only thing you will need to change will be in the process function, which we will do in the steps that follow.

Because NiFi uses Jython, you can add many Python libraries to the Jython environment, but that is beyond the scope of this book. For now, you will use the standard libraries.

4. To make a call to the SeeClickFix API, you will need to import the `urllib` libraries and `json`, as shown:

```
import urllib
import urllib2
import json
```

5. Next, you will put the code in the `process` function. The code will be a `try except` block that makes a request to the HTTP endpoint and writes out the response to `outputStream`. If there was an error, the `except` block will set `errorOccurred` to `True` and this will trigger the rest of the code to send the flowfile to the `Failure` relationship. The only line in the `try` block that is not standard Python for using `urllib` is `outputStream.write()`. This is where you write to the flowfile:

```
try:
    param = {'place_url':'bernalillo-county',
             'per_page':'100'}
    url = 'https://seeclickfix.com/api/v2/issues?' +
             urllib.urlencode(param)
    rawreply = urllib2.urlopen(url).read()
    reply = json.loads(rawreply)

    outputStream.write(bytearray(json.dumps(reply,
             indent=4).encode('utf-8')))
except:
    global errorOccurred
    errorOccurred=True

    outputStream.write(bytearray(json.dumps(reply,
             indent=4).encode('utf-8')))
```

The preceding code, when successful, will output a JSON flowfile. The contents of the flowfile will contain some metadata and an array of issues. The two pieces of metadata we will be interested in are **page** and **pages**.

You have grabbed the first 100 issues for Bernalillo County, and will pass this flowfile to two different processors – GetEveryPage and SplitJson. We will follow the SplitJson path, as this path will send the data to Elasticsearch.

Transforming the data for Elasticsearch

The following are the steps for transforming data for Elasticsearch:

1. Drag and drop the SplitJson processor to the canvas. Double-click on it to modify the properties. In the **Properties** tab, set the **JsonPath Expression** property to **$.issues**. This processor will now split the 100 issues into their own flowfiles.

2. Next, you need to add coordinates in the format expected by NiFi. We will use an x, y string named coords. To do that, drag and drop an ExecuteScript processor to the canvas. Double-click on it and click the **Properties** tab. Set the **Script Engine** to **Python**. The **Script Body** property will contain the standard boiler plate, plus the import json statement.

3. The process function will convert the input stream to a string. The input stream is the flowfile contents from the previous processor. In this case, it is a single issue. Then it will use the json library to load it as json. You then add a field named coords and assign it the value of a concatenated string of the lat and lng fields in the flowfile JSON. Lastly, you write the JSON back to the output stream as a new flowfile:

```
def process(self, inputStream, outputStream):
    try:
        text = IOUtils.toString(inputStream,
                                StandardCharsets.UTF_8)
        reply=json.loads(text)

reply['coords']=str(reply['lat'])+','+str(reply['lng'])
        d=reply['created_at'].split('T')
        reply['opendate']=d[0]
        outputStream.write(bytearray(json.dumps(reply,
                          indent=4).encode('utf-8')))
    except:
```

```
        global errorOccurred
        errorOccurred=True
        outputStream.write(bytearray(json.dumps(reply,
                         indent=4).encode('utf-8')))
```

Now you have a single issue, with a new field called `coords`, that is a string format that Elasticsearch recognizes as a geopoint. You are almost ready to load the data in Elasticsearch, but first you need a unique identifier.

4. To create the equivalent of a primary key in Elasticsearch, you can specify an ID. The JSON has an ID for each issue that you can use. To do so, drag and drop the `EvaluateJsonPath` processor on to the canvas. Double-click on it and select the **Properties** tab. Clicking the plus sign in the upper-right corner, add a property named `id` with the value of `$.id`. Remember that `$.` allows you to specify a JSON field to extract. The flowfile now contains a unique ID extracted from the JSON.

5. Drag and drop the `PutElasticsearchHttp` processor on to the canvas. Double-click on it to edit the properties. Set the **Elasticsearch URL** property to `http://localhost:9200`. In the optional **Identifier Attribute** property, set the value to **id**. This is the attribute you just extracted in the previous processor. Set the **Index** to **SCF** (short for **SeeClickFix**), and the **Type** to **doc**. Lastly, you will set the **Index Operation** property to **upsert**. In Elasticsearch, **upsert** will index the document if the ID does not already exist, and it will update if the ID exists, and the data is different. Otherwise, nothing will happen, and the record will be ignored, which is what you want if the data is already the same.

The issues are now being loaded in Elasticsearch, and if you were to check, you will have 100 documents in your `scf` index. But there are a lot more than 100 records in the SeeClickFix data for Bernalillo County; there are 44 pages of records (4,336 issues) according to the metadata from the `QuerySCF` processor.

The following section will show you how to grab all the data.

Getting every page

When you queried SeeClickFix, you sent the results to two paths. We took the `SplitJson` path. The reason for this is because on the initial query, you got back 100 issues and how many pages of issues exist (as part of the metadata). You sent the issues to the `SplitJson` path, because they were ready to process, but now you need to do something with the number of pages. We will do that by following the `GetEveryPage` path.

Drag and drop an `ExecuteScript` processor on to the canvas. Double-click on it to edit the **Properties** tab. Set the **Script Engine** property to **Python** and the **Script Body** will include the standard boiler plate – including the imports for the `urllib` and `json` libraries.

The `process` function will convert the input stream to JSON, and then it will load it using the `json` library. The main logic of the function states that if the current page is less than or equal to the total number of pages, call the API and request the next page (`next_page_url`), and then write out the JSON as a flowfile. Otherwise, it stops. The code is as follows:

```python
try:
    text = IOUtils.toString(inputStream,
                            StandardCharsets.UTF_8)
    asjson=json.loads(text)
    if asjson['metadata']['pagination']
['page']<=asjson['metadata']['pagination']['pages']:
        url = asjson['metadata']['pagination']
                            ['next_page_url']
        rawreply = urllib2.urlopen(url).read()
        reply = json.loads(rawreply)
        outputStream.write(bytearray(json.dumps(reply,
                            indent=4).encode('utf-8')))
    else:
        global errorOccurred
        errorOccurred=True
        outputStream.write(bytearray(json.dumps(asjson,
                            indent=4).encode('utf-8')))
except:
    global errorOccurred
    errorOccurred=True
    outputStream.write(bytearray(json.dumps(asjson,
                        indent=4).encode('utf-8')))
```

You will connect the relationship success for this processor to the `SplitJson` processor in the last path we took. The flowfile will be split on issues, coordinates added, the ID extracted, and the issue sent to Elasticsearch. However, we need to do this 42 times.

To keep processing pages, you need to connect the success relationship to itself. That's right; you can connect a processor to itself. When you processed the first page through this processor, the next page was 2. The issues were sent to `SplitJson`, and back to this processor, which said the current page is less than 44 and the next page is 3.

You now have an Elasticsearch index with all of the current issues from SeeClickFix. However, the number of issues for Bernalillo County is much larger than the set of current issues – there is an archive. And now that you have a pipeline pulling new issues every 8 hours, you will always be up to date, but you can backfill Elasticsearch with all of the archived issues as well. Then you will have the full history of issues.

Backfilling data

To backfill the `SCF` index with historic data only requires the addition of a single parameter to the `params` object in the `QuerySCF` processor. To do that, right-click on the `QuerySCF` processor and select **copy**. Right-click on a blank spot of canvas, and then select **paste**. Double-click the copied processor and, in the **Settings** tab, rename it as `QuerySCFArchive`. In the **Properties** tab, modify the **Script Body** parameter, changing the `params` object to the following code:

```
param = {'place_url':'bernalillo-county', 'per_page': '100',
'status':'Archived'}
```

The `status` parameter was added with the value `Archived`. Now, connect the `GenerateFlowfile` processor to this backfill processor to start it. Then, connect the processor to the `SplitJson` processor for the success relationship. This will send the issues to Elasticsearch. But you need to loop through all the pages, so connect the processor to the `GetEveryPage` processor too. This will loop through the archives and send all the issues to Elasticsearch. Once this pipeline finishes, you can stop the `QuerySCFArchive` processor.

When you have a system that is constantly adding new records – like a transactional system – you will follow this pattern often. You will build a data pipeline to extract the recent records and extract the new records at a set interval – daily or hourly depending on how often the system updates or how much in real time you need it to be. Once your pipeline is working, you will add a series of processors to grab all the historic data and backfill your warehouse. You may not need to go back to the beginning of time, but in this case, there were sufficiently few records to make it feasible.

You will also follow this pattern if something goes wrong or if you need to populate a new warehouse. If your warehouse becomes corrupted or you bring a new warehouse online, you can rerun this backfill pipeline to bring in all the data again, making the new database complete. But it will only contain current state. The next chapter deals with production pipelines and will help you solve this problem by improving your pipelines. For now, let's visualize your new Elasticsearch index in Kibana.

Building a Kibana dashboard

Now that your SeeClickFix data pipeline has loaded data in Elasticsearch, it would be nice to see the results of the data, as would an analyst. Using Kibana, you can do just that. In this section, you will build a Kibana dashboard for your data pipeline.

To open Kibana, browse to `http://localhost:5601` and you will see the main window. At the bottom of the toolbar (on the left of the screen; you may need to expand it), click the management icon at the bottom. You need to select **Create new Index Pattern** and enter `scf*`, as shown in the following screenshot:

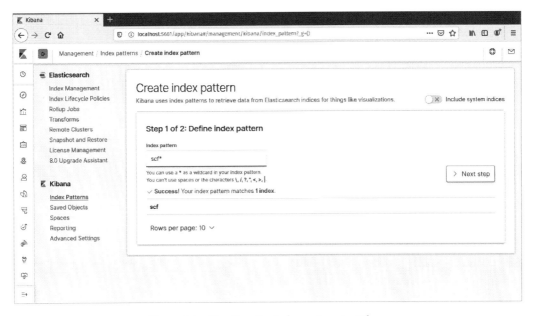

Figure 6.4 – Creating the index pattern in Kibana

When you click the next step, you will be asked to select a **Time Filter field name**. Because there are several fields with times in them, and they are in a format that is already recognizable by Elasticsearch, they will be indexed as such, and you can select a primary time filter. The field selected will be the default field used in screens such as **Discovery** when a bar chart preview of the data is displayed by time, and when you use a time filter in visualizations or dashboards. I have selected created_at, as shown in the following screenshot:

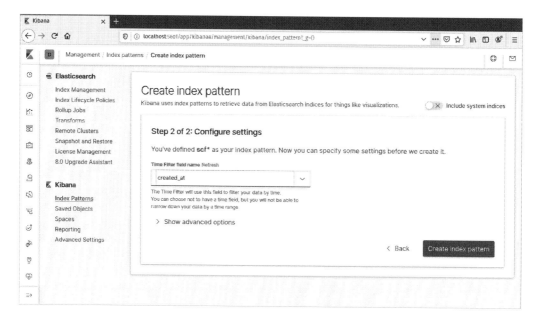

Figure 6.5 – Selecting the Time Filter field

Once you have created the index in Kibana, you can move on to visualizations.

Creating visualizations

To create visualizations, select the visualization icon in the toolbar. Select **Create Visualization** and you will see a variety of types available, as shown in the following screenshot:

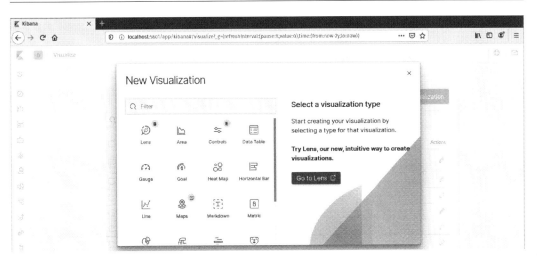

Figure 6.6 – Available visualization types

You will see the **Lens** type, which is a **Beta** visualization, as well as **Controls** and **Vega**, which are **Experimentals**. For now, select the **Vertical Bar** chart. When asked for a source, choose `scf` — this will apply to all visualizations in this chapter. Leave the y axis as **Count**, but add a new bucket and select the x axis. For **Aggregations**, choose **Date Histogram**. The field is `created_at` and the interval will be **Monthly**. You will see a chart as shown in the following screenshot (yours may vary):

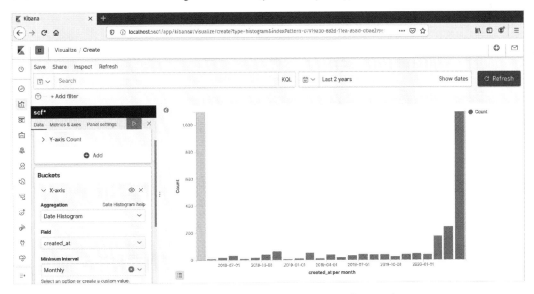

Figure 6.7 – Bar chart of created_at counts by month

Save the bar chart and name it `scf-bar`, or anything that you will be able to associate with the SeeClickFix data.

Next, select visualization again and choose metric. You will only add a custom label under the **Metrics** options. I chose **Issues**. By doing this, you remove the default count that gets placed under the numbers in the metric. This visualization is giving us a count of issues and will change when we apply filters in the dashboard. The configuration is shown in the following screenshot:

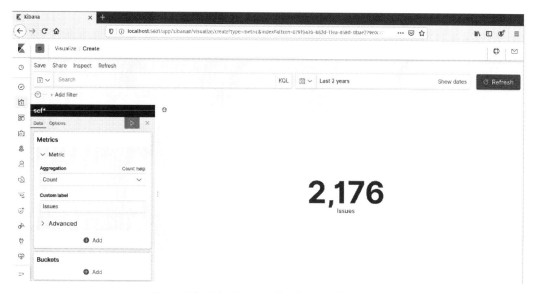

Figure 6.8 – Metrics visualization configuration

Again, save the visualization using any convention, or prefix it with `scf`, as I have done.

For the next visualization, select a pie chart – which will default to a donut. Under **Buckets**, select **Split slices**. For **Aggregations**, select **Terms**. And for **Field**, select **request_type.title.keyword**. Leave the rest of the defaults set. This will give you the top five titles. The results are shown in the following screenshot:

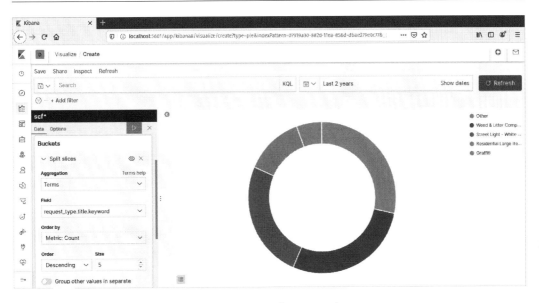

Figure 6.9 – Top five issue titles

While not a visualization, **Markdown** can add value to your dashboard by providing some context or a description. Select **Markdown** from the visualization options. You can enter Markdown in the left pane and, by clicking the run symbol, see the preview in the right pane. I have just added an H1, some text, and a bullet list, as shown in the following screenshot:

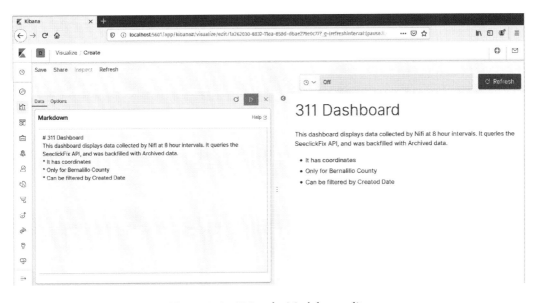

Figure 6.10 – Using the Markdown editor

The last visualization, **Map**, has an arrow because maps have their own place on the toolbar, and you can do a lot more with them than the other visualizations. For now, you can select **Map** from either location. You will select **Create Map**, and when prompted for the index pattern, select scf. Once on the map screen, select **Add Layer** and the source will be **Documents**. This allows you to select an index. The following screenshot shows what you should see:

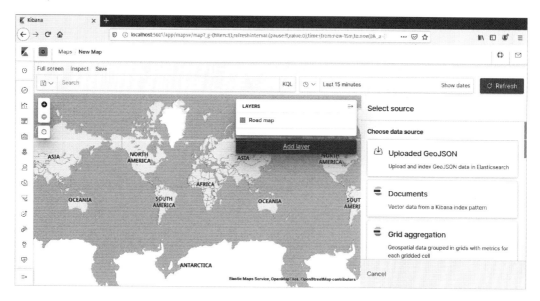

Figure 6.11 – Adding a new layer with the source being documents

When you select `scf` as the index pattern, Kibana will recognize the appropriate field and add the data to the map. Your map will be blank, and you may wonder went wrong. Kibana sets the time filter to the last 15 minutes, and you do not have data newer than the last 8 hours. Set the filter to a longer time frame, and the data will appear if the `create_at` field is in the window. The results are shown in the following screenshot:

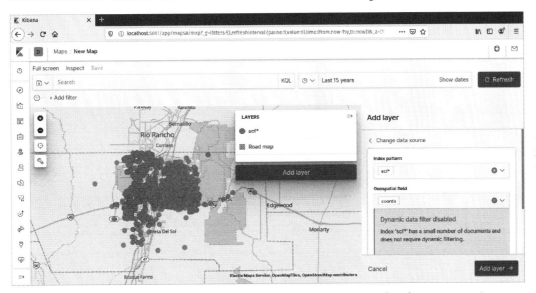

Figure 6.12 – A map visualization from an Elasticsearch index

Now that you have created visualizations from your data, you can now move on to combining them into a dashboard. The next section will show you how.

Creating a dashboard

To build a dashboard, select the dashboard icon on the toolbar. You will then select **Create a new dashboard** and add visualizations. If this is the first dashboard, you may see text asking whether you want to add an existing item. Add an item and then, in the search bar, type `scf` – or any of the names you used to save your visualizations. Adding them to the dashboard, you can then position them and resize them. Make sure to save your dashboard once it is set up. I have built the dashboard shown in the following screenshot:

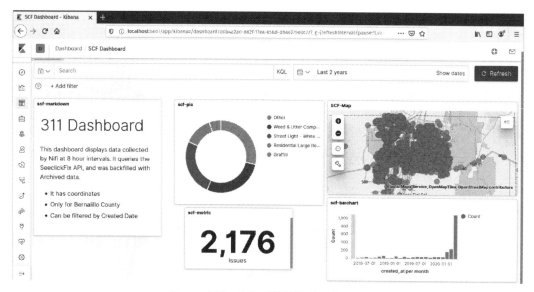

Figure 6.13 – A SeeClickFix dashboard

The dashboard has the Markdown, pie chart, map, metric, and bar chart added. I moved them around by grabbing the top of the panel and resized them by grabbing the lower-right corner and dragging. You can also click the gear icon and add a new name for your panels, so that they do not have the name that you used when you save the visualization.

With your dashboard, you can filter the data and all the visualizations will change. For example, I have clicked on the Graffiti label in the pie chart and the results are shown in the following screenshot:

Figure 6.14 – Filtering on Graffiti

Using filters is where the metric visualization comes in handy. It is nice to know what the number of records are. You can see that the map and the bar chart changed as well. You can also filter on the date range. I have selected the last 7 days in the filter, as shown in the following screenshot:

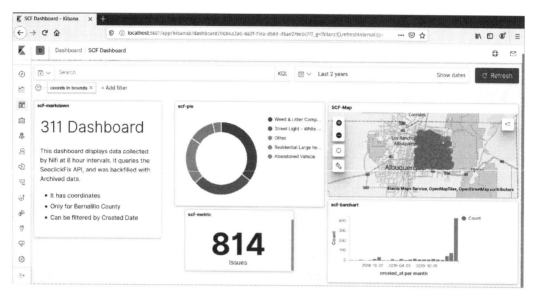

Figure 6.15 – Filtering by time in a dashboard

The time filter allows you to select **Now**, **Relative**, or **Absolute**. **Relative** is a number of days, months, years, and so on from **Now**, while **Absolute** allows you to specify a start and end time on a calendar. The results of the seven-day filter are shown in the following screenshot:

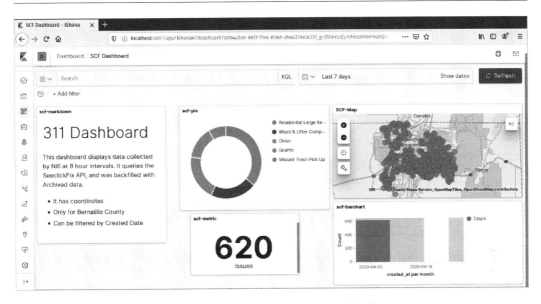

Figure 6.16 – Dashboard with a seven-day filter

The last filter I will show is the map filter. You can select an area or draw a polygon on the map to filter your dashboard. By clicking on the map tools icon, the options will appear as shown in the following screenshot:

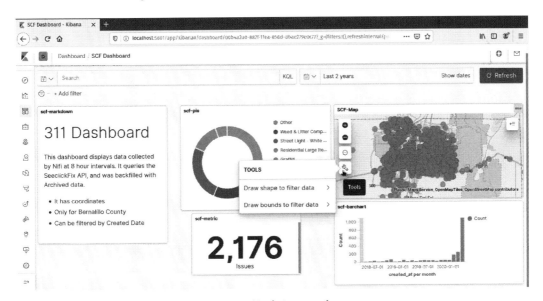

Figure 6.17 – Tools icon on the map

Using the **Draw** bounds to filter data, I drew a rectangle on the map and the results are shown in the following screenshot:

Figure 6.18 – Filtering data using the map

In the preceding dashboard, you can see the perfect rectangle of points. The map filter is one of my favorite filters.

Kibana dashboards make your data pipelines useful to non-data engineers. The work you put into moving and transforming data becomes live data that can be used by analysts and mangers to explore and learn from the data. Kibana dashboards are also an excellent way for you, the data engineer, to visualize the data you have extracted, transformed, and loaded to see whether there are any obvious issues in your data pipeline. They can be a type of debugging tool.

Summary

In this chapter, you learned how to build a data pipeline using data from a REST API. You also added a flow to the data pipeline to allow you to backfill the data, or to recreate a database with all of the data using a single pipeline.

The second half of the chapter provided a basic overview of how to build a dashboard using Kibana. Dashboards will usually be outside the responsibilities of a data engineer. In smaller firms, however, this could very well be your job. Furthermore, being able to quickly build a dashboard can help validate your data pipeline and look for any possible errors in the data.

In the next chapter, we begin a new section of this book, where you will take the skills you have learned and improve them by making your pipelines ready for production. You will learn about deployment, better validation techniques, and other skills needed when you are running pipelines in a production environment.

Section 2: Deploying Data Pipelines in Production

Section 2 builds on what you have learned and teaches you the features of production data pipelines. You will learn techniques that are similar to software engineering, such as versioning, monitoring, and logging. With these skills, you will be able to not only build, but also manage production data pipelines. Lastly, you will learn how to deploy your data pipelines in a production environment.

This section comprises the following chapters:

- *Chapter 7, Features of a Production Data Pipeline*
- *Chapter 8, Version Control Using the NiFi Registry*
- *Chapter 9, Monitoring and Logging Data Pipelines*
- *Chapter 10, Deploying Your Data Pipelines*
- *Chapter 11, Building a Production Data Pipeline*

7

Features of a Production Pipeline

In this chapter, you will learn several features that make a data pipeline ready for production. You will learn about building data pipelines that can be run multiple times without changing the results (idempotent). You will also learn what to do if transactions fail (atomicity). And you will learn about validating data in a staging environment. This chapter will use a sample data pipeline that I currently run in production.

For me, this pipeline is a bonus, and I am not concerned with errors, or missing data. Because of this, there are elements missing in this pipeline that should be present in a mission critical, or production, pipeline. Every data pipeline will have different acceptable rates of errors – missing data – but in production, your pipelines should have some extra features that you have yet to learn.

In this chapter, we're going to cover the following main topics:

- Staging and validating data
- Building idempotent data pipelines
- Building atomic data pipelines

Staging and validating data

When building production data pipelines, staging and validating data become extremely important. While you have seen basic data validation and cleaning in *Chapter 5, Cleaning, Transforming, and Enriching Data*, in production, you will need a more formal and automated way of performing these tasks. The next two sections will walk you through how to accomplish staging and validating data in production.

Staging data

In the NiFi data pipeline examples, data was extracted, and then passed along a series of connected processors. These processors performed some tasks on the data and sent the results to the next processor. But what happens if a processor fails? Do you start all over from the beginning? Depending on the source data, that may be impossible. This is where staging comes in to play. We will divide staging in to two different types: the staging of files or database dumps, and the staging of data in a database that is ready to be loaded into a warehouse.

Staging of files

The first type of staging we will discuss is the staging of data in files following extraction from a source, usually a transactional database. Let's walk through a common scenario to see why we would need this type of staging.

You are a data engineering at Widget Co – a company that has disrupted widget making and is the only online retailer of widgets. Every day, people from all over the world order widgets on the company website. Your boss has instructed you to build a data pipeline that takes sales from the website and puts them in a data warehouse every hour so that analysts can query the data and create reports.

Since sales are worldwide, let's assume the only data transformation required is the conversion of the local sales date and time to be in GMT. This data pipeline should be straightforward and is shown in the following screenshot:

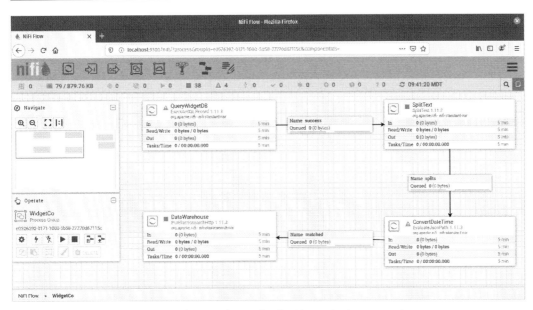

Figure 7.1 – A data pipeline to load widget sales into a warehouse

The preceding data pipeline queries the widget database. It passes the records as a single flowfile to the SplitText processor, which sends each record to the processor, which will convert the date and time to GMT. Lastly, it loads the results in the data warehouse.

But what happens when you split the records, and then a date conversion fails? You can just re-query the database, right? No, you can't, because transactions are happening every minute and the transaction that failed was canceled and is no longer in the database, or they changed their order and now want a red widget and not the five blue widgets they initially ordered. Your marketing team will not be happy because they no longer know about these changes and cannot plan for how to convert these sales.

The point of the example is to demonstrate that in a transactional database, transactions are constantly happening, and data is being modified. Running a query produces a set of results that may be completely different if you run the same query 5 minutes later, and you have now lost that original data. This is why you need to stage your extracts.

If the preceding pipeline example is used for staging, you will end up with a pipeline like the example shown in the following screenshot:

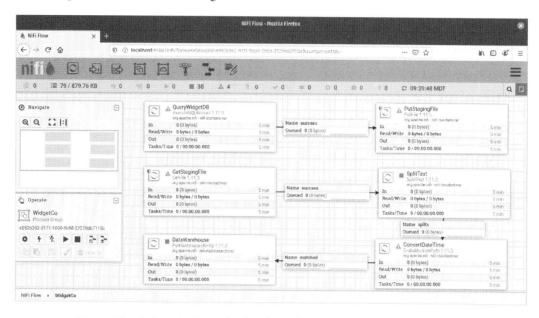

Figure 7.2 – A data pipeline to load widget sales into a warehouse using staging

The preceding data pipeline is displayed as two graphs. The first graph queries the widget database and puts the results in a file on disk. This is the staging step. From here, the next graph will load the data from the staging file, split the records into flowfiles, convert the dates and times, and finally, load it into the warehouse. If this portion of the pipeline crashes, or you need to replay your pipeline for any reason, you can then just reload the CSV by restarting the second half of the data pipeline. You have a copy of the database at the time of the original query. If, 3 months from now, your warehouse is corrupted, you could replay your data pipeline with the data at every query, even though the database is completely different.

Another benefit of having copies of database extracts in CSV files is that it reduces the load in terms of replaying your pipeline. If your queries are resource intensive, perhaps they can only be run at night, or if the systems you query belong to another department, agency, or company. Instead of having to use their resources again to fix a mistake, you can just use the copy.

In the Airflow data pipelines you have built up to this point, you have staged your queries. The way Airflow works encourages good practices. Each task has saved the results to a file, and then you have loaded that file in the next task. In NiFi, however, your queries have been sent, usually to the `SplitRecords` or `Text` processor, to the next processor in the pipeline. This is not good practice for running pipelines in production and will no longer be the case in examples from here on in.

Staging in databases

Staging data in files is helpful during the extract phase of a data pipeline. On the other end of the pipeline, the load stage, it is better to stage your data in a database, and preferably, the same database as the warehouse. Let's walk through another example to see why.

You have queried your data widget database and staged the data. The next data pipeline picks up the data, transforms it, and then loads it into the warehouse. But now what happens if loading does not work properly? Perhaps records went in and everything looks successful, but the mapping is wrong, and dates are strings. Notice I didn't say the load failed. You will learn about handling load failures later in this chapter.

Without actually loading the data into a database, you will only be able to guess what issues you may experience. By staging, you will load the data into a replica of your data warehouse. Then you can run validation suites and queries to see whether you get the results you expect – for example, you could run a `select count(*)` query from the table to see whether you get the correct number of records back. This will allow you to know exactly what issues you may have, or don't have, if all went well.

A data pipeline for Widget Co that uses staging at both ends of the pipeline should look like the pipeline in the following screenshot:

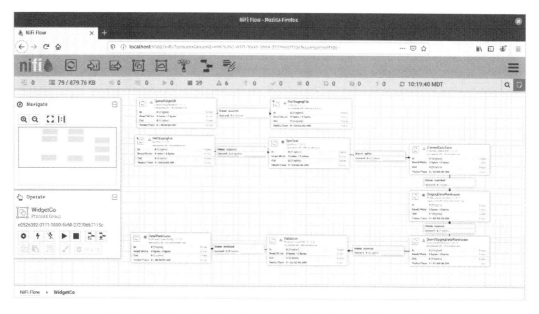

Figure 7.3 – A production using staging at both ends of the pipeline

The data pipeline in the preceding screenshot queries the widget database and stages the results in a file. The next stage picks up the file and converts the dates and times. The point of departure from the earlier example is that the data pipeline now loads the data into a replica of the data warehouse. The new segment of the data pipeline then queries this replica, performs some validation, and then loads it into the final database or warehouse.

> **ETL versus ELT**
>
> So far, you have seen Extract, Transform, and Load. However, there is a growing shift toward an Extract, Load, and Transform process. In the ELT process, data is staged in a database immediately after the extract ion without any transformations. You handle all of the transformations in the database. This is very helpful if you are using SQL-based transformation tools. There is no right or wrong way, only preferences and use cases.

By staging data at the front and end of your data pipeline, you are now better suited for handling errors and for validating the data as it moves through your pipeline. Do not think that these are the only two places where data can be staged, or that data must be staged in files. You can stage your data after every transformation in your data pipeline. Doing so will make debugging errors easier and allow you to pick up at any point in the data pipeline after an error. As your transformations become more time consuming, this may become more helpful.

You staged the extraction from the widget database in a file, but there is no reason to prevent you from extracting the data to a relational or noSQL database. Dumping data to files is slightly less complicated than loading it into a database – you don't need to handle schemas or build any additional infrastructure.

While staging data is helpful for replaying pipelines, handling errors, and debugging your pipeline, it is also helpful in the validation stages of your pipeline. In the next section, you will learn how to use Great Expectations to build validation suites on both file and database staged data.

Validating data with Great Expectations

With your data staged in either a file or a database, you have the perfect opportunity to validate it. In *Chapter 5, Cleaning, Transforming, and Enriching Data*, you used pandas to perform exploratory data analysis and gain insight into what columns existed, find counts of null values, look at ranges of values within columns, and examine the data types in each column. Pandas is powerful and, by using methods such as `value_counts` and `describe`, you can gain a lot of insight into your data, but there are tools that make validation much cleaner and make your expectations of the data much more obvious.

The library you will learn about in this section is **Great Expectations**. The following is a screenshot of the Great Expectations home page, where you can join and get involved with it:

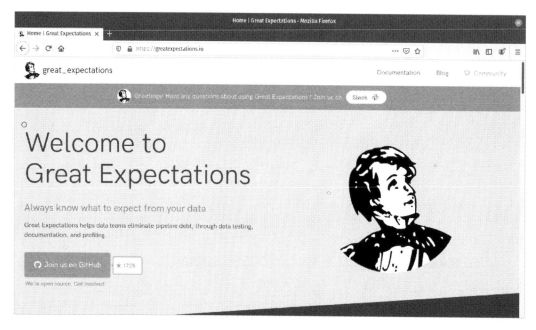

Figure 7.4 – Great Expectations Python library for validating your data, and more

Why Great Expectations? Because with Great Expectations, you can specify human-readable expectations and let the library handle the implementation. For example, you can specify that the age column should not have null values, in your code, with the following line:

```
expect_column_values_to_not_be_null('age')
```

Great Expectations will handle the logic behind doing this irrespective of whether your data is in a DataFrame or in a database. The same expectation will run on either data context.

Getting started with Great Expectations

Installing Great Expectations can be done with pip3 as shown:

```
pip3 install great_expectations
```

To view the documents that Great Expectations generates, you will also need to have Jupyter Notebook available on your machine. You can install Notebook with `pip3` as well:

```
pip3 install jupyter
```

With the requirements installed, you can now set up a project. Create a directory at `$HOME/peoplepipeline` and press *Enter*. You can do this on Linux using the following commands:

```
mkdir $HOME/peoplepipeline
cd $HOME/peoplepipeline
```

Now that you are in the project directory, before you set up Great Expectations, we will dump a sample of the data we will be working with. Using the code from *Chapter 3, Reading and Writing Files*, we will generate 1,000 records relating to people. The code is as follows:

```
from faker import Faker
import csv
output=open('people.csv','w')
fake=Faker()
header=['name','age','street','city','state','zip','lng','lat']
mywriter=csv.writer(output)
mywriter.writerow(header)
for r in range(1000):
    mywriter.writerow([fake.name(),fake.random_int(min=18,
    max=80, step=1), fake.street_address(), fake.city(),fake.
    state(),fake.zipcode(),fake.longitude(),fake.latitude()])
output.close()
```

The preceding code creates a CSV file with records about people. We will put this CSV file into the project directory.

Now you can set up Great Expectations on this project by using the command-line interface. The following line will initialize your project:

```
great_expectations init
```

You will now walk through a series of steps to configure Great Expectations. First, Great Expectations will ask you whether you are ready to proceed. Your terminal should look like the following screenshot:

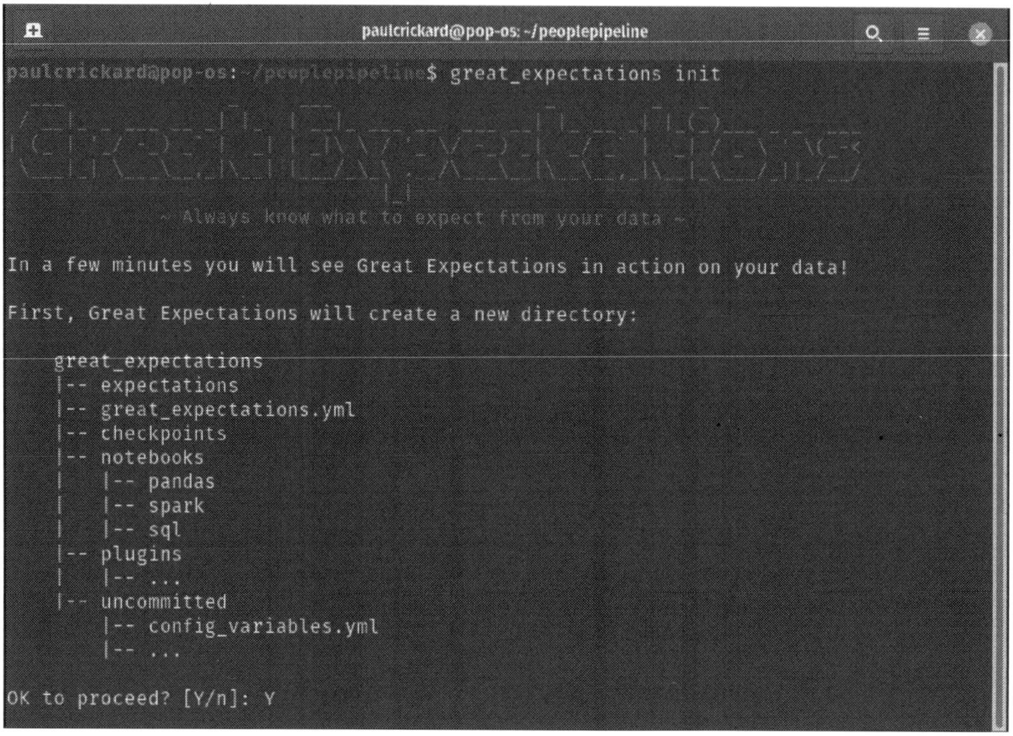

Figure 7.5 – Initializing Great Expectations on a project

Having entered *Y* and pressed *Enter*, you will be prompted with a series of questions:

```
What data would you like Great Expectations to connect
to?
What are you processing your files with?
Enter the path (relative or absolute) of a data file.
Name the new expectation suite [people.warning].
```

The answers to the questions are shown in the following screenshot, but it should be `Files`, `Pandas`, where you put your file, and whatever you would like to name it:

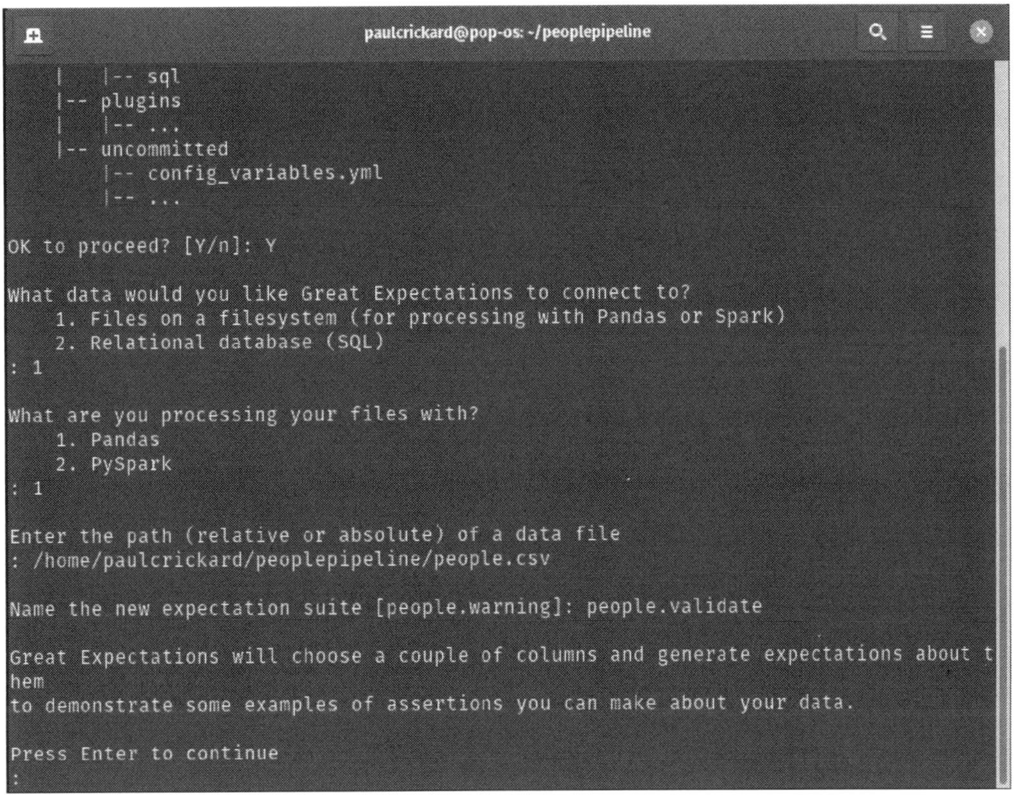

```
paulcrickard@pop-os: ~/peoplepipeline

    |    |-- sql
    |-- plugins
    |    |-- ...
    |-- uncommitted
         |-- config_variables.yml
         |-- ...

OK to proceed? [Y/n]: Y

What data would you like Great Expectations to connect to?
    1. Files on a filesystem (for processing with Pandas or Spark)
    2. Relational database (SQL)
: 1

What are you processing your files with?
    1. Pandas
    2. PySpark
: 1

Enter the path (relative or absolute) of a data file
: /home/paulcrickard/peoplepipeline/people.csv

Name the new expectation suite [people.warning]: people.validate

Great Expectations will choose a couple of columns and generate expectations about t
hem
to demonstrate some examples of assertions you can make about your data.

Press Enter to continue
:
```

Figure 7.6 – Initializing Great Expectations by answering questions

When Great Expectations has finished running, it will tell you it's done, give you a path to the document it has generated, and open the document in your browser. The documents will look like the following screenshot:

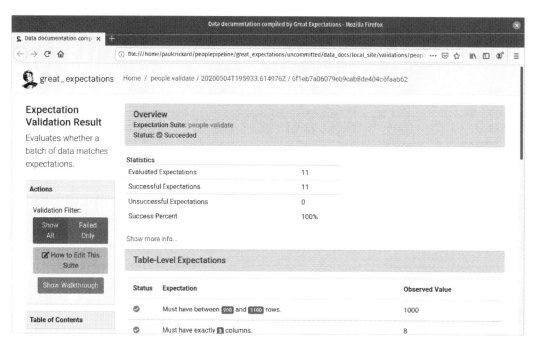

Figure 7.7 – Documentation generated by Great Expectations

The preceding screenshot shows the documentation generated for the Great Expectations Suite. You can see there are **11** expectations and we have passed all of them. The expectations are very basic, specifying how many records should exist and what columns should exist in what order. Also, in the code I specified an age range. So, **age** has a minimum and maximum value. Ages have to be greater than 17 and less than 81 to pass the validation. You can see a sample of the expectations generated by scrolling. I have shown some of mine in the following screenshot:

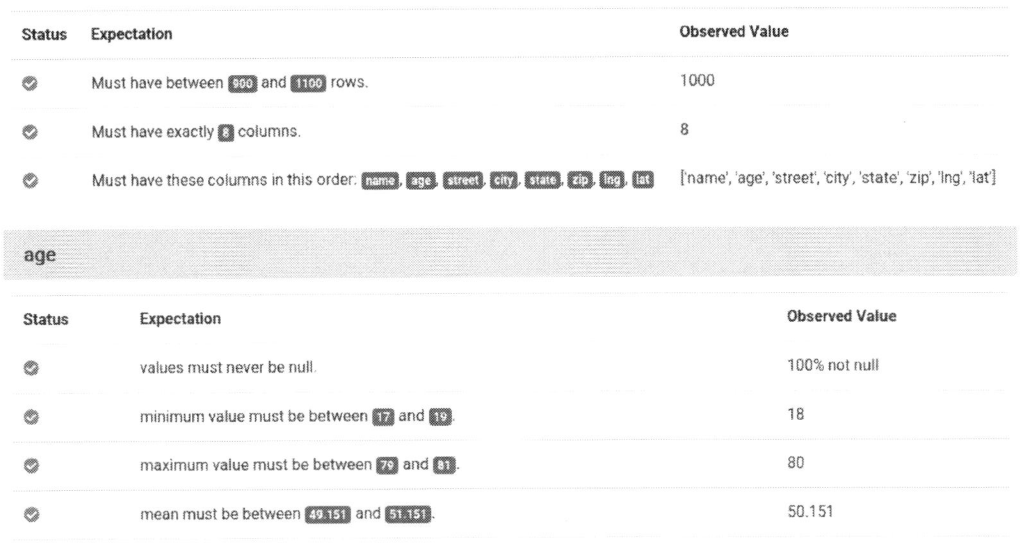

Status	Expectation	Observed Value
✓	Must have between `900` and `1100` rows.	1000
✓	Must have exactly `8` columns.	8
✓	Must have these columns in this order: `name`, `age`, `street`, `city`, `state`, `zip`, `lng`, `lat`	['name', 'age', 'street', 'city', 'state', 'zip', 'lng', 'lat']

age

Status	Expectation	Observed Value
✓	values must never be null.	100% not null
✓	minimum value must be between `17` and `19`.	18
✓	maximum value must be between `79` and `81`.	80
✓	mean must be between `49.151` and `51.151`.	50.151

Figure 7.8 – Sample generated expectations

As you can see, the expectations are very rigid – age must never be null, for example. Let's edit the expectations. You have installed Jupyter Notebook, so you can run the following command to launch your expectation suite in a single step:

```
great_expectations suite edit people.validate
```

Your browser will open a Jupyter notebook and should look like the following screenshot:

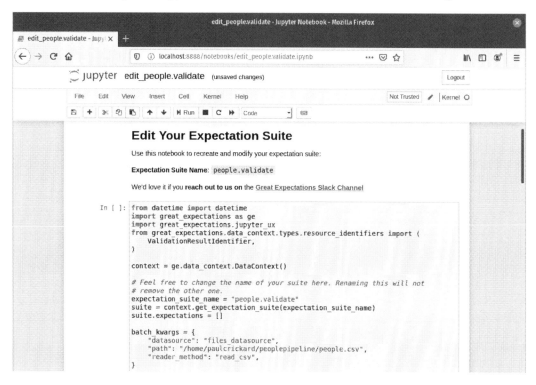

Figure 7.9 – Your expectation suite in a Jupyter notebook

Some items should stand out in the code – the expectation suite name, and the path to your data file in the `batch_kwargs` variable. As you scroll through, you will see the expectations with headers for their type. If you scroll to the `Table_Expectation(s)` header, I will remove the row count expectation by deleting the cell, or by deleting the code in the cell, as shown in the following screenshot:

Table Expectation(s)

```
In [ ]: batch.expect_table_row_count_to_be_between(max_value=1100, min_value=900)
```

```
In [ ]: batch.expect_table_column_count_to_equal(value=8)
```

```
In [ ]: batch.expect_table_columns_to_match_ordered_list(
            column_list=["name", "age", "street", "city", "state", "zip", "lng", "lat"]
        )
```

Figure 7.10 – Table Expectation(s)

The other expectation to edit is under the age header. I will remove an expectation, specifically, the expect_quantile_values_to_be_between expectation. The exact line is shown in the following screenshot:

age

```
In [ ]: batch.expect_column_values_to_not_be_null("age")
```

```
In [ ]: batch.expect_column_min_to_be_between("age", max_value=19, min_value=17)
```

```
In [ ]: batch.expect_column_max_to_be_between("age", max_value=81, min_value=79)
```

```
In [ ]: batch.expect_column_mean_to_be_between("age", max_value=51.151, min_value=49.151)
```

```
In [ ]: batch.expect_column_median_to_be_between("age", max_value=52.0, min_value=50.0)
```

```
In [ ]: batch.expect_column_quantile_values_to_be_between(
            "age",
            quantile_ranges={
                "quantiles": [0.05, 0.25, 0.5, 0.75, 0.95],
                "value_ranges": [[21, 23], [34, 36], [50, 52], [64, 66], [76, 78]],
            },
        )
```

Figure 7.11 – Age expectations with the quantile expectations to be removed

You can continue to remove expectations, or you can add new ones, or even just modify the values of existing expectations. You can find a glossary of available expectations at https://docs.greatexpectations.io/en/latest/reference/glossary_of_expectations.html.

Once you have made all of the changes and are satisfied, you can run the entire notebook to save the changes to your expectation suite. The following screenshot shows how to do that – select **Cell | Run All**:

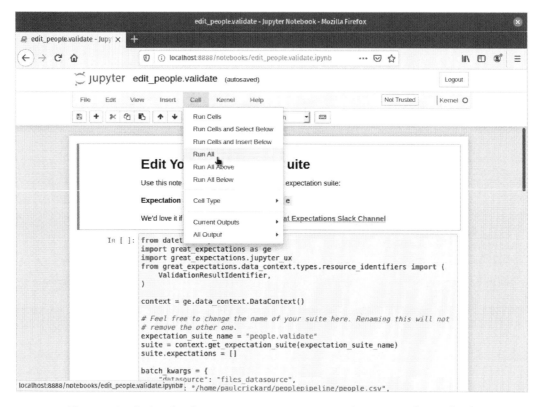

Figure 7.12 – Saving the changes to your expectation suite by running the notebook

Now that you have an expectation suite, it is time to add it to your pipeline. In the next two sections, you will learn how to add it alongside your pipeline for use with NiFi or embed the code into your pipeline for use with Airflow.

Great Expectations outside the pipeline

So far, you have validated data while you edited the expectation suite inside a Jupyter notebook. You could continue to do that using a library such as Papermill, but that is beyond the scope of this book. In this section, however, you will create a tap and run it from NiFi.

> **Papermill**
>
> Papermill is a library created at Netflix that allows you to create parameterized Jupyter notebooks and run them from the command line. You can change parameters and specify an output directory for the resultant notebook. It pairs well with another Netflix library, Scrapbook. Find them both, along with other interesting projects, including Hydrogen, at `https://github.com/nteract`.

A tap is how Great Expectations creates executable Python files to run against your expectation suite. You can create a new tap using the command-line interface, as shown:

```
great_expectations tap new people.validate
peoplevalidatescript.py
```

The preceding command takes an expectation suite and the name of a Python file to create. When it runs, it will ask you for a data file. I have pointed it to the `people.csv` file that you used in the preceding section when creating the suite. This is the file that the data pipeline will overwrite as it stages data:

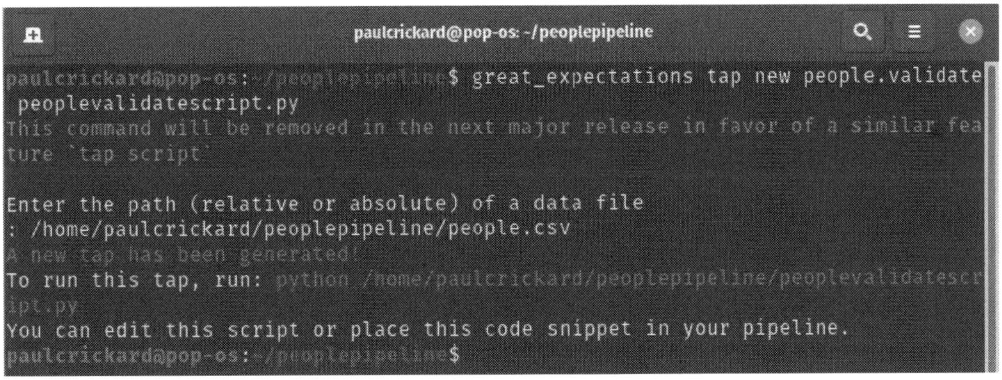

Figure 7.13 – Result of the Python file at the specified location

If you run the tap, you should see that it succeeded, as shown in the following screenshot:

Figure 7.14 – Great Expectation tap run

You are now ready to build a pipeline in NiFi and validate your data using Great Expectations. The next section will walk you through the process.

Great Expectations in NiFi

Combining NiFi and Great Expectations requires a few modifications to the tap you created in the previous section. First, you will need to change all the exits to be 0. If you have a system.exit(1) exit, NiFi processors will crash because the script failed. We want the script to close successfully, even if the results are not, because the second thing you will change are the print statements. Change the print statements to be a JSON string with a result key and a pass or fail value. Now, even though the script exits successfully, we will know in NiFi whether it actually passed or failed. The code of the tap is shown in the following code block, with the modifications in bold:

```python
import sys
from great_expectations import DataContext
context = DataContext("/home/paulcrickard/peoplepipeline/great_
expectations")
suite = context.get_expectation_suite("people.validate")
batch_kwargs = {
    "path": "/home/paulcrickard/peoplepipeline/people.csv",
    "datasource": "files_datasource",
    "reader_method": "read_csv",
}
batch = context.get_batch(batch_kwargs, suite)
results = context.run_validation_operator(
                              "action_list_operator", [batch])
if not results["success"]:
    print('{"result":"fail"}')
    sys.exit(0)

print('{"result":"pass"}')
sys.exit(0)
```

With the changes to the tap complete, you can now build a data pipeline in NiFi. The following screenshot is the start of a data pipeline using the tap:

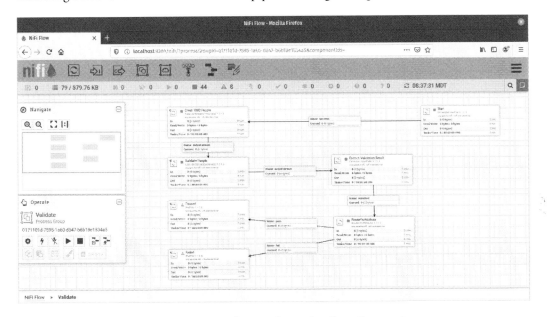

Figure 7.15 – A NiFi data pipeline using Great Expectations

The preceding data pipeline creates 1,000 records and saves it as a CSV file. It then runs the tap on the data and reads in the result — the pass or fail JSON from the script. Lastly, it extracts the result and routes the flowfile to either a pass or fail processor. From there, your data pipeline can continue, or it can log the error. You will walk through the pipeline in the following steps:

1. The data pipeline starts by generating a fake flowfile without any data to trigger the next processor. You could replace this processor with one that queries your transactional database, or that reads files from your data lake. I have scheduled this processor to run every hour.

2. Once the empty flowfile is received, the `ExecuteStreamCommand` processor calls the `loadcsv.py` Python script. This file is from *Chapter 3, Reading and Writing Files*, and uses `Faker` to create 1,000 fake people records. The `ExecuteStreamCommand` processor will read the output from the script. If you had print statements, each line would become a flowfile. The script has one output, and that is `{"status":"Complete"}`.

3. To configure the processor to run the script, you can set the **Working Directory** to the path of your Python script. Set **Command Path** to python3 – if you can run the command with the full path, you do not need to enter it all. Lastly, set **Command Arguments** to the name of the Python file – loadcsv.py. When the processor runs, the output flowfile is shown in the following screenshot:

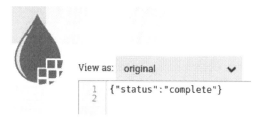

Figure 7.16 – The flowfile shows the JSON string

4. The next processor is also an ExecuteStreamCommand processor. This time, the script will be your tap. The configuration should be the same as in the previous step, except **Command Argument** will be peoplevalidatescript.py. Once the processor completes, the flowfile will contain JSON with a result of pass or fail. The pass flowfile is shown in the following screenshot:

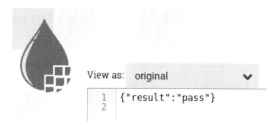

Figure 7.17 – Result of the tap, validation passed

5. The value of the result is extracted in the next processor – EvaluateJsonPath. Adding a new property with the plus button, name it result and set the value to $.result. This will extract the pass or fail value and send it as a flowfile attribute.

6. The next process is `RouteOnAttribute`. This processor allows you to create properties that can be used as a relationship in a connection to another processor, meaning you can send each property to a different path. Creating two new properties – `pass` and `fail`, the values are shown in the following code snippet:

```
${result:startsWith('pass')}
${result:startsWith('fail')}
```

7. The preceding command uses the NiFi expression language to read the value of the result attribute in the flowfile.

8. From here, I have terminated the data pipeline at a `PutFile` processor. But you would now be able to continue by connecting a `pass` and `fail` path to their respective relationships in the previous processor. If it passed, you could read the staged file and insert the data into the warehouse.

In this section, you connected Great Expectations to your data pipeline. The tap was generated using your data, and because of this, the test passed. The pipeline ended with the file being written to disk. However, you could continue the data pipeline to route success to a data warehouse. In the real world, your tests will fail on occasion. In the next section, you will learn how to handle failed tests.

Failing the validation

The validation will always pass because the script we are using generates records that meet the validations rules. What if we changed the script? If you edit the `loadcsv.py` script and change the minimum and maximum age, we can make the validation fail. The edit is shown as follows:

```
fake.random_int(min=1, max=100, step=1)
```

This will create records that are below the minimum and above the maximum—hopefully, because it is random, but 1,000 records should get us there. Once you have edited the script, you can rerun the data pipeline. The final flowfile should have been routed to the `fail` path. Great Expectations creates documents for your validations. If you remember, you saw them initially when you created the validation suite. Now you will have a record of both the passed and failed runs. Using your browser, open the documents. The path is within your project folder. For example, my docs are at the following path:

```
file:///home/paulcrickard/peoplepipeline/great_expectations/
uncommitted/data_docs/local_site/validations/people/
validate/20200505T145722.862661Z/6f1eb7a06079eb9cab8de404c6faa
b62.html
```

The documents should show all your validations runs. The documents will look like the following screenshot:

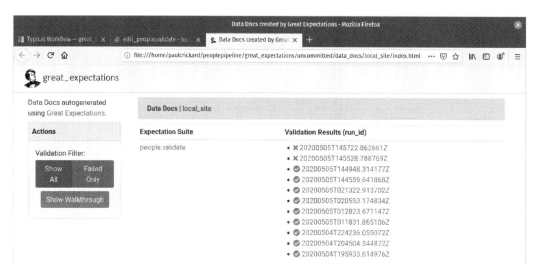

Figure 7.18 – Results of multiple validation runs

The preceding screenshot shows all of the validation runs. You can see the red **x** indicating failures. Click on one of the failed runs to see which expectations were not met. The results should be that both the minimum and maximum age were not met. You should see that this is the case, as shown in the following screenshot:

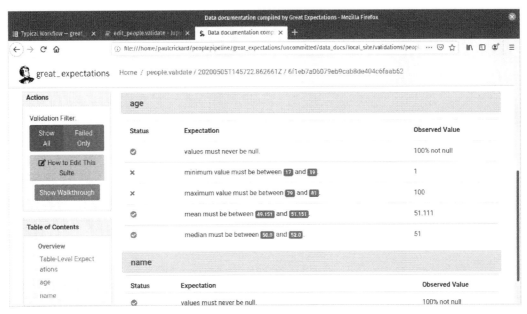

Figure 7.19 – Age expectations have not been met

In this section, you have created a Great Expectations suite and specified expectations for your data. Previously, you would have had to do this manually using DataFrames and a significant amount of code. Now you can use human-readable statements and allow Great Expectations to do the work. You have created a tap that you can run inside your NiFi data pipeline — or that you can schedule using Cron or any other tool.

A quick note on Airflow

In the preceding example, you ran the validation suite outside of your pipeline – the script ran in the pipeline, but was called by a processor. You can also run the code inside the pipeline without having to call it. In Apache Airflow, you can create a validation task that has the code from the tap. To handle the failure, you would need to raise an exception. To do that, import the library in your Airflow code. I have included the libraries that you need to include on top of your standard boilerplate in the following code block:

```
import sys
from great_expectations import DataContext
from airflow.exceptions import AirflowException
from airflow import DAG
from airflow.operators.bash_operator import BashOperator
from airflow.operators.python_operator import PythonOperator
```

After importing all of the libraries, you can write your task, as shown in the following code block:

```
def validateData():
    context = DataContext("/home/paulcrickard/peoplepipeline/
great_expectations")
    suite = context.get_expectation_suite("people.validate")

    batch_kwargs = {
    "path": "/home/paulcrickard/peoplepipeline/people.csv",
    "datasource": "files_datasource",
    "reader_method": "read_csv",
}

    batch = context.get_batch(batch_kwargs, suite)
    results = context.run_validation_operator(
                        "action_list_operator", [batch])

    if not results["success"]:
        raise AirflowException("Validation Failed")
```

The preceding code will throw an error, or it will end if the validation succeeded. However, choosing to handle the failure is up to you. All you need to do is check whether results["success"] is True. You can now code the other functions, create the tasks using PythonOperator, and then set the downstream relationships as you have in all the other Airflow examples.

The following sections will discuss two other features of a production data pipeline – idempotence and atomicity.

Building idempotent data pipelines

A crucial feature of a production data pipeline is that it is idempotent. Idempotent is defined as *denoting an element of a set that is unchanged in value when multiplied or otherwise operated on by itself.*

In data science, this means that when your pipeline fails, which is not a matter of *if*, but *when*, it can be rerun and the results are the same. Or, if you accidently click run on your pipeline three times in a row by mistake, there are not duplicate records – even if you accidently click run multiple times in a row.

In *Chapter 3, Reading and Writing Files*, you created a data pipeline that generated 1,000 records of people and put that data in an Elasticsearch database. If you let that pipeline run every 5 minutes, you would have 2,000 records after 10 minutes. In this example, the records are all random and you may be OK. But what if the records were rows queried from another system?

Every time the pipeline runs, it would insert the same records over and over again. How you create idempotent data pipelines depends on what systems you are using and how you want to store your data.

In the SeeClickFix data pipeline from the previous chapter, you queried the SeeClickFix API. You did not specify any rolling time frame that would only grab the most recent records, and your backfill code grabbed all the archived issues. If you run this data pipeline every 8 hours, as it was scheduled, you will grab new issues, but also issues you already have.

The SeeClickFix data pipeline used the `upsert` method in Elasticsearch to make the pipeline idempotent. Using the `EvaluteJsonPath` processor, you extracted the issue ID and then used that as the `Identifier Attribute` in the `PutElasticsearchHttp` processor. You also set the **Index Operation** to `upsert`. This is the equivalent of using an update in SQL. No records will be duplicated, and records will only be modified if there have been changes.

Another way to make the data pipeline idempotent, and one that is advocated by some functional data engineering advocates, is to create a new index or partition every time your data pipeline is run. If you named your index with the datetime stamped as a suffix, you would get a new index with distinct records every time the pipeline runs. This not only makes the data pipeline idempotent; it creates an immutable object out of your database indexes. An index will never change; just new indexes will be added.

Building atomic data pipelines

The final feature of a production data pipeline that we will discuss in this chapter is atomicity. Atomicity means that if a single operation in a transaction fails, then all of the operations fail. If you are inserting 1,000 records into the database, as you did in *Chapter 3, Reading and Writing Files*, if one record fails, then all 1,000 fail.

In SQL databases, the database will roll back all the changes if record number 500 fails, and it will no longer attempt to continue. You are now free to retry the transaction. Failures can occur for many reasons, some of which are beyond your control. If the power or the network goes down while you are inserting records, do you want those records to be saved to the database? You would then need to determine which records in a transaction succeeded and which failed and then retry only the failed records. This would be much easier than retrying the entire transaction.

In the NiFi data pipelines you have built, there was no atomicity. In the SeeClickFix example, each issue was sent as a flowfile and upserted in Elasticsearch. The only atomicity that existed is that every field in the document (issue) succeeded or failed. But we could have had a situation where all the issues failed except one, and that would have resulted in the data pipeline succeeding.

Elasticsearch does not have atomic transactions, so any data pipeline that implements Elasticsearch would need to handle that within the logic. For example, you could track every record that is indexed in Elasticsearch as well as every failure relationship. If there is a failure relationship during the run, you would then delete all the successfully indexed issues. An example data pipeline is shown in the following screenshot:

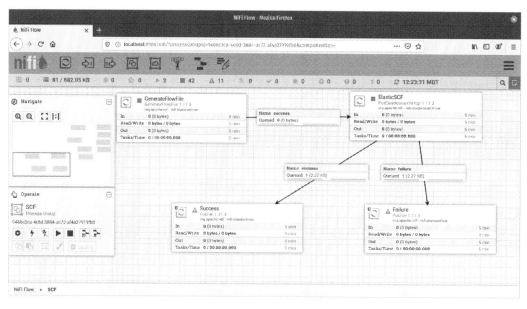

Figure 7.20 – Building atomicity into a data pipeline

The preceding data pipeline created two flowfiles; one succeeded and one failed. The contents of both are put in files on disk. From here, your data pipeline could list the files in the failed directory. If there was one or more, it could then read the success files and remove them from Elasticsearch.

This is not elegant, but atomicity is important. Debugging data pipeline failures when the failure is only partial is extremely difficult and time consuming. The extra work required to incorporate atomicity is well worth it.

SQL databases have atomicity built into the transactions. Using a library such as psycopg2, you can roll multiple inserts, updates, or deletes into a single transaction and guarantee that the results will either be that all operations were successful, or the transaction failed.

Creating data pipelines that are idempotent and atomic requires additional work when creating your data pipeline. But without these two features, you will have data pipelines that will make changes to your results if accidently run multiple times (not idempotent) or if there are records that are missing (not atomic). Debugging these issues is difficult, so the time spent on making your data pipelines idempotent and atomic is well spent.

Summary

In this chapter, you learned three key features of production data pipelines: staging and validation, idempotency, and atomicity. You learned how to use Great Expectations to add production-grade validation to your data pipeline staged data. You also learned how you could incorporate idempotency and atomicity into your pipelines. With these skills, you can build more robust, production-ready pipelines.

In the next chapter, you will learn how to use version control with the NiFi registry.

8
Version Control with the NiFi Registry

In the previous chapters, you built several data pipelines, but we have left out a very important component—version control. Any good software developer will almost always set up version control on their project before they start writing any code. Building data pipelines for production is no different. Data engineers use many of the same tools and processes as software engineers. Using version control allows you to make changes without the fear of breaking your data pipeline. You will always be able to roll back changes to previous versions. The NiFi registry also allows you to connect new NiFi instances and have full access to all your existing data pipelines. In this chapter, we're going to cover the following main topics:

- Installing and configuring the NiFi Registry
- Using the Registry in NiFi
- Versioning your data pipelines
- Using git-persistence with the NiFi Registry

Installing and configuring the NiFi Registry

When you hear about version control, you are probably used to hearing about Git. Later in this chapter, we will use Git, but Apache NiFi has a sub-project that can handle all of our version control needs—the NiFi Registry:

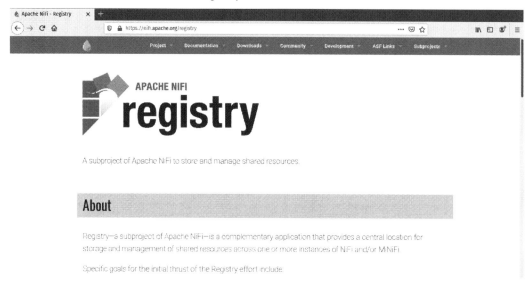

Figure 8.1 – The NiFi Registry home page

Let's now install the Registry.

Installing the NiFi Registry

To install the NiFi Registry, go to the website at `https://nifi.apache.org/ registry` and scroll to **Releases**. The following screenshot shows the available releases:

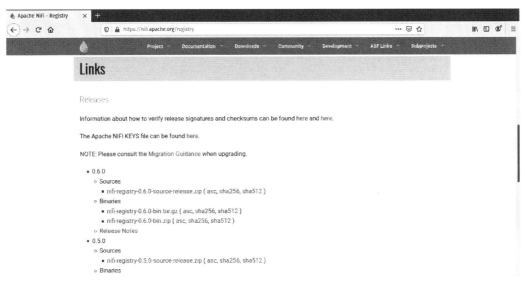

Figure 8.2 – The NiFi Registry

You will see a source release and two binaries for the current version, which, at the time of writing, is 0.6.0. On Windows, you can download the zip version, but since I am on Linux, I will download the `nifi-registry-0.6.0-bin.tar.gz` file.

Once the file is downloaded, move it to your home directory, extract the contents, then delete the archive using the following lines:

```
mv Downloads/nifi-r* ~/
tar -xvzf nifi-registry-0.6.0-bin.tar.gz
rm nifi-registry-0.6.0-bin.tar.gz
```

You will now have a folder named `nifi-registry-0.6.0`. To run the Registry using the default settings (HTTP on port `18080`), from the directory, use the following command:

```
sudo ./bin/nifi-registry.sh start
```

Once you have launched the Registry, browse to it at `http://localhost:18080/ nifi-registry`. You should see the following screen:

Figure 8.3 – The NiFi Registry

As you can see, it is blank, and the user is anonymous. You have not changed any defaults or added any authentication, and you have not added any data pipelines yet.

The NiFi Registry uses buckets to hold your data pipelines. A bucket is similar to a folder. You can either group similar pipelines, or create a folder for each source, or for destinations, or however you see fit to meet your needs and use cases. The next section will walk you through configuring the NiFi Registry.

Configuring the NiFi Registry

With the Registry up and running, you will need to create a folder to hold your data pipelines. To create a folder, click the wrench in the top-right corner of the screen. A popup will appear on the screen. Click the **NEW BUCKET** button. On the next popup, enter the bucket name, as shown in the following screenshot:

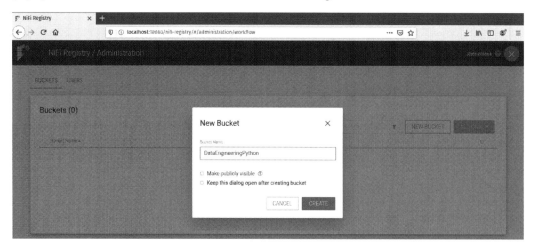

Figure 8.4 – Creating a new bucket

Once the bucket is created, you will see it on the main registry screen. Your registry should now look like the following screenshot:

Figure 8.5 – Registry with the new bucket

Now that you have the Registry deployed and a bucket created, you are ready to register it with NiFi and start versioning your data pipelines. The next section will walk you through this.

Using the Registry in NiFi

The Registry is up and running, and now you need to tell NiFi about it so that you can start using it to version your data pipelines. The NiFi GUI will handle all of the configuration and versioning. In the next section, you will add the Registry to NiFi.

Adding the Registry to NiFi

To add the Registry to NiFi, click on the waffle menu in the top-right corner of the window, then select **Controller Settings** from the drop-down menu, as shown in the following screenshot:

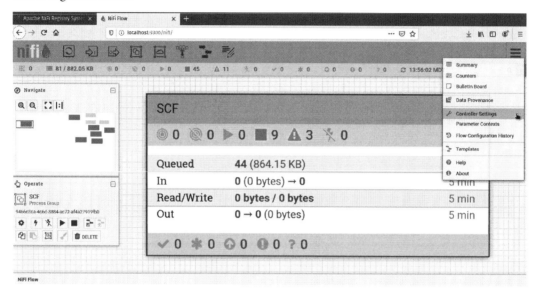

Figure 8.6 – Controller Settings in Nifi

In the **Controller Settings** popup, there are several tabs. You will select the last tab—**Registry Clients**. Clicking the plus sign at the top right of the window, you will add your Registry as shown in the following screenshot:

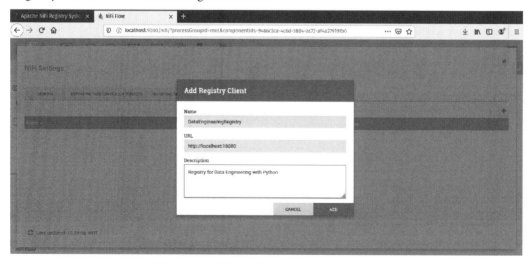

Figure 8.7 – Adding the NiFi Registry to NiFi

After clicking the **ADD** button, you will have your Registry connected to NiFi. Close the window and you will be in your main NiFi canvas. You are now ready to version your data pipelines.

Versioning your data pipelines

You can use the NiFi Registry to version your data pipelines inside of a processor group. I have NiFi running and the canvas zoomed in to the `SeeClickFix` processor group from *Chapter 6, Building a 311 Data Pipeline*. To start versioning this data pipeline, right-click on the title bar of the processor group and select **Version | Start version control**, as shown in the following screenshot:

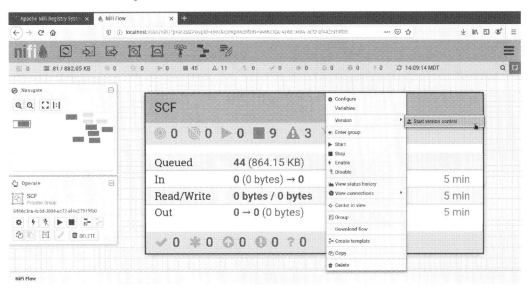

Figure 8.8 – Starting version control on a processor group

Your processor group is now being tracked by version control. You will see a green checkmark on the left of the processor group title box, as shown in the following screenshot:

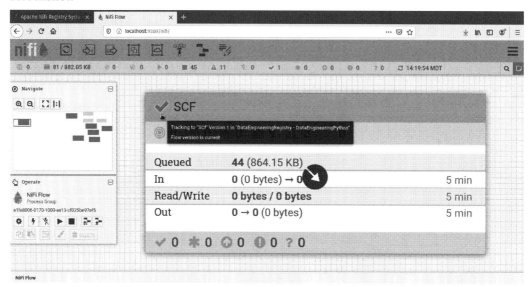

Figure 8.9 – Processor group using version control

If you browse back to the NiFi Registry, you will see that **Scf-DataEngineeringPython** is being tracked. You will also see the details by expanding the bar. The details show your description and the version notes (**First Commit**), as well as some identifiers. The results are shown in the following screenshot:

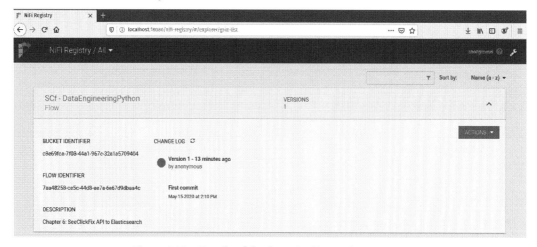

Figure 8.10 – Details of the data pipeline in the Registry

You are not tracking a data pipeline in the Registry. In the next section, you will make changes and update the Registry.

Editing a versioned pipeline

In a normal workflow, you would create a processor group and add it to the Registry (in other words, start versioning the processor). You would then make changes, and then commit those changes to the Registry and always make sure you were using the appropriate version.

Let's make a change to the SeeClickFix data pipeline. Your pipeline is running, and everything is working perfectly. Then your supervisor says that there is a new warehouse that needs to start receiving SeeClickFix data. You don't need to build a new data pipeline; you just need to add the warehouse to your current pipeline. Entering the processor group, I have added a `NewDataWarehouse` processor alongside the original. The changes are highlighted in the following screenshot:

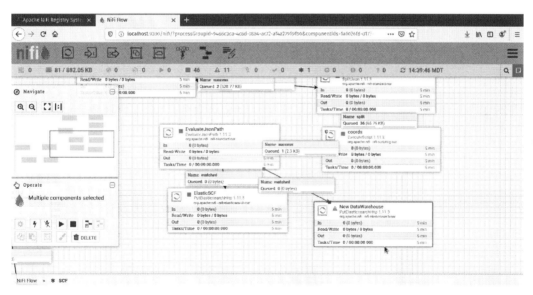

Figure 8.11 – Adding a new data warehouse to the data pipeline

Exit the processor group back to the main canvas. Looking at the title bar of the processor group, you will see the green checkmark is gone and you have an asterisk. Hovering over it will show you local changes made, as shown in the following screenshot:

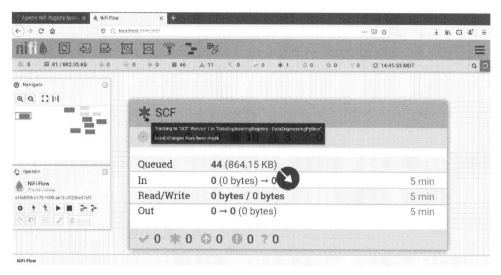

Figure 8.12 – Local changes have been made inside the processor group

After making any changes, you need to commit those changes, and add them to the Registry. Right-click on the title bar and select **Version**. Before committing the local changes, let's view the changes. Select **Show Local Changes**. The following screenshot shows the changes:

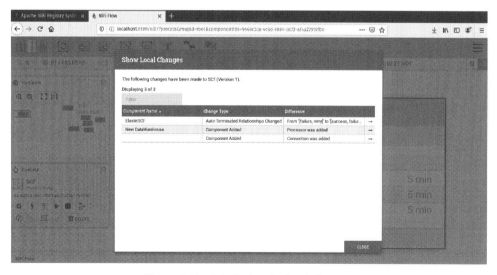

Figure 8.13 – Displaying the local changes

As you can see in the preceding screenshot, a processor and a relationship were added. Now you can select **Version | Commit Local Changes** to add them to the Registry. You will be prompted to add a description. Once saved, you will now have a green checkmark in the title bar. The NiFi Registry will now show that you have two versions and will show the details of the most recent version.

With multiple versions, you can now right-click on the title bar and select **Version | Change Version**. Changing to **Version 1** will result in an orange circle with an upward arrow in it alerting you that you are not using the most current version.

With the processor group tracked in version control, you can make changes, roll them back, and commit new changes. If you make a mistake, you can roll back your work and start again. But you can also import a processor that other users may have created in their local development copy of NiFi. The next section will show you how.

Importing a processor group from the NiFi Registry

Let's imagine that you and another worker are building data pipelines in your own local copies of NiFi. You both commit your changes to the NiFi Registry, just like software developers do with Git. Now you have been tasked with fixing an issue your coworker is struggling with. How can you use their work? You could have them export a template, and you could import it. This was how things used to be done before the Registry. But now, you will use the Registry.

Drag a processor group to the NiFi canvas. Notice that underneath the textbox for naming the group, there is now an option to import, as shown in the following screenshot:

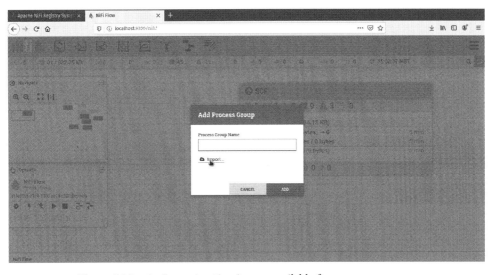

Figure 8.14 – An Import option is now available for processor groups

Now that NiFi has access to the NiFi Registry, it has added the option to import processor groups. By clicking **Import**, you will be able to select a registry, a bucket, and a flow. In the following screenshot, I have selected the **SCf** flow:

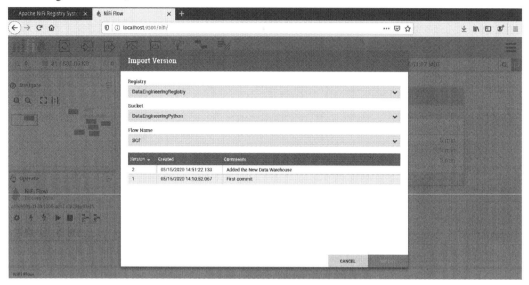

Figure 8.15 – Selecting the flow and version

After importing the flow, you can see it is now added to the canvas. In the previous section, I changed the processor group back to **Version 1**, so you can see that I have that version, with the orange circle and arrow, as well as the imported current version with the green check mark.

When you bring in a new data engineer, or set up a new NiFi instance, you can import all the production pipelines into the new environment. This guarantees everyone is working from the same source, but also that all changes are tracked and shared between development environments.

Using git-persistence with the NiFi Registry

Just like software developers, you can also use Git to version control your data pipelines. The NiFi Registry allows you to use git-persistence with some configuration. To use Git with your data pipelines, you need to first create a repository.

Log in to GitHub and create a repository for your data pipelines. I have logged in to my account and have created the repository as shown in the following screenshot:

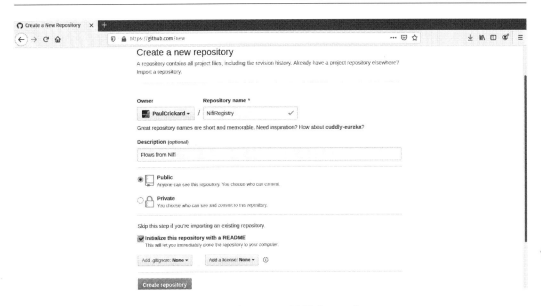

Figure 8.16 – Creating a GitHub repository

After creating a repository, you will need to create an access token for the registry to use to read and write to the repository. In the GitHub **Settings**, go to **Developer settings**, then **Personal access tokens**, then click the **Generate a personal access token** hyperlink shown in the following screenshot:

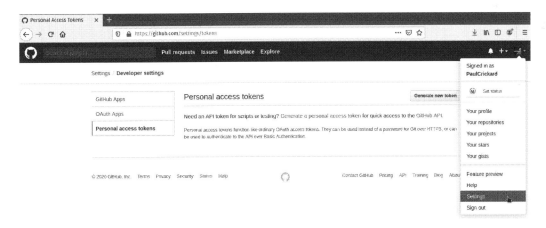

Figure 8.17 – The setting to create an access token

You can then add a note for the token so you can remember what service is using it. Then select the scope access—check the repo heading. The following screenshot shows the settings:

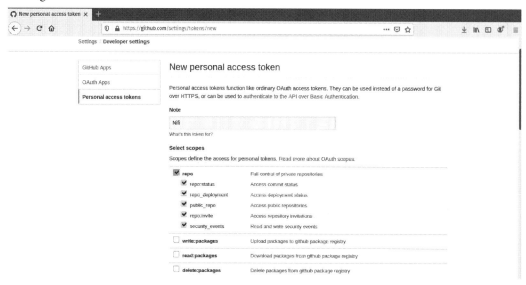

Figure 8.18 – Giving the access token scope

Now, clone the repository to your local filesystem. You can get the link from the GitHub repository by clicking the **Clone or Download** button. Then, run the following command in your terminal to clone it:

```
git clone https://github.com/PaulCrickard/NifiRegistry.git
```

You will see some output and should now have the repository as a folder in the current directory. The output of the command is shown in the following screenshot:

```
paulcrickard@pop-os: $ git clone https://github.com/PaulCrickard/NifiRegistry.git
Cloning into 'NifiRegistry'...
remote: Enumerating objects: 3, done.
remote: Counting objects: 100% (3/3), done.
Unpacking objects: 100% (3/3), done.
remote: Total 3 (delta 0), reused 0 (delta 0), pack-reused 0
```

Figure 8.19 – Cloning the GitHub repository

You will need to enter the GitHub information into the NiFi Registry. You can do this in the `providers.xml` file in the `conf` directory. You will edit the file towards the top under the header named `flowPersistenceProvider`. The configuration is shown in the following screenshot:

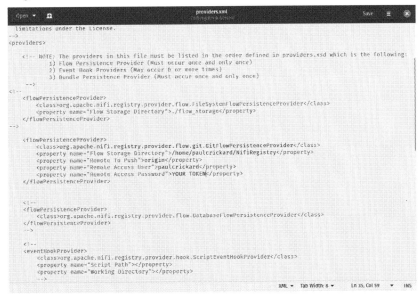

Figure 8.20 – Adding GitHub information to the Registry in providers.xml

After modifying the `providers.xml` file, you will need to restart the Registry. You can restart it using the following command:

```
sudo ./bin/nifi-registry.sh start
```

When the Registry restarts, go to your NiFi canvas and add a third data warehouse to the `SeeClickFix` processor group. When you exit the group, you will see that there are local changes that have not been committed—the green checkmark is gone and there is an asterisk. Right-click on the title menu and select **Version** then **Commit Local Version**. It will take a little longer this time as the files are being sent to your GitHub repository.

Looking at the NiFi Registry, you can see that I now have three versions, as shown in the following screenshot:

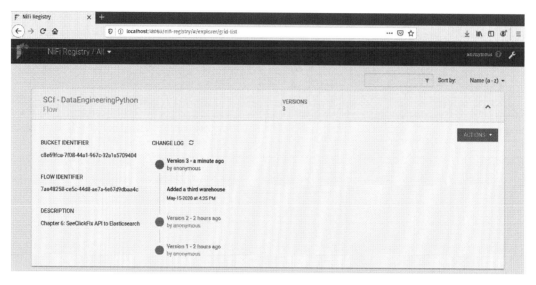

Figure 8.21 – Version 3 is in the Registry

Browsing to the repository, you will see there is a folder created for the name of the bucket in the Registry, and then the flow data has been added. The following screenshot shows the contents of the folder:

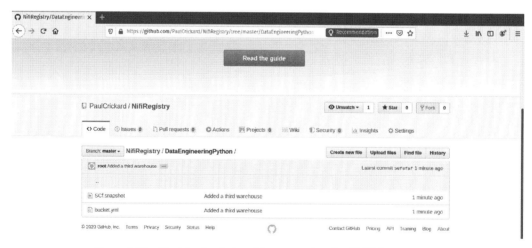

Figure 8.22 – Registry bucket and flows saved to the GitHub repository

Now your data pipelines are using version control through the NiFi Registry and persisted in Git on your local disk and GitHub online.

Congratulations, you now have a fully functional NiFi registry and have saved your data pipelines to a Git repository. At some point in your career, you will be asked to run a data pipeline like you did several months ago. Instead of looking through your files and trying to remember what you did way back then, you will now be able to browse to your NiFi Registry and select the proper version of the data pipeline. And if your server crashes and everything is lost? You can now reinstall NiFi and connect it to your Git-repository-backed NiFi Registry to recover all of your hard work.

Summary

In this chapter, you have learned one of the most important features of production data pipelines: version control. A software developer would not write code without using version control and neither should a data engineer. You have learned how to install and configure the Nifi Registry and how to start tracking version on processor groups. Lastly, you are now able to persist the version to GitHub. Any changes to your data pipelines will be saved and if you need to roll back, you can. As your team grows, all the data engineers will be able to manage the data pipelines and be sure they have the latest versions, all while developing locally.

In the next chapter, you will learn about logging and monitoring your data pipelines. If something goes wrong, and it will, you will need to know about it. Good logging and monitoring of data pipelines will allow you to catch errors when they happen and debug them to restore your data flows.

9
Monitoring Data Pipelines

You now know how to build data pipelines that are production ready—they are idempotent, use atomic transactions, and are version controlled. They are ready to start running in production, but before you can deploy them, you need to be able to monitor them. There will be errors in the code, in the data, in the network, or in other areas outside your control. You will need to know when errors happen, and when things are running as they should.

In this chapter, we're going to cover the following main topics:

- Monitoring NiFi in the GUI
- Monitoring NiFi using processors
- Monitoring NiFi with Python and the REST API

Monitoring NiFi using the GUI

The NiFi GUI provides several ways to monitor your data pipelines. Using the GUI is the simplest way to start monitoring your NiFi instance.

Monitoring NiFi with the status bar

Much of the information you need is on the status bar. The status bar is below the component toolbar and looks like the following screenshot:

Figure 9.1 – Component and status toolbars

Starting at the left of the status bar, let's look at what is being monitored:

- **Active thread**: This lets you know how many threads are running. You can get a sense of tasks and load.

- **Total queued data**: The number of flowfiles and the combined size on disk.

- **Transmitting remote process groups and not transmitting remote process groups**: You can run NiFi on multiple machines or instances on the same machine and allow process groups to communicate. These icons tell you whether they are or are not communicating.

- **Running components, stopped components, invalid components, and disabled components**: These show you the state of your components. Running does not necessarily mean that a component is currently processing data, but that it is on and scheduled to do so.

- **Up-to-date versioned process groups, locally modified versioned process groups, stale versioned process groups, locally modified and stale versioned process groups, and sync failure versioned process groups**: This group of icons show the versioning information of your processor groups. From here you can tell if you have uncommitted changes or are using older versions.

- **Last refresh**: This lets you know when the data in the toolbar is valid for. The refresh is usually every five minutes.

The status bar gives you the monitoring information for all of your processors, but there is also a status toolbar on every processor group and for each processor. You can see the status of the same metrics in the **SCF** processor group, as shown in the following screenshot:

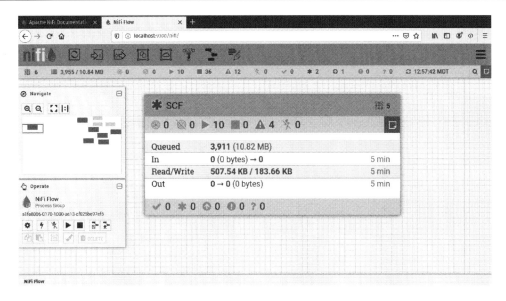

Figure 9.2 – Processor group monitoring

The **In** and **Out** metrics show if there is data flowing into the process group from another processor or group. You will learn how to connect processor groups in the next chapter. The versioning information is not on the toolbar but to the left of the title of the processor group. The red square on the right of the processor group is a **bulletin**. This provides information on errors within the processor group. Hovering over it shows the error, as shown in the following screenshot:

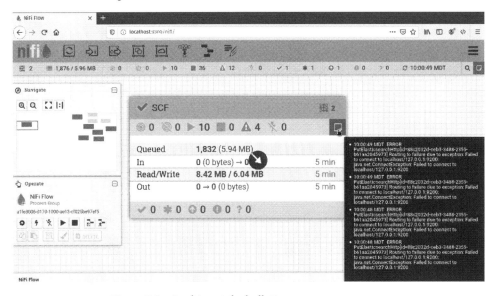

Figure 9.3 – Looking at the bulletin on a processor group

I currently do not have Elasticsearch running and as a result, the processor that sends data to Elasticsearch is failing with a connection timeout. If you enter the processor group, you can see the bulletin on the specific processor, as shown in the following screenshot:

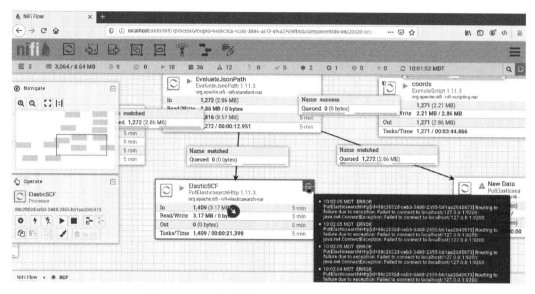

Figure 9.4 – The bulletin on a specific processor

To change the bulletin messages, you can adjust the level in the processor configuration under **Settings**. The **Bulletin Level** dropdown allows you to show more or less based on severity, as shown in the following screenshot:

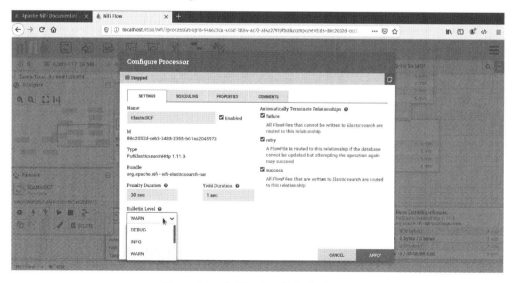

Figure 9.5 – Setting the Bulletin Level

You can see the bulletin information for all your NiFi processors using the **Bulletin Board**, which is accessed from the waffle menu in the upper-right corner of NiFi. Selecting the **Bulletin Board** will show all the messages, as shown in the following screenshot:

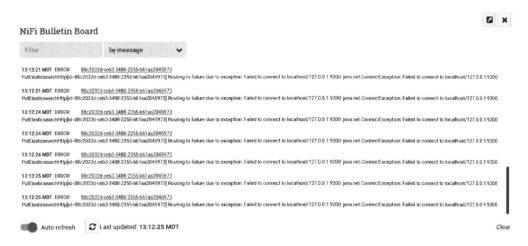

Figure 9.6 – Bulletin Board showing all the notices

Within each processor group, every processor also has status information, as shown in the following screenshot:

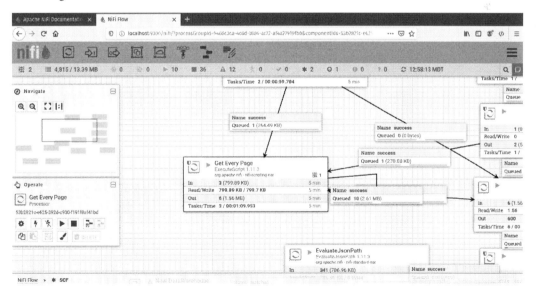

Figure 9.7 – Status of a single processor

The **In** and **Out** metrics in a processor show how much data (the flowfiles size) has passed through the processor in the last five minutes.

Using counters

Similar to bulletins, you can create increment- or decrement-counters. Counters don't tell you that something succeeded or failed, but they can give you an idea of how many flowfiles are being processed at any point in a data pipeline.

In the **SCF** processor group, I have inserted an `UpdateCounter` processor between the `EvaluateJsonPath` and `ElasticSCF` processors. This means that before a flowfile is inserted into Elasticsearch, the counter will be updated. The flow is shown in the following screenshot:

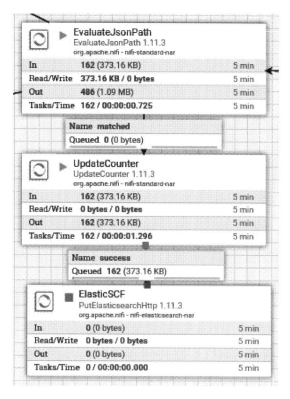

Figure 9.8 – The UpdateCounter processor added to the data pipeline

As you can see in the preceding screenshot, 162 flowfiles were sent through the processor. You will see the results of this later in this section. But first, to configure the processor, you will need to specify **Counter Name** and **Delta**. **Delta** is the number to increment or decrement by. I have configured the processor as shown in the following screenshot:

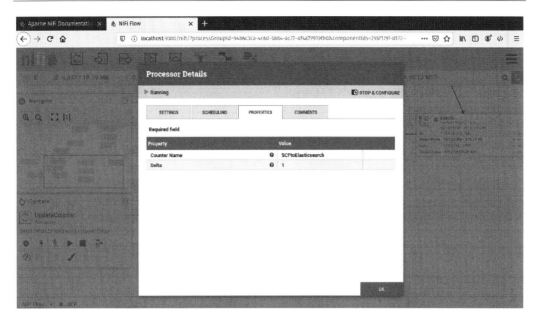

Figure 9.9 – Configuration of the UpdateCounter processor

When you have configured the processor and ran the data pipeline, you will have a count. Earlier, 162 records passed through the data pipeline when I ran it. To see your counters, click the waffle menu in the top-right corner of the NiFi window and select **Counters**, as shown in the following screenshot:

Figure 9.10 – NiFi Counters

The preceding screenshot shows the counts of the counter and an aggregate. If we had other UpdateCounter processors that updated the same counter, it would aggregate those values.

Using the GUI is an excellent way to quickly see how your processor groups and processors are running. But you can also use processors to monitor the data pipeline.

In the previous section, you learned about the NiFi bulletin. You can use background tasks to monitor NiFi and post that data to the NiFi bulletin using reporting tasks. Reporting tasks are like processors that run in the background and perform a task. The results will appear in the bulletin or you can send it to other locations.

To create a reporting task, in the waffle menu, select **Controller Settings**, then navigate to the **Reporting Task** tab. The list should be blank, but you can add a new task using the plus sign on the right-hand corner of the window. You will see a list of tasks that are available. Single-click on one to see the description. You should see a list similar to the following screenshot:

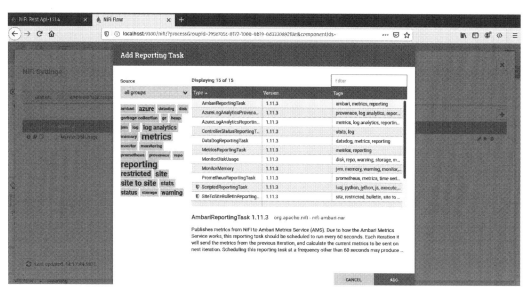

Figure 9.11 – Reporting tasks available in NiFi

For this example, double click the **MonitorDiskUsage** task. It will appear on the list with the ability to edit. Click the pencil to edit, set the **Threshold** to **1%**, and set the directory to your NiFi directory. The configuration will look like the following screenshot:

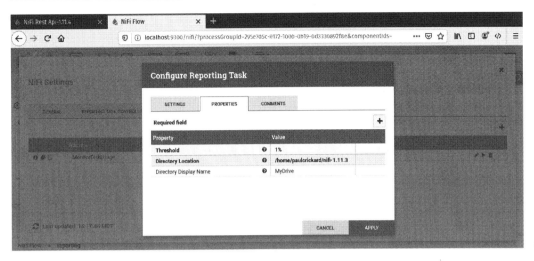

Figure 9.12 – Configuring the MonitorDiskUsage task

You can use a percentage or a value such as 20 gigabytes. I have set it to 1% so that it will post to the bulletin. I chose the NiFi directory because it contains all the logs and repositories.

Running the **Reporting Task** processor, you should see a bulletin in the main NiFi window. The message will be that the **MonitorDiskUsage** task exceeded the 1% threshold. The following screenshot shows the bulletin:

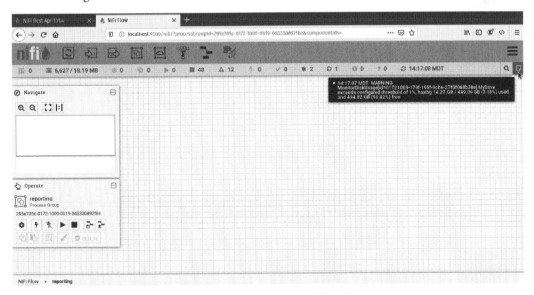

Figure 9.13 – The Reporting Task bulletin

You can create reporting tasks for many other metrics. Using the GUI is useful and convenient, but you will most likely not be able to sit in front of NiFi watching it all day. This would be horribly inefficient. A better method would be to have NiFi send you a message. You can do this using processors. The next section will show you how.

Monitoring NiFi with processors

Instead of relying on watching the NiFi GUI, you can insert a processor into your data pipeline to report what is happening with the pipeline. For example, you can use the `PutSlack` processor to send messages on failures or success.

To send Slack messages, you will need to create an app in your Slack workspace. You can do this by browsing to `https://api.slack.com/apps`. Click **Create New App**, as shown in the following screenshot:

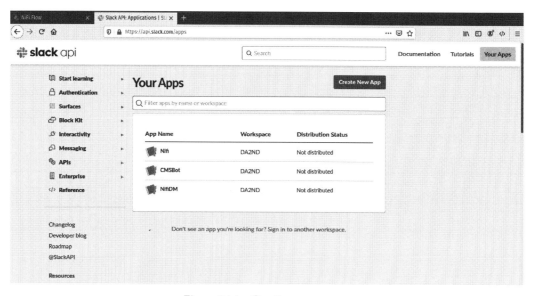

Figure 9.14 – Creating a new app

Slack will ask you to name your app and then select a workspace, as shown in the following screenshot:

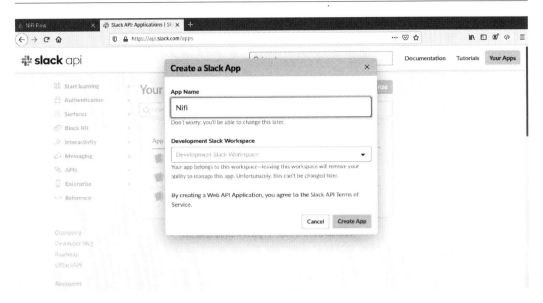

Figure 9.15 – Specifying a name and workspace for your app

When finished, you will be redirected to the app page. Under the **Features** heading, click **Incoming Webhooks** and turn it on, as shown in the following screenshot:

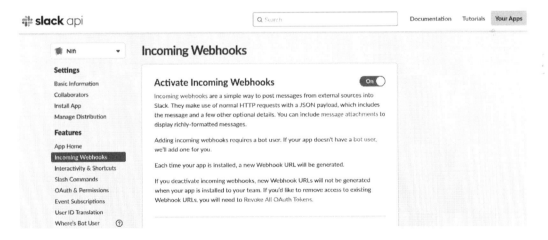

Figure 9.16 – Activating Incoming Webhooks

You will be asked to select a channel for the webhook. I selected myself so that the channel becomes a direct message to me. You can create a channel for the data pipeline so that multiple people can join and see the messages. Once you have completed this step, scroll to the bottom of the page to see the new webhook. Click the copy button and open NiFi. It is time to add PutSlack to your data pipeline.

In NiFi, I have opened the **SCF** processor group. I found the **ElasticSCF** processor—the processor that sends the issues in to Elasticsearch. Drag and drop the processor icon in the control toolbar to the canvas and select **PutSlack**. Create a connection between **ElasticSCF** and **PutSlack** for the relationship failure, as shown in the following screenshot:

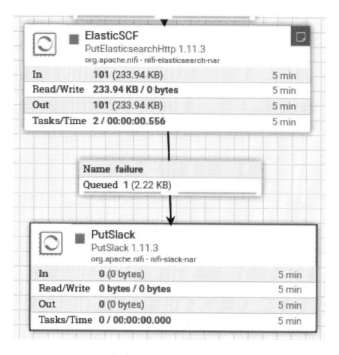

Figure 9.17 – PutSlack added to the end of the data pipeline

To configure the PutSlack processor, paste the copied URL to the **Webhook URL** property. NiFi will hide the URL because it is a sensitive property. The **Username** property is whatever you want Slack to display when the message is sent. You can also set an icon or an emoji. The **Webhook Text** property is the message that will be sent. You can set the message to plain text saying that the processor failed, or because the **Webhook Text** property accepts the NiFi expression language, you can use a combination of a flowfile attribute with text. I have configured the processor as shown in the following screenshot:

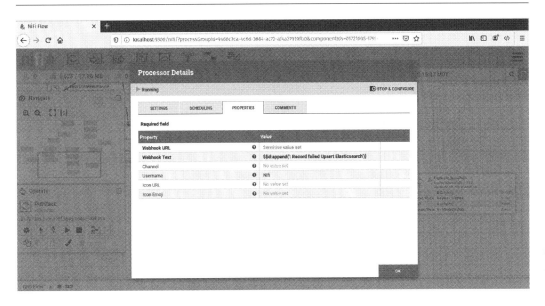

Figure 9.18 – PutSlack configuration

I used the append method of the NiFi expression language. The statement is as follows:

```
${id:append(': Record failed Upsert Elasticsearch')}
```

The preceding statement gets the id property, ${id}, and calls append, :append(). Inside the append() method is the text. The result will be a message like the one shown in the following screenshot:

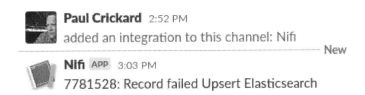

Figure 9.19 – Slack direct message from NiFi

The preceding screenshot is my direct messages. You can see that I added the NiFi integration to the workspace, then received a message from NiFi. The message is the ID of the **SeeClickFix** issue and some text saying that it failed. I can now take action.

You can use processors to send emails, write files, or perform many other actions that you could use to monitor your data pipeline. You can also write your own monitoring applications outside of NiFi using Python. The next section will cover the NiFi REST API.

Using Python with the NiFi REST API

Using Python and the NiFi REST API, you could write your own monitoring tools, or wire up a dashboard. The NiFi REST API documentation is located at `https://nifi.apache.org/docs/nifi-docs/rest-api/index.html`. You can see all of the different endpoints by type and some information about each of them. This section will highlight some of the endpoints that you have covered in this chapter but by using the GUI.

The first thing we can look at are the system diagnostics. System diagnostics will show you your resource usage. You can see heap size, threads, repository usage, and several other metrics. To call the endpoint with requests, you can use the following code:

```
r=requests.get('http://localhost:9300/nifi-api/system-
diagnostics')
data=r.json()
data['systemDiagnostics']['aggregateSnapshot']['maxHeap']
#'512 MB'
data['systemDiagnostics']['aggregateSnapshot']['totalThreads']
#108
data['systemDiagnostics']['aggregateSnapshot']
['heapUtilization']
#'81.0%'
```

Other endpoints of interest are the processor groups. Using this endpoint, you can find basic information about any processor group. You will need to get the ID of the group in NiFi. You can find this in the URL as the `processGroupId` parameter. With it, you can use the process-groups endpoint, as shown in the following code:

```
pg=requests.get('http://localhost:9300/nifi-api/process-
groups/9466c3ca-4c6d-3884-ac72-af4a27919fb0')
pgdata=pg.json()
pgdata['component']['name']
#'SCF'
pgdata['status']
```

The `status` object holds most of the pertinent information that you would find in the status toolbar. The output is as follows:

```
{'id': '9466c3ca-4c6d-3884-ac72-af4a27919fb0', 'name': 'SCF',
'statsLastRefreshed': '16:11:16 MDT', 'aggregateSnapshot':
{'id': '9466c3ca-4c6d-3884-ac72-af4a27919fb0', 'name': 'SCF',
```

```
'versionedFlowState': 'LOCALLY_MODIFIED', 'flowFilesIn':
0, 'bytesIn': 0, 'input': '0 (0 bytes)', 'flowFilesQueued':
6481, 'bytesQueued': 18809602, 'queued': '6,481 (17.94 MB)',
'queuedCount': '6,481', 'queuedSize': '17.94 MB', 'bytesRead':
0, 'read': '0 bytes', 'bytesWritten': 0, 'written': '0
bytes', 'flowFilesOut': 0, 'bytesOut': 0, 'output': '0 (0
bytes)', 'flowFilesTransferred': 0, 'bytesTransferred':
0, 'transferred': '0 (0 bytes)', 'bytesReceived': 0,
'flowFilesReceived': 0, 'received': '0 (0 bytes)',
'bytesSent': 0, 'flowFilesSent': 0, 'sent': '0 (0 bytes)',
'activeThreadCount': 0, 'terminatedThreadCount': 0}}
```

Using the processors endpoint, you can look specifically at a single processor. You can use the `status` object to look at the status toolbar information, as shown in the following code:

```
p=requests.get('http://localhost:9300/nifi-api/
processors/8b63e4d0-eff2-3093-f4ad-0f1581e56674')
pdata=p.json()
pdata['component']['name']
#'Query SCF - Archive'
pdata['status']
```

Using the NiFi API, you can even look into the queues and download flowfiles. To get the contents of a flowfile you need to follow these steps:

1. Make a listing request to the queue:

    ```
    q=requests.post('http://localhost:9300/nifi-api/flowfile-
    queues/295fc119-0172-1000-3949-54311cdb478e/listing-
    requests')
    qdata=q.json()
    listid=qdata['listingRequest']['id']
    # '0172100b-179f-195f-b95c-63ea96d151a3'
    ```

2. Then you will get the status of the listing request by passing the request (`listid`):

    ```
    url="http://localhost:9300/nifi-api/flowfile-
    queues/295fc119-0172-1000-3949-54311cdb478e/listing-
    requests/"+listid
    ff=requests.get(url)
    ffdata=ff.json()
    ffid=ffdata['listingRequest']['flowFileSummaries'][0]
    ```

```
['uuid']
#'3b2dd0fa-dfbe-458b-83e9-ea5f9dbb578f'
```

3. Lastly, you will call the flowfiles endpoint, pass the flowfile ID (`ffid`), and then request the content. The flowfile is JSON, so the result will be JSON:

```
ffurl="http://localhost:9300/nifi-api/flowfile-
queues/295fc119-0172-1000-3949-54311cdb478e/
flowfiles/"+ffid+"/content"
download=requests.get(ffurl)
download.json()
```

You now have the contents of an entire flowfile:

```
{'request_type': {'related_issues_url': 'https://
seeclickfix.com/api/v2/issues?lat=35.18151754051&lng=-
106.689667822892&request_types=17877&sort=distance',
'title': 'Missed Trash Pick Up', 'url': 'https://
seeclickfix.com/api/v2/request_types/17877',
'organization': 'City of Albuquerque', 'id': 17877},
'shortened_url': None, 'rating': 2, 'description': 'Yard
waste in bags', 'created_at': '2020-05-08T17:15:57-
04:00', 'opendate': '2020-05-08', 'media': {'image_
square_100x100': None, 'image_full': None, 'video_
url': None, 'representative_image_url': 'https://
seeclickfix.com/assets/categories/trash-f6b4bb46a3084
21d38fc042b1a74691fe7778de981d59493fa89297f6caa86a1.
png'}, 'private_visibility': False, 'transitions':
{}, 'point': {'coordinates': [-106.689667822892,
35.18151754051], 'type': 'Point'}, 'updated_at':
'2020-05-10T16:31:42-04:00', 'id': 7781316, 'lat':
35.18151754051, 'coords': '35.1815175405,-106.689667823',
'summary': 'Missed Trash Pick Up', 'address': '8609 Tia
Christina Dr Nw Albuquerque NM 87114, United States',
'closed_at': '2020-05-08T17:24:55-04:00', 'lng':
-106.689667822892, 'comment_url': 'https://seeclickfix.
com/api/v2/issues/7781316/comments', 'reporter':
{'role': 'Registered User', 'civic_points': 0, 'avatar':
{'square_100x100': 'https://seeclickfix.com/assets/
no-avatar-100-5e06fcc664c6376bbf654cbd67df857ff81918c5f5c
6a2345226093147382de9.png', 'full': 'https://seeclickfix.
com/assets/no-avatar-100-5e06fcc664c6376bbf654cbd67d
f857ff81918c5f5c6a2345226093147382de9.png'}, 'html_
url': 'https://seeclickfix.com/users/347174', 'name':
'Gmom', 'id': 347174, 'witty_title': ''}, 'flag_url':
```

```
'https://seeclickfix.com/api/v2/issues/7781316/flag',
'url': 'https://seeclickfix.com/api/v2/issues/7781316',
'html_url': 'https://seeclickfix.com/issues/7781316',
'acknowledged_at': '2020-05-08T17:15:58-04:00', 'status':
'Archived', 'reopened_at': None}
```

4. You can clear queues by making a `drop` request:

```
e=requests.post('http://localhost:9300/nifi-api/flowfile-
queues/295fc119-0172-1000-3949-54311cdb478e/drop-
requests')
```

```
edata=e.json()
```

5. You can pass the listing request ID to the end of the preceding URL to see that it worked. Or you can open NiFi and browse to the queue and you will see that it is empty.

6. You can read the NiFi bulletin by calling the bulletin board endpoint:

```
b=requests.get('http://localhost:9300/nifi-api/flow/
bulletin-board')
```

```
bdata=b.json()
```

```
bdata
```

The result is a single message saying I do not have Elasticsearch running. The output is as follows:

```
{'bulletinBoard': {'bulletins': [{'id': 2520, 'groupId':
'9466c3ca-4c6d-3884-ac72-af4a27919fb0', 'sourceId':
'e5fb7c4b-0171-1000-ac53-9fd365943393', 'timestamp':
'17:15:44 MDT', 'canRead': True, 'bulletin': {'id': 2520,
'category': 'Log Message', 'groupId': '9466c3ca-4c6d-
3884-ac72-af4a27919fb0', 'sourceId': 'e5fb7c4b-0171-1000-
ac53-9fd365943393', 'sourceName': 'ElasticSCF', 'level':
'ERROR', 'message': 'PutElasticsearchHttp[id=e5fb7c4b-
0171-1000-ac53-9fd365943393] Routing to failure due to
exception: Failed to connect to localhost/127.0.0.1:9200:
java.net.ConnectException: Failed to connect to
localhost/127.0.0.1:9200', 'timestamp': '17:15:44
MDT'}}], 'generated': '17:16:20 MDT'}}
```

7. You can also read the counters you created earlier. The following code will send a
    `get` request to the counter endpoint:

```
c=requests.get('http://localhost:9300/nifi-api/counters')
cdata=c.json()
cdata
```

In the following code block, you will see that I have added an additional counter:

```
{'counters': {'aggregateSnapshot': {'generated':
'17:17:17 MDT', 'counters': [{'id': '6b2fdf54-a984-
38aa-8c56-7aa4a544e8a3', 'context': 'UpdateCounter
(01721000-179f-195f-6715-135d1d999e33)', 'name':
'SCFSplit', 'valueCount': 1173, 'value': '1,173'}, {'id':
'b9884362-c70e-3634-8e53-f0151396be0b', 'context': "All
UpdateCounter's", 'name': 'SCFSplit', 'valueCount':
1173, 'value': '1,173'}, {'id': 'fb06d19f-682c-3f85-9ea2-
f12b090c4abd', 'context': "All UpdateCounter's", 'name':
'SCFtoElasticsearch', 'valueCount': 162, 'value': '162'},
{'id': '72790bbc-3115-300d-947c-22d889f15a73', 'context':
'UpdateCounter (295f179f-0172-1000-ee63-c25c545f224e)',
'name': 'SCFtoElasticsearch', 'valueCount': 162, 'value':
'162'}]}}}
```

8. Lastly, you can also get information on your reporting tasks. You can see the results
    in the bulletin, but this endpoint allows you to see their state; in this case, I have
    them stopped. The following code shows you how:

```
rp=requests.get('http://localhost:9300/nifi-api/
reporting-tasks/01721003-179f-195f-9cbe-27f0f068b38e')
rpdata=rp.json()
rpdata
```

The information about the reporting task is as follows:

```
{'revision': {'clientId': '2924cbec-0172-1000-ab26-
103c63d8f745', 'version': 8}, 'id': '01721003-179f-195f-
9cbe-27f0f068b38e', 'uri': 'http://localhost:9300/
nifi-api/reporting-tasks/01721003-179f-195f-9cbe-
27f0f068b38e', 'permissions': {'canRead': True,
'canWrite': True}, 'bulletins': [], 'component':
{'id': '01721003-179f-195f-9cbe-27f0f068b38e',
'name': 'MonitorDiskUsage', 'type': 'org.apache.nifi.
controller.MonitorDiskUsage', 'bundle': {'group':
'org.apache.nifi', 'artifact': 'nifi-standard-nar',
```

```
'version': '1.12.1'}, 'state': 'STOPPED', 'comments':
'', 'persistsState': False, 'restricted': False,
'deprecated': False, 'multipleVersionsAvailable': False,
'schedulingPeriod': '5 mins', 'schedulingStrategy':
'TIMER_DRIVEN', 'defaultSchedulingPeriod': {'TIMER_
DRIVEN': '0 sec', 'CRON_DRIVEN': '* * * * * ?'},
'properties': {'Threshold': '1%', 'Directory Location':
'/home/paulcrickard/nifi-1.12.1', 'Directory Display
Name': 'MyDrive'}, 'descriptors': {'Threshold': {'name':
'Threshold', 'displayName': 'Threshold', 'description':
'The threshold at which a bulletin will be generated to
indicate that the disk usage of the partition on which
the directory found is of concern', 'defaultValue':
'80%', 'required': True, 'sensitive': False, 'dynamic':
False, 'supportsEl': False, 'expressionLanguageScope':
'Not Supported'}, 'Directory Location': {'name':
'Directory Location', 'displayName': 'Directory
Location', 'description': 'The directory path of
the partition to be monitored.', 'required': True,
'sensitive': False, 'dynamic': False, 'supportsEl':
False, 'expressionLanguageScope': 'Not Supported'},
'Directory Display Name': {'name': 'Directory Display
Name', 'displayName': 'Directory Display Name',
'description': 'The name to display for the directory in
alerts.', 'defaultValue': 'Un-Named', 'required': False,
'sensitive': False, 'dynamic': False, 'supportsEl':
False, 'expressionLanguageScope': 'Not Supported'}},
'validationStatus': 'VALID', 'activeThreadCount': 0,
'extensionMissing': False}, 'operatePermissions':
{'canRead': True, 'canWrite': True}, 'status':
{'runStatus': 'STOPPED', 'validationStatus': 'VALID',
'activeThreadCount': 0}}
```

With these NiFi endpoints, you can collect information on your system, on process groups, on processors, and on queues. You can use this information to build your own monitoring systems or create dashboards. The API has a lot of potential—you could even call the API using NiFi itself.

Summary

In this chapter, you have learned how to use the NiFi GUI to monitor your data pipelines using the status bar, the bulletin, and counters. You also learned how to add processors that can send information to you inside your data pipeline. With the `PutSlack` processor, you were able to send yourself direct messages when there was a failure, and you passed data from the flowfile in the message with the NiFi expression language. Lastly, you learned how to use the API to write your own monitoring tools and grab the same data as is in the NiFi GUI—even reading the contents of a single flowfile.

In the next chapter, you will learn how to deploy your production pipelines. You will learn how to use processor groups, templates, versions, and variables to allow you to import data pipelines to a production NiFi instance with minimal configuration.

10
Deploying Data Pipelines

In software engineering, you will usually have **development**, **testing**, and **production** environments. The testing environment may be called **quality control** or **staging** or some other name, but the idea is the same. You develop in an environment, then push it to another environment that will be a clone of the production environment and if everything goes well, then it is pushed into the production environment. The same methodology is used in data engineering. So far, you have built data pipelines and run them on a single machine. In this chapter, you will learn methods for building data pipelines that can be deployed to a production environment.

In this chapter, we're going to cover the following main topics:

- Finalizing your data pipelines for production
- Using the NiFi variable registry
- Deploying your data pipelines

Finalizing your data pipelines for production

In the last few chapters, you have learned about the features and methods for creating production data pipelines. There are still a few more features needed before you can deploy your data pipelines—backpressure, processor groups with input and output ports, and funnels. This section will walk you through each one of these features.

Backpressure

In your data pipelines, each processor or task will take different amounts of time to finish. For example, a database query may return hundreds of thousands of results that are split into single flowfiles in a few seconds, but the processor that evaluates and modifies the attributes within the flowfiles may take much longer. It doesn't make sense to dump all of the data into the queue faster than the downstream processor can actually process it. Apache NiFi allows you to control the number of flowfiles or the size of the data that is sent to the queue. This is called **backpressure**.

To understand how backpressure works, let's make a data pipeline that generates data and writes it to a file. The data pipeline is shown in the following screenshot:

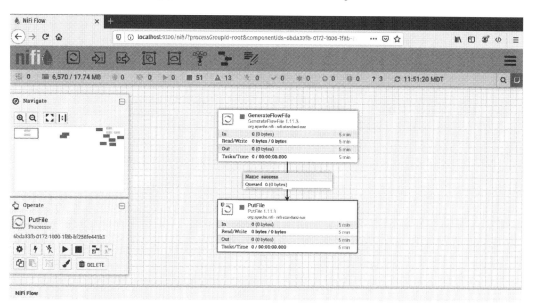

Figure 10.1 – A data pipeline to generate data and write the flowfiles to a file

The preceding data pipeline a creates connection between the `GenerateFlowFile` processor and the `PutFile` processor for the success relationship. I have configured the `PutFile` processor to write files to `/home/paulcrickard/output`. The `GenerateFlowFile` processor is using the default configuration.

If you run the data pipeline by starting the `GenerateFlowFile` processor only, you will see that the queue has 10,000 flowfiles and is red, as shown in the following screenshot:

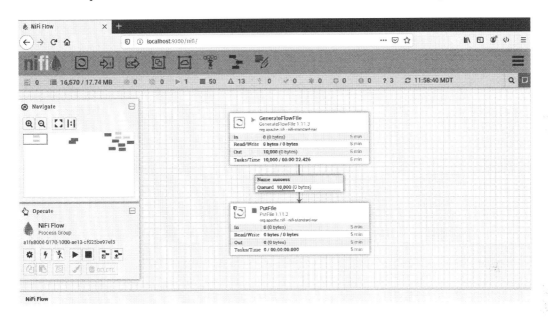

Figure 10.2 – A full queue with 10,000 flowfiles

If you refresh NiFi, the number of flowfiles in the queue will not increase. It has 10,000 flowfiles and cannot hold anymore. But is 10,000 the maximum number?

Queues can be configured just like the processors that feed them. Right-click on the queue and select **Configure**. Select the **SETTINGS** tab, and you will see the following options:

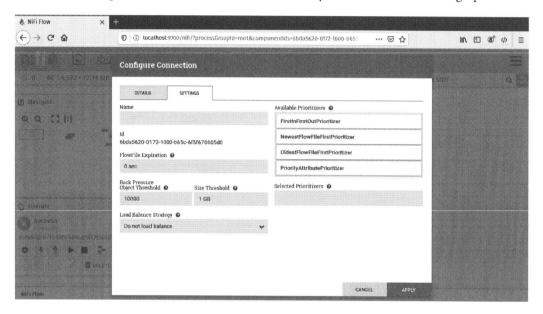

Figure 10.3 – Queue configuration settings

You will notice that **Back Pressure Object Threshold** is set to `10000` flowfiles and that **Size Threshold** is set to `1 GB`. The `GenerateFlowFile` processor set the size of each flowfile to 0 bytes, so the object threshold was hit before the size threshold. You can test hitting the size threshold by changing the **File Size** property in the `GenerateFlowFile` processor. I have changed it to 50 MB. When I start the processor, the queue now stops at 21 flowfiles because it has exceeded 1 GB of data. The following screenshot shows the full queue:

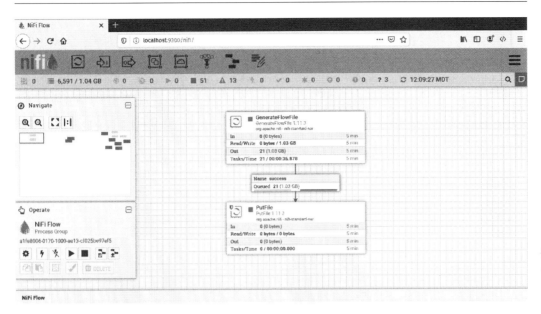

Figure 10.4 – Queue that has the size threshold

By adjusting **Object Threshold** or **Size Threshold**, you can control the amount of data that gets sent to a queue and create backpressure slowing down an upstream processor. While loading the queues does not break your data pipeline, it will run much more smoothly if the data flows in a more even manner.

The next section will zoom out on your data pipelines and show other techniques for improving the use of processor groups.

Improving processor groups

Up to this point, you have used processor groups to hold a single data pipeline. If you were to push all of these data pipelines to production, what you would soon realize is that you have a lot of processors in each processor group doing the same exact task. For example, you may have several processors that SplitJson used followed by an `EvaluateJsonPath` processor that extracts the ID from a flowfile. Or, you might have several processors that insert flowfiles in to Elasticsearch.

You would not have several functions in code that do the exact same thing on different variables; you would have one that accepted parameters. The same holds true for data pipelines, and you accomplish this using processor groups with the input and output ports.

To illustrate how to break data pipelines into logical pieces, let's walk through an example:

1. In NiFi, create a processor group and name it `Generate Data`.

2. Inside the processor group, drag the `GenerateFlowFile` processor to the canvas. I have set the **Custom Text** property in the configuration to `{"ID":123}`.

3. Next, drag an output port to the canvas. You will be prompted for **Output Port Name** and **Send To**. I have named it `FromGeneratedData` and **Send To** is set to **Local connections**.

4. Lastly, connect the `GenerateFlowfile` processor to **Output Port**. You will have a warning on the output port that it is invalid because it has no outgoing connections. We will fix that in the next steps.

5. Exit the processor group.

6. Create a new processor group and name it `Write Data`.

7. Enter the processor group and drag the `EvaluateJsonPath` processor to the canvas. Configure it by creating a property ID with the value of `$.{ID}`, and set the **Destination** property to **flowfile-attribute**.

8. Next, drag the `UpdateAttribute` processor to the canvas and create a new property filename and set the value to `${ID}`.

9. Now, drag the `PutFile` processor to the canvas. Set the **Directory** property to any location you have permissions to edit. I have set mine to `/home/paulcrickard/output`.

10. Lastly, drag an **Input Port** to the canvas and make it the first processor in the data pipeline. The completed pipeline should look like the following screenshot:

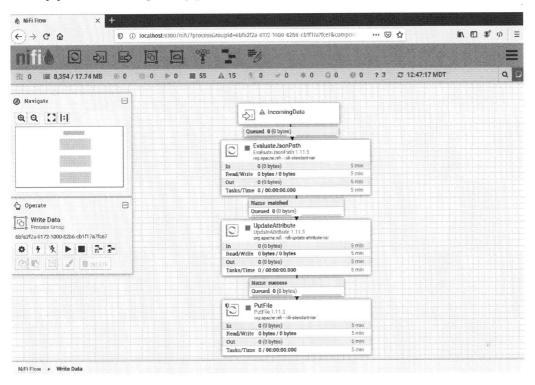

Figure 10.5 – A data pipeline that starts with an input port

11. Exit the processor group. You should now have two processor groups on the canvas—Generate Data and Write Data. You can connect these processor groups just like you do with single processors. When you connect them by dragging the arrow from Generate Data to Write Data, you will be prompted to select which ports to connect, as shown in the following screenshot:

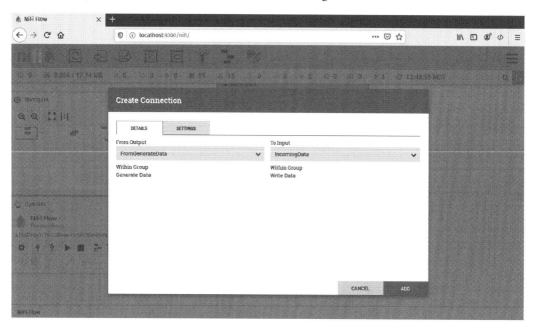

Figure 10.6 – Connecting two processor groups

12. The default values will work because you only have one output port and one input port. If you had more, you could use the drop-down menus to select the proper ports. This is where naming them something besides input and output becomes important. Make the names descriptive.

13. With the processor groups connected, start the Generate Data group only. You will see the queue fill up with flowfiles. To see how the ports work, enter the Write Data processor group.

14. Start only the incoming data input port. Once it starts running, the downstream queue will fill with flowfiles.

15. Right-click the queue and select **List queue**. You can see that the flowfiles are coming from the `Generate Data` processor group. You can now start the rest of the processor.

16. As the data pipeline runs, you will have a file, `123`, created in your output directory.

You have successfully connected two processor groups using input and output ports. In production, you can now have a single process group to write data to a file and it can receive data from any processor group that needs to write data, as shown in the following screenshot:

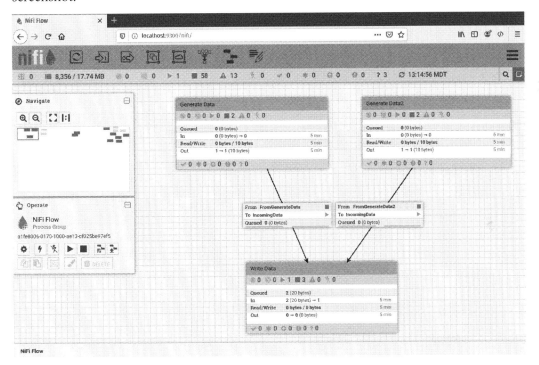

Figure 10.7 – Two processor groups utilizing the Write Data processor group

In the preceding data pipeline, I made a copy of `Generate Data` and configured the **Custom Text** property to `{"ID":456}` and set the run schedule to an hour so that I would only get one flowfile from each processor—`Generate Data` and `Generate Data2`. Running all of the processor groups, you list the queue and confirm that one flowfile comes from each processor group, and your output directory now has two files—`123` and `456`.

Using the NiFi variable registry

When you are building your data pipelines, you are hardcoding variables—with the exception of some expression language where you extract data from the flowfile. When you move the data pipeline to production, you will need to change the variables in your data pipeline, and this can be time consuming and error prone. For example, you will have a different test database than production. When you deploy your data pipeline to production, you need to point to production and change the processor. Or you can use the variable registry.

Using the `postgresToelasticsearch` processor group from *Chapter 4, Working with Databases*, I will modify the data pipeline to use the NiFi variable registry. As a reminder, the data pipeline is shown in the following screenshot:

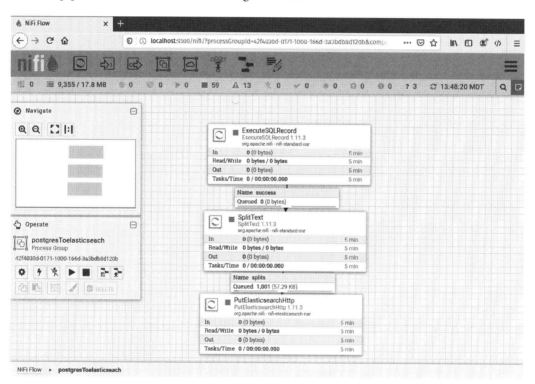

Figure 10.8 – A data pipeline to query PostgreSQL and save the results to Elasticsearch

From outside the processor group, right-click on it and select **Variables**. To add a new variable, you can click the plus sign and provide a name and a value. These variables are now associated with the processor group.

Just like functions in programming, variables have a scope. Variables in a processor group are local variables. You can right-click on the NiFi canvas and create a variable, which you can consider global in scope. I have created two local variables, `elastic` and `index`, and one global, `elastic`. When I open the variables in the group, it looks like the following screenshot:

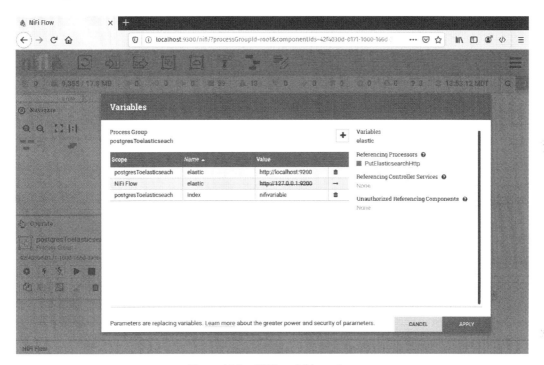

Figure 10.9 – NiFi variable registry

In the preceding screenshot, you can see the scopes. The scope of **postgresToelasticsearch** is the processor group, or local variables. The **NiFi Flow** scope is the global variables. Because I have two variables named `elastic`, the local variable takes precedence.

You can now reference these variables using the expression language. In the `PutElasticsearchHttp` process, I have set the **Elasticsearch URL** to `${elastic}` and the **Index** to `${index}`. These will populate with the local variables—`http://localhost:9200` and `nifivariable`.

Running the data pipeline, you can see the results in Elasticsearch. There is now a new index with the name `nifivariable` and 1,001 records. The following screenshot shows the result:

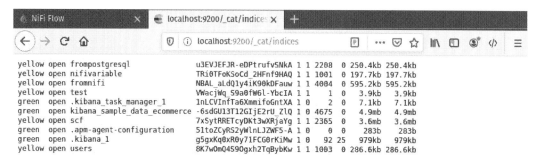

Figure 10.10 – The new index, nifivariable, is the second row

You have now put the finishing touches on production pipelines and have completed all the steps needed to deploy them. The next section will teach you different ways to deploy your data pipelines.

Deploying your data pipelines

There are many ways to handle the different environments—**development**, **testing**, **production**—and how you choose to do that is up to what works best with your business practices. Having said that, any strategy you take should involve using the NiFi registry.

Using the simplest strategy

The simplest strategy would be to run NiFi over the network and split the canvas into multiple environments. When you have promoted a process group, you would move it in to the next environment. When you needed to rebuild a data pipeline, you would add it back to development and modify it, then update the production data pipeline to the newest version. Your NiFi instance would look like the following screenshot:

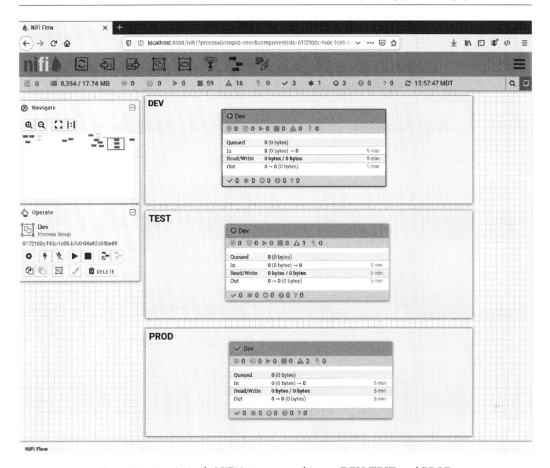

Figure 10.11 – A single NiFi instance working as DEV, TEST, and PROD

Notice in the preceding screenshot that only PROD has a green checkmark. The DEV environment created the processor group, then changes were committed, and they were brought into TEST. If any changes were made, they were committed, and the newest version was brought in to PROD. To improve the data pipeline later, you would bring the newest version into DEV and start the process over until PROD has the newest version as well.

While this will work, if you have the resources to build out a separate NiFi instance, you should.

Using the middle strategy

The middle strategy utilizes the NiFi registry but also adds a production NiFi instance. I have installed NiFi on another machine, separate from the one I have used through this book, that is also running the NiFi registry—this could also live on a separate machine.

After launching my new NiFi instance, I added the NiFi registry as shown in the following screenshot:

Figure 10.12 – Adding the NiFi registry to another NiFi instance

On the development machine, the registry was created using localhost. However, other machines can connect by specifying the IP address of the host machine. After reading it, the NiFi instance has access to all the versioned data pipelines.

Drag a processor group to the canvas and select **Import**. You can now select the processor group that has been promoted to production, as shown in the following screenshot:

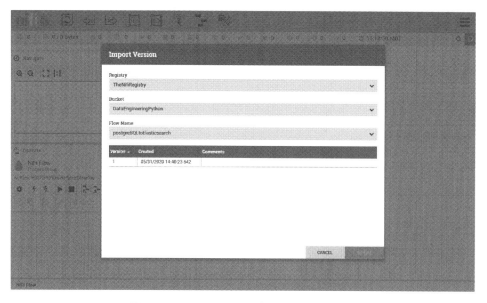

Figure 10.13 – Importing the processor group

Once you import the processor, it will come over with the variables that were defined in the development environment. You can overwrite the values of the variables. Once you change the variables, you will not need to do it again. You can make the changes in the development environment and update the production environment and the new variables will stay. The updated variables are shown in the following screenshot:

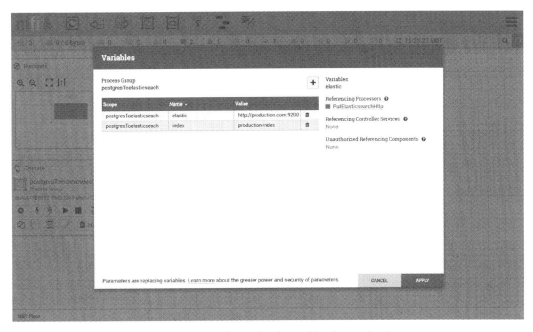

Figure 10.14 – Updating local variables for production

In the development environment, you can change the processor and commit the local changes. The production environment will now show that there is a new version available, as shown in the following screenshot:

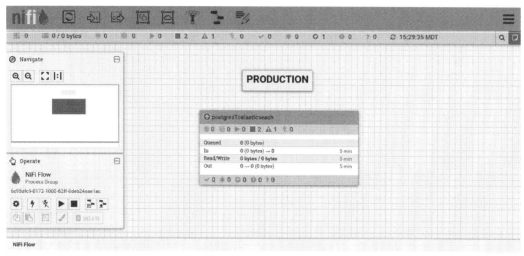

Figure 10.15 – Production is now no longer using the current version

You can right-click the processor group and select the new version. The following screenshot shows version 2:

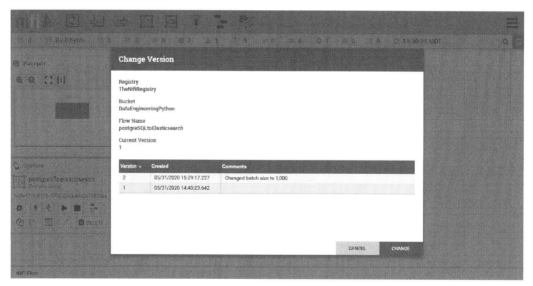

Figure 10.16 – A new version

After selecting the new version, the production environment is now up to date. The following screenshot shows the production environment. You can right-click on the processor group to see that the variable still points to the production values:

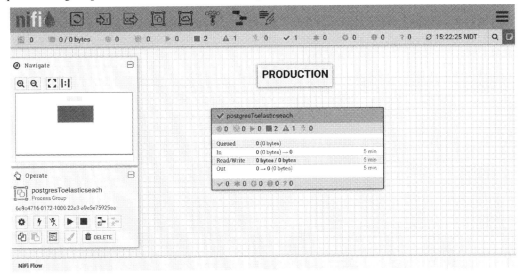

Figure 10.17 – Production is up to date

This strategy should work for most users' needs. In this example, I used development and production environments, but you can add TEST and use the same strategy here, just change the local variables to point to your test databases.

The preceding strategies used a single NiFi registry, but you can use a registry per environment.

Using multiple registries

A more advanced strategy for managing development, test, and production would be to use multiple NiFi registries. In this strategy, you would set up two NiFi registries—one for development and one for test and production. You would connect the development environment to the development registry and the test and production environments to the second registry.

When you have promoted a data pipeline to test, an administrator would use the NiFi CLI tools to export the data pipeline and import it in to the second NiFi registry. From there, you could test and promote it to development. You would import the version from the second registry to the production environment, just like you did in the middle strategy. This strategy makes mistakes much more difficult to handle as you cannot commit data pipelines to test and production without manually doing so. This is an excellent strategy but requires many more resources.

Summary

In this chapter, you learned how to finalize your data pipelines for deployment into production. By using processor groups for specific tasks, much like functions in code, you could reduce the duplication of processors. Using input and output ports, you connected multiple processor groups together. To deploy data pipelines, you learned how NiFi variables could be used to declare global and locally scoped variables.

In the next chapter, you will use all the skills you have learned in this section to create and deploy a production data pipeline.

11
Building a Production Data Pipeline

In this chapter, you will build a production data pipeline using the features and techniques that you have learned in this section of the book. The data pipeline will be broken into processor groups that perform a single task. Those groups will be version controlled and they will use the NiFi variable registry so that they can be deployed in a production environment.

In this chapter, we're going to cover the following main topics:

- Creating a test and production environment
- Building a production data pipeline
- Deploying a data pipeline in production

Creating a test and production environment

In this chapter, we will return to using PostgreSQL for both the extraction and loading of data. The data pipeline will require a test and production environment, each of which will have a staging and a warehouse table. To create the databases and tables, you will use **PgAdmin4**.

Creating the databases

To use PgAdmin4, perform the following steps:

1. Browse to `http://localhostw/pgadmin4/l`, enter your username and password, and then click the **Login** button. Once logged in, expand the server icon in the left panel.

2. To create the databases, right-click on the databases icon and select **Create** | **Database**. Name the database `test`.

3. Next, you will need to add the tables. To create the staging table, right-click on **Tables** | **Create** | **Table**. On the **General** tab, name the table `staging`. Then, select the **Columns** tab. Using the plus sign, create the fields shown in the following screenshot:

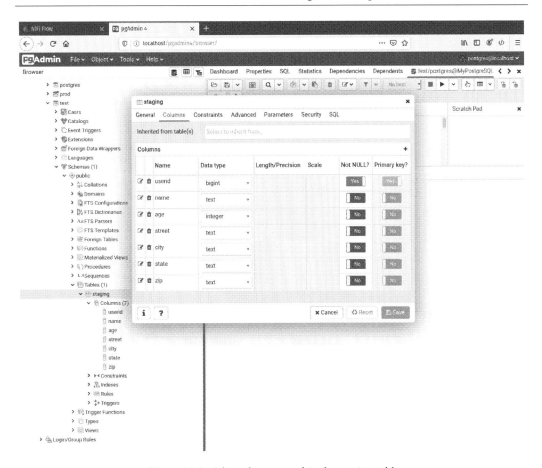

Figure 11.1 – The columns used in the staging table

4. Save the table when you are done. You will need to create this table once more for the test database and twice more for the production database. To save some time, you can use **CREATE Script** to do this for you. Right-click on the staging table, and then select **Scripts | CREATE Script**, as shown in the following screenshot:

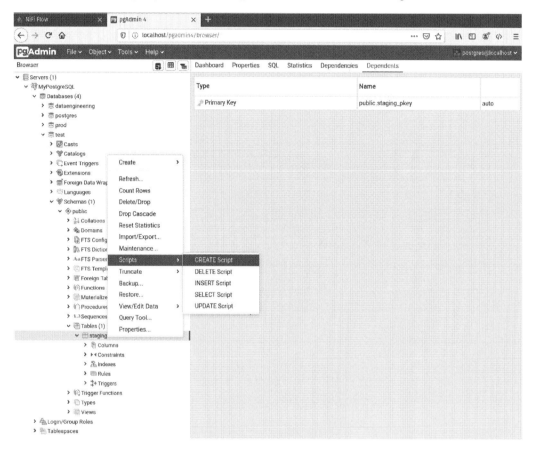

Figure 11.2 – Generating the CREATE script

5. A window will open in the main screen with the SQL required to generate the table. By changing the name from `staging` to `warehouse`, you can make the warehouse table in test, which will be identical to staging. Once you have made the change, click the play button in the toolbar.

6. Lastly, right-click on **Databases** and create a new database named `production`. Use the script to create both the tables.

Now that you have the tables created for the test and production environments, you will need a data lake.

Populating a data lake

A **data lake** is usually a place on disk where files are stored. Usually, you will find data lakes using Hadoop for the **Hadoop Distributed File System** (**HDFS**) and the other tools built on top of the Hadoop ecosystem. In this chapter, we will just drop files in a folder to simulate how reading from the data lake would work.

To create the data lake, you can use Python and the Faker library. Before you write the code, create a folder to act as the data lake. I have created a folder named `datalake` in my home directory.

To populate the data lake, you will need to write JSON files with information about an individual. This is similar to the JSON and CSV code you wrote in the first section of this book. The steps are as follows:

1. Import the libraries, set the data lake directory, and set `userid` to 1. The `userid` variable is going to be a primary key, so we need it to be distinct – incrementing will do that for us:

```
from faker import Faker
import json
import os
os.chdir("/home/paulcrickard/datalake")
fake=Faker()
userid=1
```

2. Next, create a loop that generates a data object containing the user ID, name, age, street, city, state, and zip of a fake individual. The `fname` variable holds the first and last name of a person without a space in the middle. If you had a space, Linux would wrap the file in quotes:

```
for i in range(1000):
    name=fake.name()
    fname=name.replace(" ","-")+'.json'
    data={
        "userid":userid,
        "name":name,
        "age":fake.random_int(min=18, max=101, step=1),
        "street":fake.street_address(),
        "city":fake.city(),
        "state":fake.state(),
```

```
            "zip":fake.zipcode()
        }
```

3. Lastly, dump the JSON object and then write it to a file named after the person. Close the file and let the loop continue:

```
        datajson=json.dumps(data)
        output=open(fname,'w')
        userid+=1
        output.write(datajson)
        output.close()
```

Run the preceding code and you will have 1,000 JSON files in your data lake. Now you can start building the data pipeline.

Building a production data pipeline

The data pipeline you build will do the following:

- Read files from the data lake.
- Insert the files into staging.
- Validate the staging data.
- Move staging to the warehouse.

The final data pipeline will look like the following screenshot:

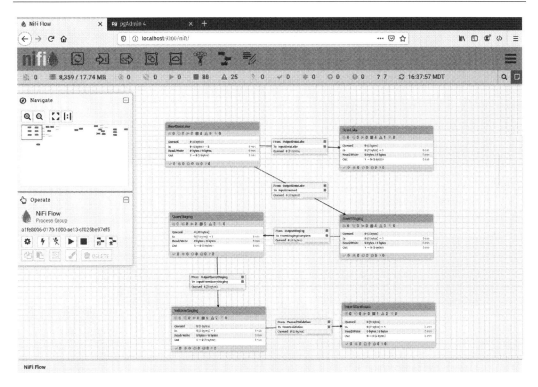

Figure 11.3 – The final version of the data pipeline

We will build the data pipeline processor group by processor group. The first processor group will read the data lake.

Reading the data lake

In the first section of this book, you read files from NiFi and will do the same here. This processor group will consist of three processors – `GetFile`, `EvaluateJsonPath`, and `UpdateCounter` – and an output port. Drag the processors and port to the canvas. In the following sections, you will configure them.

GetFile

The GetFile processor reads files from a folder, in this case, our data lake. If you were reading a data lake in Hadoop, you would switch out this processor for the GetHDFS processor. To configure the processor, specify the input directory; in my case, it is /home/paulcrickard/datalake. Make sure **Keep Source File** is set to **True**. If you wanted to move the processed files and drop them somewhere else, you could do this as well. Lastly, I have set **File Filter** to a regex pattern to match the JSON file extension – ^.*\.([jJ][sS][oO][nN]??)$. If you leave the default, it will work, but if there are other files in the folder, NiFi will try to grab them and will fail.

EvaluateJsonPath

The EvaluateJsonPath processor will extract the fields from the JSON and put them into flowfile attributes. To do so, set the **Destination** property to **flowfile-attribute**. Leave the rest of the properties as the default. Using the plus sign, create a property for each field in the JSON. The configuration is shown in the following screenshot:

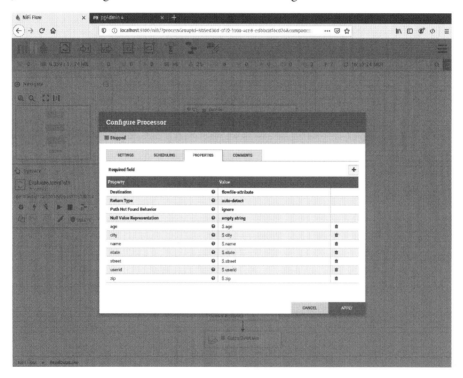

Figure 11.4 – The configuration for the EvaluateJsonPath processor

This would be enough to complete the task of reading from the data lake, but we will add one more processor for monitoring.

UpdateCounter

This processor allows you to create an increment counter. As flowfiles pass through, we can hold a count of how many are being processed. This processor does not manipulate or change any of our data, but will allow us to monitor the progress of the processor group. We will be able to see the number of FlowFiles that have moved through the processor. This is a more accurate way than using the GUI display, but it only shows the number of records in the last 5 minutes. To configure the processor, leave the **Delta** property set to 1 and set the **Counter Name** property to datalakerecordsprocessed.

To finish this section of the data pipeline, drag an output port to the canvas and name it OutputDataLake. Exit the processor group and right-click, select **Version**, and start version control. I set **Flow Name** to ReadDataLake, wrote a short description and version comments, and then performed a save.

> **NiFi-Registry**
>
> I have created a new bucket named DataLake. To create buckets, you can browse to the registry at http://localhost:18080/nifi-registry/. Click the wrench in the right corner and then click the **NEW BUCKET** button. Name and save the bucket.

The first processor group is complete. You can use this processor group any time you need to read from the data lake. The processor group will hand you every file with the fields extracted. If the data lake changed, you would only need to fix this one processor group to update all of your data pipelines.

Before continuing down the data pipeline, the next section will take a small diversion to show how you can attach other processor groups.

Scanning the data lake

The goal of the data pipeline is to read the data lake and put the data in the data warehouse. But let's assume there is another department at our company that needs to monitor the data lake for certain people – maybe VIP customers. Instead of building a new data pipeline, you can just add their task to the ReadDataLake processor group.

The `ScanLake` processor group has an input port that is connected to the output of the `ReadDataLake` processor. It uses the `ScanContent` processor attached to the `EvaluateJsonPath` processor, which is terminated at the `PutSlack` processor, as well as sending the data through to an output port. The flow is shown in the following screenshot:

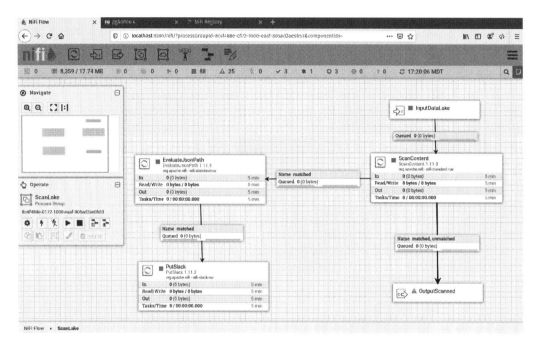

Figure 11.5 – The ScanLake processor group

The previous chapter used the `PutSlack` processor and you are already familiar with the `EvaluateJsonPath` processor. `ScanContent`, however, is a new processor. The `ScanContent` processor allows you to look at fields in the flowfile content and compare them to a dictionary file – a file with content on each line that you are looking for. I have put a single name in a file at `/home/paulcrickard/data.txt`. I configured the processor by setting the path as the value of the **Dictionary File** property. Now, when a file comes through that contains that name, I will get a message on Slack.

Inserting the data into staging

The data we read was from the data lake and will not be removed, so we do not need to take any intermediary steps, such as writing data to a file, as we would have done had the data been from a transactional database. But what we will do is place the data in a staging table to make sure that everything works as we expect before putting it in the data warehouse. To insert the data into staging only requires one processor, `PutSQL`.

PutSQL

The PutSQL processor will allow you to execute an INSERT or UPDATE operation on a database table. The processor allows you to specify the query in the contents of a flowfile, or you can hardcode the query to use as a property in the processor. For this example, I have hardcoded the query in the **SQL Statement** property, which is shown as follows:

```
INSERT INTO ${table} VALUES ('${userid}',
'${name}',${age},'${street}','${city}','${state}','${zip}');
```

The preceding query takes the attributes from the flowfile and passes them into the query, so while it is hardcoded, it will change based on the flowfiles it receives. You may have noticed that you have not used ${table} in any of the EvaluateJsonPath processors. I have declared a variable using the NiFi registry and added it to the processor group scope. The value of the table will be staging for this test environment, but will change later when we deploy the data pipeline to production.

You will also need to add a **Java Database Connection** (**JDBC**) pool, which you have done in earlier chapters of this book. You can specify the batch size, the number of records to retrieve, and whether you want the processor to roll back on failure. Setting **Rollback on Failure** to **True** is how you can create atomicity in your transactions. If a single flowfile in a batch fails, the processor will stop and nothing else can continue.

I have connected the processor to another UpdateCounter processor. This processor creates and updates InsertedStaging. The counter should match datalakerecordsprocessor when everything has finished. The UpdateCounter processor connects to an output port named OutputStaging.

Querying the staging database

The next processor group is for querying the staging database. Now that the data has been loaded, we can query the database to make sure all the records have actually made it in. You could perform other validation steps or queries to see whether the results match what you would expect – if you have data analysts, they would be a good source of information for defining these queries. In the following sections, you will query the staging database and route the results based on whether it meets your criteria.

ExecuteSQLRecord

In the previous processor group, you used the PutSQL processor to insert data into the database, but in this processor group, you want to perform a select query. The select query is shown as follows:

```
select count(*) from ${table}
```

The preceding query is set as the value of the optional SQL `select` query property. The `${table}` is a NiFi variable registry variable assigned to the processor group and has a value of `staging`. You will need to define a JDBC connection and a record writer in the processor properties. The record writer is a JSON record set writer. The return value of the processor will be a JSON object with one field – `count`. This processor is sent to an `EvaluateJsonPath` processor to extract the count as `recordcount`. That processor is then sent to the next processor.

RouteOnAttribute

The `RouteOnAttribute` processor allows you to use expressions or values to define where a flowfile goes. To configure the processor, I have set the **Routing strategy** to **Route to Property name**. I have also created a property named `allrecords` and set the value to a NiFi expression, shown as follows:

```
${recordcount:ge( 1000 )}
```

The preceding expression evaluates the `recordcount` attribute to see whether it is greater than or equal to 1,000. If it is, it will route on this relationship. I have attached the output to an output port named `OutputQueryStaging`.

Validating the staging data

The previous processor group did some validation and you could stop there. However, Great Expectations is an excellent library for handling validation for you. You learned about Great Expectations in *Chapter 7, Features of a Production Pipeline*, but I will cover it quickly again here.

To use Great Expectations, you need to create a project folder. I have done that in the following code snippet and initialized Great Expectations:

```
mkdir staging
great_expectations init
```

You will be prompted to create your validation suite. Choose **Relational database (SQL)**, then **Postgres**, and provide the required information. The prompts will look like the following screenshot:

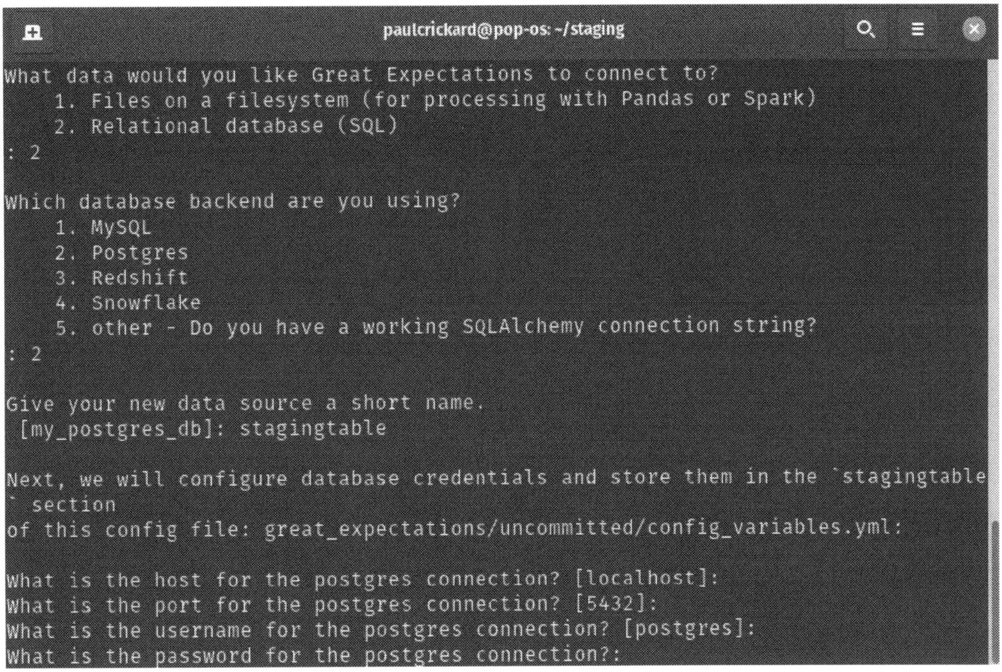

Figure 11.6 – Configuring Great Expectations to work with PostgreSQL

When it is finished, Great Expectations will attempt to connect to the database. If successful, it will provide the URL for your documents. Since the table is empty, it will not create a very detailed validation suite. You can edit the suite using the following command:

```
great_expectations suite edit staging.validation
```

This will launch a Jupyter notebook with the code for the suite. I have deleted one line that sets the number of rows between 0 and 0, as shown in the following screenshot:

Figure 11.7 – Editing the Great Expectations suite

After deleting the highlighted line, run all the cells in the notebook. Now you can refresh your documents and you will see that the expectation on the row number is no longer part of the suite, as shown in the following screenshot:

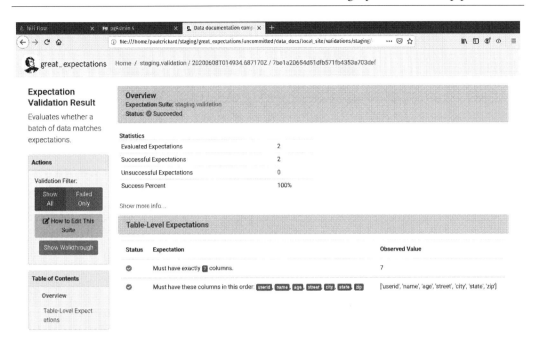

Figure 11.8 – Great Expectations documents for the suite

Now that the suite is complete, you need to generate a file that you can run to launch the validation. Use the following command to create a tap using the `staging.validation` suite and output the `sv.py` file:

```
great_expectations tap new staging.validation sv.py
```

Now you can run this file to validate the test database staging table.

The first processor receives flowfiles from an input port that is connected to the output port of the `QueryStaging` processor group. It connects to an `ExecuteStreamCommand` processor.

ExecuteStreamCommand

The `ExecuteStreamCommand` will execute a command and listen for output, streaming the results. Since the `sv.py` file only prints a single line and exits, there is no stream, but if your command had multiple outputs, the processor would grab them all as they were output.

To configure the processor, set the **Command Arguments** property to `sv.py`, the **Command Path** to **Python3**, and the working directory to the location of the `sv.py` file.

The processor connects to an `EvaluateJsonPath` processor that extracts `$.result` and sends it to a `RouteOnAttribute` processor. I have configured a single property and accorded it the value `pass`:

```
${result:startsWith('pass')}
```

The preceding expression checks the result attribute to see whether it matches `pass`. If so, the processor sends the flowfile to an output port.

Insert Warehouse

You have made it to the last processor group – **Insert Warehouse**. The data has been staged and validated successfully and is ready to move to the warehouse. This processor group uses an `ExecuteSQLRecord` and a `PutSQL` processor.

ExecuteSQLRecord

`ExecuteSQLProcessor` performs a select operation on the staging table. It has a variable table defined in the NiFi variable registry pointing to staging. The query is a `select *` query, as shown:

```
select * from ${table}
```

This query is the value of the SQL `select` query property. You will need to set up a `Database Pooling Connection` service and a `Record Writer` service. `Record Writer` will be a `JsonRecordSetWriter` and you will need to make sure that you set **Output Grouping** to **One Line per Object**. This processor sends the output to the `SplitText` processor, which connects to the `EvalueJsonPath` processor, which is a direct copy of the one from the `ReadDataLake` processor group that connects to the final `PutSQL` processor.

PutSQL

The `PutSQL` processor puts all of the data from the `staging` table into the final data warehouse table. You can configure the batch size and the rollback on failure properties. I have set the SQL Statement property to the same as when it was inserted into `staging`, except the variable for the table has been changed to `warehouse` and we set it to `warehouse` in the NiFi variable registry. The query is as follows:

```
INSERT INTO ${warehouse} VALUES ('${userid}',
'${name}',${age},'${street}','${city}','${state}','${zip}');
```

I have terminated the processor for all relationships as this is the end of the data pipeline. If you start all the processor groups, you will have data in your `staging` and `warehouse` tables. You can check your counters to see whether the records processed are the same as the number of records inserted. If everything worked correctly, you can now deploy your data pipeline to production.

Deploying a data pipeline in production

In the previous chapter, you learned how to deploy data to production, so I will not go into any great depth here, but merely provide a review. To put the new data pipeline into production, perform the following steps:

1. Browse to your production NiFi instance. I have another instance of NiFi running on port `8080` on localhost.

2. Drag and drop processor groups to the canvas and select **Import**. Choose the latest version of the processor groups you just built.

3. Modify the variables on the processor groups to point to the database production. The table names can stay the same.

You can then run the data pipeline and you will see that the data is populated in the production database `staging` and `warehouse` tables.

The data pipeline you just built read files from a data lake, put them into a database table, ran a query to validate the table, and then inserted them into the warehouse. You could have built this data pipeline with a handful of processors and been done, but when you build for production, you will need to provide error checking and monitoring. Spending the time up front to build your data pipelines properly will save you a lot of time when something changes or breaks in production. You will be well positioned to debug and modify your data pipeline.

Summary

In this chapter, you learned how to build and deploy a production data pipeline. You learned how to create TEST and PRODUCTION environments and built the data pipeline in TEST. You used the filesystem as a sample data lake and learned how you would read files from the lake and monitor them as they were processed. Instead of loading data into the data warehouse, this chapter taught you how to use a staging database to hold the data so that it could be validated before being loaded into the data warehouse. Using Great Expectations, you were able to build a validation processor group that would scan the staging database to determine whether the data was ready to be loaded into the data warehouse. Lastly, you learned how to deploy the data pipeline into PRODUCTION. With these skills, you can now fully build, test, and deploy production batch data pipelines.

In the next chapter, you will learn how to build Apache Kafka clusters. Using Kafka, you will begin to learn how to process data streams. This data is usually near real time, as opposed to the batch processing you have been currently working with. You will install and configure the cluster to run on a single machine, or multiple devices if you have them.

Section 3: Beyond Batch – Building Real-Time Data Pipelines

In this section, you will learn about the differences between batch processing – what you have currently been doing – and stream processing. You will learn about a new set of tools that allow you to stream and process data in real time. First, you will learn how to build an Apache Kafka cluster to stream real-time data. To process this data, you will use an Apache Spark cluster that you will build and deploy. Lastly, you will learn two more advanced NiFi topics – how to stream data to NiFi from an Internet of Things device using MiNiFi, and how to cluster NiFi for more processing power.

This section comprises the following chapters:

- *Chapter 12, Building an Apache Kafka Cluster*
- *Chapter 13, Streaming Data with Kafka*
- *Chapter 14, Data Processing with Apache Spark*
- *Chapter 15, Real-Time Edge Data – Kafka, Spark, and MiNiFi*

12
Building a Kafka Cluster

In this chapter, you will move beyond batch processing – running queries on a complete set of data – and learn about the tools used in stream processing. In stream processing, the data may be infinite and incomplete at the time of a query. One of the leading tools in handling streaming data is Apache Kafka. Kafka is a tool that allows you to send data in real time to topics. These topics can be read by consumers who process the data. This chapter will teach you how to build a three-node Apache Kafka cluster. You will also learn how to create and send messages (**produce**) and read data from topics (**consume**).

In this chapter, we're going to cover the following main topics:

- Creating ZooKeeper and Kafka clusters
- Testing the Kafka cluster

Creating ZooKeeper and Kafka clusters

Most tutorials on running applications that can be distributed often only show how to run a single node and then you are left wondering how you would run this in production. In this section, you will build a three-node ZooKeeper and Kafka cluster. It will run on a single machine. However, I will split each instance into its own folder and each folder simulates a server. The only modification when running on different servers would be to change localhost to the server IP.

The next chapter will go into detail on the topic of Apache Kafka, but for now it is enough to understand that Kafka is a tool for building real-time data streams. Kafka was developed at LinkedIn and is now an Apache project. You can find Kafka on the web at `http://kafka.apache.org`. The website is shown in the following screenshot:

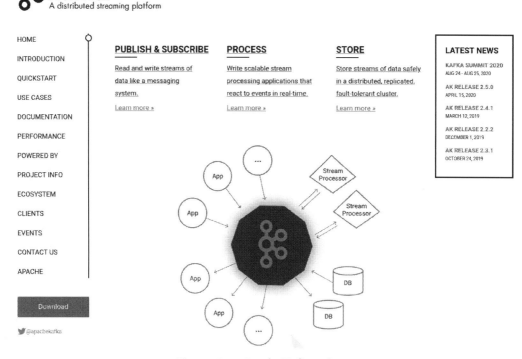

Figure 12.1 – Apache Kafka website

Kafka requires another application, ZooKeeper, to manage information about the cluster, to handle discovery, and to elect leaders. You can install and build a ZooKeeper cluster on your own, but for this example, you will use the ZooKeeper scripts provided by Kafka. To learn more about ZooKeeper, you can find it at `http://zookeeper.apache.org`. The website is shown in the following screenshot:

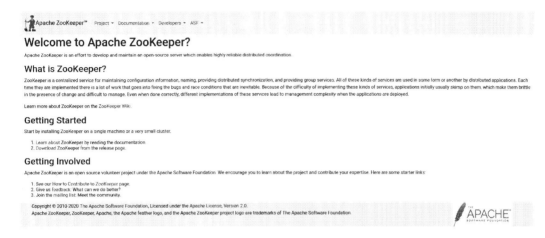

Figure 12.2 – The Apache ZooKeeper website

The following section will walk you through building the cluster.

Downloading Kafka and setting up the environment

You can download Apache Kafka from the website under the **Downloads** section – which is useful if you want a previous version – or you can use `wget` to download it from the command line. From your home directory, run the following commands:

```
Wget https://downloads.apache.org/kafka/2.5.0/kafka_2.12-
2.5.0.tgz
```

```
tar -xvzf kafka_2.12-2.5.0.tgz
```

The preceding commands download the current Kafka version and extract it into the current directory. Because you will run three nodes, you will need to create three separate folders for Kafka. Use the following commands to create the directories:

```
cp kafka_2.12-2.5.0 kafka_1
```

```
cp kafka_2.12-2.5.0 kafka_2
```

```
cp kafka_2.12-2.5.0 kafka_3
```

You will now have three Kafka folders. You will also need to specify a log directory for each instance of Kafka. You can create three folders using the `mkdir` command, as shown:

```
mkdir logs_1
mkdir logs_2
mkdir logs_2
```

Next, you will need a `data` folder for ZooKeeper. Create the directory, and then enter it using `cd`, as shown:

```
mkdir data
cd data
```

You will run three ZooKeeper instances, so you will need to create a folder for each instance. You can do that using `mkdir`, as shown:

```
mkdir zookeeper_1
mkdir zookeeper_2
mkdir zookeeper_3
```

Each ZooKeeper instance needs an ID. It will look for a file named `myid` with an integer value in it. In each folder, create the corresponding `myid` file with the correct value. The following commands will create the file:

```
echo 1 > zookeeper_1/myid
echo 2 > zookeeper_2/myid
echo 3 > zookeeper_3/myid
```

You have completed the prerequisite tasks for configuring ZooKeeper and Kafka. Now you can edit the configuration files for both. The next section will walk you through the process.

Configuring ZooKeeper and Kafka

The configuration files for both ZooKeeper and Kafka are in the Kafka directory in the `conf` folder. Since you have three Kafka directories, I will walk through using `Kafka_1` and the steps will need to be applied to every other directory.

From the `~/kafka_1/conf` directory, you will need to edit the `zookeeper.properties` file. You will edit the data directory and the servers, as well as adding properties. The configuration file is shown in the following code block, with the modifications in bold (for the full file, refer to the GitHub repo):

```
# the directory where the snapshot is stored.
dataDir=/home/paulcrickard/data/zookeeper_1
# the port at which the clients will connect
clientPort=2181
# disable the per-ip limit on the number of connections since
this is a non-production config
maxClientCnxns=0
# Disable the adminserver by default to avoid port conflicts.
# Set the port to something non-conflicting if choosing to
enable this
admin.enableServer=false
# admin.serverPort=8080
tickTime=2000
initLimit=5
syncLimit=2
server.1=localhost:2666:3666
server.2=localhost:2667:3667
server.3=localhost:2668:3668
```

After making the changes, you can save the file. You will now need to modify this file in the `kafka_2` and `kafka_3` directories. Note that the `dataDir` setting will end in `zookeeper_2` and `zookeeper_3`, respectively. Also, the port number should increment by one to `2182` and `2183`. Everything else will remain the same. Again, the only reason you are changing the directory and ports is so that you can run three servers on a single machine. On three distinct servers, you would leave the settings as they are, only changing localhost to the IP address of the server.

Now that ZooKeeper is configured, you can configure Kafka. In the same `conf` directory, open the `server.properties` file. The file is shown with the edits in bold (for the full file, refer to the GitHub repo):

```
############################# Server Basics
#############################
# The id of the broker. This must be set to a unique integer
for each broker.
```

```
broker.id=1
############################ Socket Server Settings
############################
# The address the socket server listens on. It will get the
value returned from
# java.net.InetAddress.getCanonicalHostName() if not
configured.
#    FORMAT:
#       listeners = listener_name://host_name:port
#    EXAMPLE:
#       listeners = PLAINTEXT://your.host.name:9092
listeners=PLAINTEXT://localhost:9092
############################ Log Basics
############################
# A comma separated list of directories under which to store
log files
log.dirs=/home/paulcrickard/logs_1
############################ Zookeeper
############################
# Zookeeper connection string (see zookeeper docs for details).
# This is a comma separated host:port pairs, each corresponding
to a zk
# server. e.g. "127.0.0.1:3000,127.0.0.1:3001,127.0.0.1:3002".
# You can also append an optional chroot string to the urls to
specify the
# root directory for all kafka znodes.
zookeeper.connect=localhost:2181,localhost:2182,localhost:2183
```

For each Kafka directory, you will modify the server.properties file to have a broker ID of 1, 2, and 3. You can use any integer, but I am keeping them the same as the folder names. Also, you will set the listeners to localhost:9092, localhost:9093, and localhost:9094. The log.dirs property will be set to each of the log_1, log_2, and log_3 folders. All three configurations will have the same value for the zookeeper.connect property.

You have created all the necessary directories to simulate three servers and have configured both ZooKeeper and Kafka. You can now move on to starting the clusters.

Starting the ZooKeeper and Kafka clusters

To run the servers, you will need to open six terminals – you will not run them in the background.

Docker

You could use Docker Compose to run multiple containers and launch everything with a single file. Containers are an excellent tool, but beyond the scope of this book.

In the first three terminals, you will launch the ZooKeeper cluster. In each terminal, enter the Kafka folder for each instance. Run the following command:

```
bin/zookeeper-server-start.sh config/zookeeper.properties
```

When you start all of the servers, a lot of text will scroll by as the servers look for others and hold an election. Once they connect, the text will stop, and the cluster will be ready.

To start the Kafka cluster, enter an instance of the kafka directory in each of the three remaining terminals. You can then run the following command in each terminal:

```
bin/kafka-server-start.sh config/server.properties
```

When you are finished, you will have a line in each terminal that should look like the following line:

```
INFO [ZookeeperClient Kafka server] Connected. (kafka.
zookeeper.zookeeperClient)
```

You now have two clusters of three nodes running for both ZooKeeper and Kafka. To test out the clusters and make sure everything is working properly, the next section will create a topic, a consumer and, a producer, and send some messages.

Testing the Kafka cluster

Kafka comes with scripts to allow you to perform some basic functions from the command line. To test the cluster, you can create a topic, create a producer, send some messages, and then create a consumer to read them. If the consumer can read them, your cluster is running.

To create a topic, run the following command from your `kafka_1` directory:

```
bin/kafka-topics.sh --create --zookeeper
localhost:2181,localhost:2182,localhost:2183 --replication-
factor 2 --partitions 1 --topic dataengineering
```

The preceding command runs the `kafka-topics` script with the `create` flag. It then specifies the ZooKeeper cluster IP addresses and the topic. If the topic was created, the terminal will have printed the following line:

```
created topic dataengineering
```

You can verify this by listing all the topics in the Kafka cluster using the same script, but with the `list` flag:

```
bin/kafka-topics.sh -list --zookeeper
localhost:2181,localhost:2182,localhost:2183
```

The result should be a single line: `dataengineering`. Now that you have a topic, you can send and receive messages on it. The next section will show you how.

Testing the cluster with messages

In the next chapters, you will use Apache NiFi and Python to send and receive messages, but for a quick test of the cluster, you can use the scripts provided to do this as well. To create a producer, use the following command:

```
bin/kafka-console-producer.sh --broker-list
localhost:9092,localhost:9093,localhost:9094 --topic
dataengineering
```

The preceding command uses the `kafka-console-producer` script with the `broker-list` flag that passes the `kafka` cluster servers. Lastly, it takes a topic, and since we only have one, it is `dataengineering`. When it is ready, you will have a > prompt to type messages into.

To read the messages, you will need to use the `kafka-console-consumer` script. The command is as shown:

```
bin/kafka-console-consumer.sh --zookeeper
localhost:2181,localhost:2182,localhost:2183 --topic
dataengineering -from-beginning
```

The consumer passes the `zookeeper` flag with the list of servers. It also specifies the topic and the `from-beginning` flag. If you had already read messages, you could specify an `offset` flag with the index of the last message so that you start from your last position.

Putting the producer and consumer terminals next to each other, you should have something like the following screenshot:

Figure 12.3 – Producer and consumer

In the preceding screenshot, you will notice that I typed *first message* and *second message* twice. When the consumer turned on, it read all the messages on the topic. Once it has read them all, it will await new messages. If you type a message in the producer, it will show up in the consumer window after a short lag.

You now have a fully functional Kafka cluster and are ready to move on to stream processing with NiFi and Python in the next chapter.

Summary

In this chapter, you learned how to create a Kafka cluster, which required the creation of a ZooKeeper cluster. While you ran all of the instances on a single machine, the steps you took will work on different servers too. Kafka allows the creation of real-time data streams and will require a different way of thinking than the batch processing you have been doing.

The next chapter will explain the concepts involved in streams in depth. You will also learn how to process streams in both NiFi and Python.

13
Streaming Data with Apache Kafka

Apache Kafka opens up the world of real-time data streams. While there are fundamental differences in stream processing and batch processing, how you build data pipelines will be very similar. Understanding the differences between streaming data and batch processing will allow you to build data pipelines that take these differences into account.

In this chapter, we're going to cover the following main topics:

- Understanding logs
- Understanding how Kafka uses logs
- Building data pipelines with Kafka and NiFi
- Differentiating stream processing from batch processing
- Producing and consuming with Python

Understanding logs

If you have written code, you may be familiar with software logs. Software developers use logging to write output from applications to a text file to store different events that happen within the software. They then use these logs to help debug any issues that arise. In Python, you have probably implemented code similar to the following code:

```
import logging
logging.basicConfig(level=0,filename='python-log.log',
filemode='w', format='%(levelname)s - %(message)s')
logging.debug('Attempted to divide by zero')
logging.warning('User left field blank in the form')
logging.error('Couldn't find specified file')
```

The preceding code is a basic logging example that logs different levels – debug, warning, and error – to a file named python-log.log. The code will produce the following output:

```
DEBUG - Attempted to divide by zero
WARNING - User left field blank in the form
ERROR - Couldn't find specified file
```

The messages are logged to the file in the order in which they occur. You do not, however, know the exact time the event happened. You can improve on this log by adding a timestamp, as shown in the following code:

```
logging.basicConfig(level=0,filename='python-log.log',
filemode='w', format='%(asctime)s - %(levelname)s - %(message)
s')
logging.info('Something happened')
logging.info('Something else happened, and it was bad')
```

The results of the preceding code are shown in the following code block. Notice that now there is a timestamp. The log is ordered, as was the previous log. However, the exact time is known in this log:

```
2020-06-21 10:55:40,278 - INFO - Something happened
2020-06-21 10:55:40,278 - INFO - Something else happened, and
it was bad
```

In the preceding logs, you should notice that they follow a very specific format, or schema, which is defined in `basicConfig`. Another common log that you are probably familiar with is the `web` log.

Web server logs are like software logs; they report events – usually requests – in chronological order, with a timestamp and the event. These logs follow a very specific format and have many tools available for parsing them. Databases also use logs internally to help in replication and to record modifications in a transaction.

If applications, web servers, and databases all use logs, and they are all slightly different, what exactly is a log?

A **log** is an ordered collection of events, or records, that is append only.

That is all there is to it. Simple. To the point. And yet an extremely powerful tool in software development and data processing. The following diagram shows a sample log:

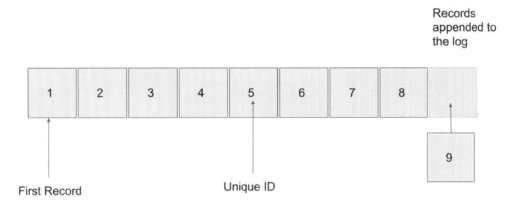

Figure 13.1 – An example of a log

The preceding diagram shows individual records as blocks. The first record is on the left. Time is represented by the position of records in the log. The record to the right of another record is newer. So, record **3** is newer than record **2**. Records are not removed from the log but appended to the end. Record **9** is added to the far right of the log, as it is the newest record – until record 10 comes along.

Understanding how Kafka uses logs

Kafka maintains logs that are written to by producers and read by consumers. The following sections will explain topics, consumers, and producers.

Topics

Apache Kafka uses logs to store data – records. Logs in Kafka are called **topics**. A topic is like a table in a database. In the previous chapter, you tested your Kafka cluster by creating a topic named `dataengineering`. The topic is saved to disk as a log file. Topics can be a single log, but usually they are scaled horizontally into partitions. Each partition is a log file that can be stored on another server. In a topic with partitions, the message order guarantee no longer applies to the topic, but only each partition. The following diagram shows a topic split into three partitions:

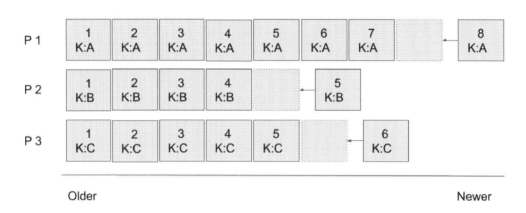

Figure 13.2 – A Kafka topic with three partitions

The preceding topic – **Transactions** – has three partitions labeled **P1**, **P2**, and **P3**. Within each partition, the records are ordered, with the records to the left being older than the records to the right – the larger the number in the box, the newer the record. You will notice that the records have **K:A** in **P1** and **K:B** and **K:C** in **P2** and **P3**, respectively. Those are the keys associated with the records. By assigning a key, you guarantee that the records containing the same keys will go to the same partition. While the order of records in the topic may be out of order, each partition is in order.

Kafka producers and consumers

Kafka producers send data to a topic and a partition. Records can be sent round-robin to partitions or you can use a key to send data to specific partitions. When you send messages with a producer, you can do it in one of three ways:

- **Fire and Forget**: You send a message and move on. You do not wait for an acknowledgment back from Kafka. In this method, records can get lost.

- **Synchronous**: Send a message and wait for a response before moving on.

- **Asynchrous**: Send a message and a callback. You move on once the message is sent, but will get a response at some point that you can handle.

Producers are fairly straightforward – they send messages to a topic and partition, maybe request an acknowledgment, retry if a message fails – or not – and continue. Consumers, however, can be a little more complicated.

Consumers read messages from a topic. Consumers run in a poll loop that runs indefinitely waiting for messages. Consumers can read from the beginning – they will start at the first message in the topic and read the entire history. Once caught up, the consumer will wait for new messages.

If a consumer reads five messages, the offset is five. The offset is the position of the consumer in the topic. It is a bookmark for where the consumer left off. A consumer can always start reading a topic from the offset, or a specified offset – which is stored by Zookeeper.

What happens when you have a consumer on the `dataengineering` topic, but the topic has three partitions and is writing records faster than you can read it? The following diagram shows a single consumer trying to consume three partitions:

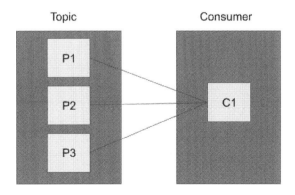

Figure 13.3 – Single consumer reading multiple partitions

Using consumer groups, you can scale the reading of Kafka topics. In the preceding diagram, the consumer **C1** is in a consumer group, but is the only consumer. By adding additional consumers, the topics can be distributed. The following diagram shows what that looks like:

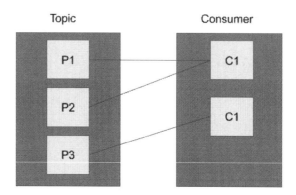

Figure 13.4 – Two consumers in a consumer group consuming three partitions

The preceding diagram shows that there are still more partitions than consumers in the group, meaning that one consumer will be handling multiple partitions. You can add more consumers, as shown in the following diagram:

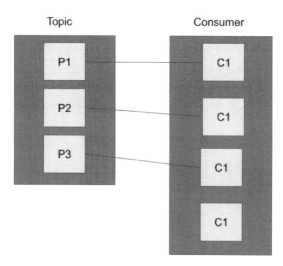

Figure 13.5 – More consumers than partitions leave one idle

In the preceding diagram, there are more consumers in the consumer group than partitions. When there are more consumers than partitions, consumers will sit idle. Therefore, it is not necessary to create more consumers than the number of partitions.

You can, however, create more than one consumer group. The following diagram shows what this looks like:

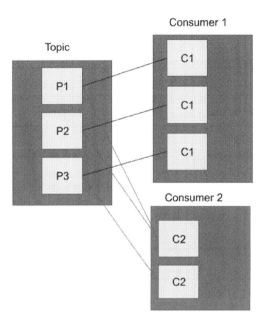

Figure 13.6 – Multiple consumer groups reading from a single topic

Multiple consumer groups can read from the same partition. It is good practice to create a consumer group for every application that needs access to the topic.

Now that you understand the basics of working with Kafka, the next section will show you how to build data pipelines using NiFi and Kafka.

Building data pipelines with Kafka and NiFi

To build a data pipeline with Apache Kafka, you will need to create a producer since we do not have any production Kafka clusters to connect to. With the producer running, you can read the data like any other file or database.

The Kafka producer

The Kafka producer will take advantage of the production data pipeline from *Chapter 11, Project — Building a Production Data Pipeline*. The producer data pipeline will do little more than send the data to the Kafka topic. The following screenshot shows the completed producer data pipeline:

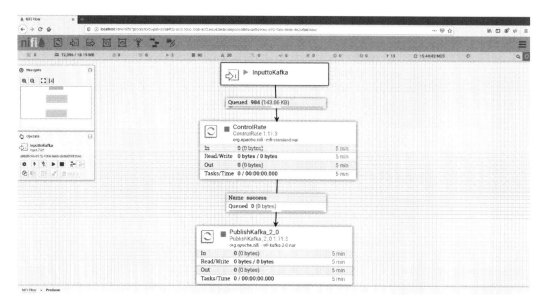

Figure 13.7 – The NiFi data pipeline

To create the data pipeline, perform the following steps:

1. Open a terminal. You need to create the topic before you can send messages to it in NiFi. Enter the following command:

    ```
    bin/kafka-topics.sh --create --bootstrap-server
    localhost:9092 --replication-factor 1 --partitions 3
    --topic users
    ```

    The preceding command is slightly different than the one used in the previous chapter to test the cluster. The difference is that the partitions flag is set to 3. This will allow you to test using Consumer Groups in the next section.

2. Drag an input port and connect it to the output from the ReadDataLake processor group, as shown in the following screenshot:

Figure 13.8 – Connecting the input port to an output port

3. Next, drag and drop the `ControlRate` processor to the canvas. The `ControlRate` processor will allow us to slow down the data flow with more control than just using backpressure in the queue. This will allow you to make it appear that data is streaming into the Kafka topic instead of just being there all at once. If you did write it all in one pass, once you had read it, the pipeline would stop until you added more data.

4. To configure the `ControlRate` processor, set the **Rate Control Criteria** property to `flowfile count`. Set **Maximum Rate** to `1`. These two properties allow you to specify the amount of data passing through. Since you used the flowfile count, the maximum rate will be an integer of the number of flowfiles to let through. If you used the default option, you would set **Maximum Rate** to a file size on disk such as `1 MB`. Lastly, specify how frequently to allow the maximum rate through in the **Time Duration** property. I have left it at 1 minute. Every minute, one flowfile will be sent to the user's Kafka topic.

5. To send the data to Kafka, drag and drop the `PublishKafka_2_0` processor to the canvas. There are multiple Kafka processors for different versions of Kafka. To configure the processor, you will set the **Kafka Brokers** property to `localhost:9092`, `localhost:9093`, and `localhost:9094`. A Kafka broker is a Kafka server. Since you are running a cluster, you will enter all of the IPs as a comma-separated string – just as you did in the command-line example in the previous chapter. Enter **Topic Name** as users and the **Delivery Guarantee** property to **Guarantee Replication Delivery**.

You now have a Kafka producer configured in NiFi that will take the output from `ReadDataLake` and send each record to Kafka at one-minute intervals. To read the topic, you will create a NiFi data pipeline.

The Kafka consumer

As a data engineer, you may or may not need to set up the Kafka cluster and producers. However, as you learned at the beginning of this book, the role of the data engineer varies widely, and building the Kafka infrastructure could very well be part of your job. With Kafka receiving messages on a topic, it is time to read those messages.

The completed data pipeline is shown in the following screenshot:

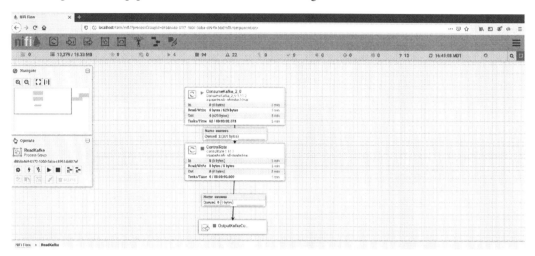

Figure 13.9 – Consuming a Kafka topic in NiFi

To create the data pipeline, perform the following steps:

1. Drag and drop the `ConsumeKafka_2_0` processor to the canvas. To configure the processor, set the Kafka brokers to your cluster – `localhost:9092`, `localhost:9093`, and `localhost:9094`. Set **Topic Name** to `users` and **Offset** to `Earliest`. Lastly, set **Group ID** to `NiFi Consumer`. The **Group ID** property defines the consumer group that the consumer (processor) will be a part of.

2. Next, I have added the `ControlRate` processor to the canvas. The `ControlRate` processor will slow down the reading of the records already on the topic. If the topic is not too large, you could just use backpressure on the queue so that once you have processed the historical data, the new records will move in real time.

3. To configure the `ControlRate` processor, set **Rate Control Criteria** to `flowfile count`, **Maximum Rate** to `1`, and **Time Duration** to `1` minute.

4. Add an output port to the canvas and name it. I have named it
`OutputKafkaConsumer`. This will allow you to connect this processor group to
others to complete a data pipeline.

5. Start the processor group, and you will see records processed every minute. You are
reading a Kafka topic with a single consumer in a consumer group. If you recall,
when you created the topic, you set the number of partitions to three. Because there
are multiple partitions, you can add more consumers to the group. To do that, you
just need to add another `ConsumeKafka_2_0` processor and configure it.

6. Drag another `ConsumeKafka_2_0` processor to the canvas. Configure it
with the same Kafka brokers – `localhost:9092`, `localhost:9093`, and
`localhost:9094` – and the same topic – `users`. Set **Group ID** to `NiFi`
`Consumer`.

7. Now that both processors have the same group ID, they will be members of
the same consumer group. With two consumer and three partitions, one of the
consumers will read two partitions and the other will read one. You can add another
`ConsumeKafka_2_0` processor if the topic is streaming large amounts of data, but
any more than three would sit idle.

The new data pipeline is shown in the following screenshot:

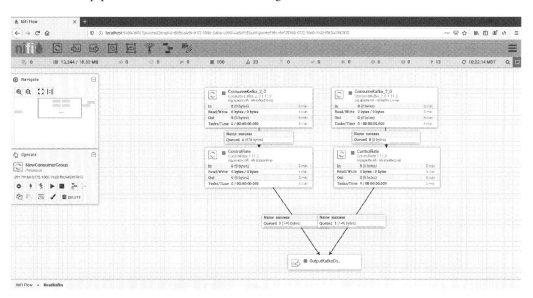

Figure 13.10 – Consuming a Kafka with multiple consumers in a consumer group

Running the processor group, you will start to see records flow through both `ConsumerKafka_2_0` processors. The configuration of the producer will determine which partition records are sent to and how many will flow through your consumer. Because of the default settings and the number of partitions to consumers, you will probably see two flowfiles processed by one consumer for every one flowfile processed by the other.

Just as you can add more consumers to a consumer group, you can have more than one consumer group read a topic – the number of consumer groups is in no way related to the number of partitions.

To add another consumer group to the data pipeline, drag and drop another `ConsumeKafka_2_0` processor. Set **Kafka Brokers** to `localhost:9092`, `localhost:9093`, and `localhost:9094`, and set **Topic** to `users`. The group ID is the name of the consumer group. Set it to anything other than `NiFi Consumer` – since this consumer group already exists. I have set **Group ID** to `NiFi Consumer2` – hardly creative or original, but it gets the job done. The data pipeline will now look like the following screenshot:

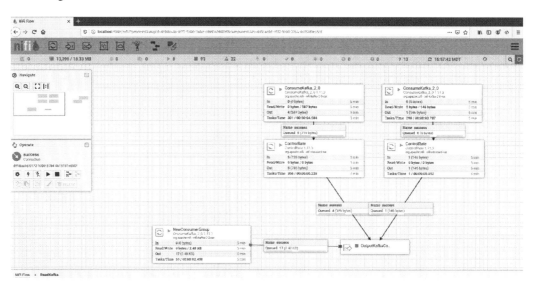

Figure 13.11 – Two consumer groups in NiFi

In the preceding screenshot, you will notice that there is no `ControlRate` processor on the second consumer group. Once started, the processor will consume the entire history of the topic and send the records downstream. There were 17 records in the topic. The other queues are much smaller because the topic is being throttled.

You can now connect the processor group to any other processor group to create a data pipeline that reads from Apache Kafka. In the following screenshot, I have connected the ReadKafka processor group to the production data pipeline from *Chapter 11, Project – Building a Production Data Pipeline*:

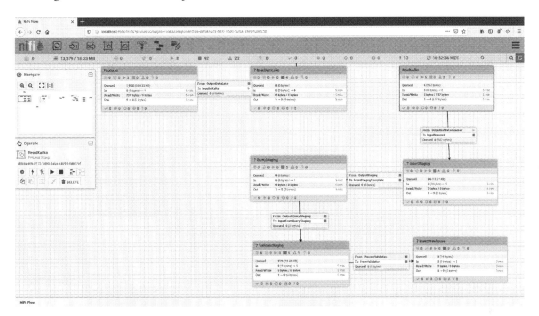

Figure 13.12 – The completed data pipeline

Instead of reading the data from the data lake, the new data pipeline reads the data from the Kafka topic users. The records are sent to the staging processor group to continue the data pipeline. The end result is that the PostgreSQL production table will have all of the records from the Kafka topic. The reading of the data lake is now a Kafka producer.

Creating producers and consumers in NiFi only requires the use of a single processor – PublishKafka or ConsumeKafka. The configuration is dependent on the Kafka cluster you will publish to or read from. In NiFi, Kafka is just another data input. How you process the data once received will be no different than if you ran a database query. There are some differences in the nature of the data that you must take into consideration, and the next section will discuss them.

Differentiating stream processing from batch processing

While the processing tools don't change whether you are processing streams or batches, there are two things you should keep in mind while processing streams – **unbounded** and **time**.

Data can be bounded or unbounded. Bounded data has an end, whereas unbounded data is constantly created and is possibly infinite. Bounded data is last year's sales of widgets. Unbounded data is a traffic sensor counting cars and recording their speeds on the highway.

Why is this important in building data pipelines? Because with bounded data, you will know everything about the data. You can see it all at once. You can query it, put it in a staging environment, and then run Great Expectations on it to get a sense of the ranges, values, or other metrics to use in validation as you process your data.

With unbounded data, it is streaming in and you don't know what the next piece of data will look like. This doesn't mean you can't validate it – you know that the speed of a car must be within a certain range and can't have the value h – it will be an integer between 0 and 200-ish.

On bounded data, you can query the average or maximum of a field. On unbounded data, you will need to keep recalculating these values as data streams through the data pipeline. In the next chapter, you will learn about Apache Spark and how it can help in processing unbounded, or streaming, data.

You may be thinking that yes, last year's sales numbers are bounded, but this year's are not. The year is not over, and the data is still streaming in. This brings up the second thing you should keep in mind when dealing with streams and that is time. Bounded data is complete over a time period or a window. And windowing is a method of making unbounded data bounded.

There are three common windows – **fixed**, **sliding**, and **session**:

- **Fixed** – Sometimes called **tumbling windows, these**re windows that covers a fixed time and records do not overlap. If you specify a one-minute window, the records will fall within each interval, as shown in the following diagram:

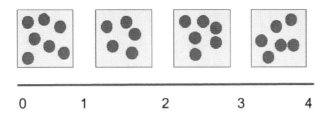

Figure 13.13 – Data in fixed windows

- **Sliding** – This is a window in which the window is defined, such as 1 minute, but the next window starts in less than the window length – say, every 30 seconds. This type of window will have duplicates and is good for rolling averages. A sliding window is shown in the following diagram:

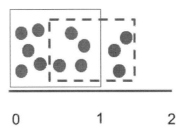

Figure 13.14 – Data in sliding windows

The diagram shows two windows, one starting at 0 that is extended for 1 minute. The second window overlaps at 0:30 and extends for 1 minute until 1:30.

- **Session** – Sessions will not have the same window of time but are events. For example, a user logs in to shop, their data is streamed for that login session, and the session is defined by some piece of data in the records, called a session token.

When discussing windows and time, you must also consider what time to use – **Event**, **Ingest**, or **Processing**. The three different times could have different values and whichever you choose depends on your use case:

- **Event Time** is when the event happens. This may be recorded in the record before it is sent to Kafka. For example, at 1:05, a car was recorded travelling 55 mph.

- **Ingest Time** is the time that the data is recorded in a Kafka topic. The latency between the event and the recording could fluctuate depending on network latency.

- **Processing Time** is the time in which you read the data from the Kafka topic and did something with it – such as processed it through your data pipeline and put it in the warehouse.

By recognizing that you may be working with unbounded data, you will avoid problems in your data pipelines by not trying to analyze all the data at once, but by choosing an appropriate windowing and also by using the correct time for your use case.

Producing and consuming with Python

You can create producers and consumers for Kafka using Python. There are multiple Kafka Python libraries – Kafka-Python, PyKafka, and Confluent Python Kafka. In this section, I will use Confluent Python Kafka, but if you want to use an open source, community-based library, you can use Kafka-Python. The principles and structure of the Python programs will be the same no matter which library you choose.

To install the library, you can use `pip`. The following command will install it:

```
pip3 install confluent-kafka
```

Once the library has finished installing, you can use it by importing it into your applications. The following sections will walk through writing a producer and consumer.

Writing a Kafka producer in Python

To write a producer in Python, you will create a producer, send data, and listen for acknowledgements. In the previous examples, you used `Faker` to create fake data about people. You will use it again to generate the data in this example. To write the producer, perform the following steps:

1. Import the required libraries and create a faker:

   ```
   from confluent_kafka import Producer
   from faker import Faker
   import json
   import time

   fake=Faker()
   ```

2. Next, create the producer by specifying the IP addresses of your Kafka cluster:

   ```
   p=Producer({'bootstrap.
   servers':'localhost:9092,localhost:9093,localhost:9094'})
   ```

3. You can list the topics available to publish to as follows:

```
p.list_topics().topics
```

4. There are different settings for acknowledgments and how you handle them, but for now, create a callback that will receive an error (`err`) and an acknowledgment (`msg`). In every call, only one of them will be true and have data. Using an `if` statement, check whether there is an error, otherwise, you can print the message:

```
def receipt(err,msg):
    if err is not None:
        print('Error: {}'.format(err))
    else:
        print('{} : Message on topic {} on partition
        {} with value of {}'.format(time.strftime('%Y-
        %m-%d %H:%M:%S',time.localtime(msg.timestamp()
        [1]/1000)), msg.topic(), msg.partition(),
        msg.value().decode('utf-8')))
```

The code that prints the message prints several pieces of data within the message object. The message has a timestamp in milliseconds. To convert it to seconds so that you can print the local datetime, divide by 1,000. It then print the topic that the message was published on – your producer can write to any topic, so if you are writing to multiple topics within a single producer, you will want to know which topic worked or had an error. It also prints the partition (`0`, `1`, `2`) and then the value of the message. The messages come back as bytes so you can decode them to `utf-8`.

5. Next, create the producer loop. The code loops through a range creating a fake data object. The object is the same as in *Chapter 3, Working with Files*. It then dumps the dictionary so that it can be sent to Kafka:

```
for i in range(10):
    data={'name':fake.name(),'age':fake.random_
        int(min=18, max=80, step=1),'street':fake.
        street_address(),'city':fake.city(),
        'state':fake.state(),'zip':fake.zipcode()}
    m=json.dumps(data)
```

6. Before sending the data to Kafka, call `poll()` to get any acknowledgments for previous messages. Those will be sent to the callback (`receipt`). Now you can call `produce()` and pass the topic name, the data, and the function to send acknowledgments to:

```
p.poll(0)
p.produce('users',m.encode('utf-8'),callback=receipt)
```

7. To finish, flush the producer. This will also get any existing acknowledgements and send them to `receipt()`:

```
p.flush()
```

The results of the preceding code will be messages sent to the `user` topic on the Kafka cluster, and the terminal will print the acknowledgments, which will look like the following output:

```
2020-06-22 15:29:30 : Message on topic users on partition 1
with value of {'name': 'Willie Chambers', 'age': 66, 'street':
'13647 Davis Neck Suite 480', 'city': 'Richardside', 'state':
'Nebraska', 'zip': '87109'}
```

Now that you can send data to a Kafka topic, the next section will show you how to consume it.

Writing a Kafka consumer in Python

To create a consumer in Python, you create the consumer pointing to the Kafka cluster, select a topic to listen to, and then enter a loop that listens for new messages. The code that follows will walk you through how to write a Python consumer:

1. First, import the `Consumer` library and create the consumer. You will pass the IP addresses of your Kafka cluster, the consumer group name – this can be anything you want, but if you add multiple consumers to the group, they will need the same name, and Kafka will remember the offset where this consumer group stopped reading the topic – and lastly, you will pass the offset reset, or where you want to start reading:

```
from confluent_kafka import Consumer


c=Consumer({'bootstrap.servers':
'localhost:9092,localhost:9093,localhost9093','group.
id':'python-consumer','auto.offset.reset':'earliest'})
```

2. You can get a list of topics available to subscribe to as well as the number of partitions for a particular topic:

```
c.list_topics().topics
t.topics['users'].partitions
```

3. Once you know which topic you want to consume, you can subscribe to it:

```
c.subscribe(['users'])
```

4. To receive messages, create an infinite loop – if you want to listen forever. You can always start and stop using the offset to pick up where you left off. Call `poll()` to get the message. The result will be one of three things – nothing yet, an error, or a message. Using the `if` statements, check for a nothing, an error, or decode the message and do something with the data, which in this case is to print it. When you are done, close the connection:

```
while True:
    msg=c.poll(1.0) #timeout

    if msg is None:
        continue

    if msg.error():
        print('Error: {}'.format(msg.error()))
        continue

    data=msg.value().decode('utf-8')
    print(data)
c.close()
```

The results will be several JSON objects scrolling through the terminal and will look like the following output:

```
{'name': 'Joseph Vaughn', 'age': 39, 'street': '978 Jordan
Extensions Suite 684', 'city': 'Zunigamouth', 'state':
'Michigan', 'zip': '38090'}
```

This is a basic example of consuming a topic with Python, but should give you an idea of the architecture and how to start building more complex consumers.

Summary

In this chapter, you learned the basics of Apache Kafka – from what is a log and how Kafka uses it, to partitions, producers, and consumers. You learned how Apache NiFi can create producers and consumers with a single processor. The chapter took a quick detour to explain how streaming data is unbounded and how time and windowing work with streams. These are important considerations when working with streaming data and can result in errors if you assume you have all the data at one time. Lastly, you learned how to use Confluent Python Kafka to write basic producers and consumers in Python.

Equipped with these skills, the next chapter will show you how to build a real-time data pipeline.

14
Data Processing with Apache Spark

In the previous chapter, you learned how to add streaming data to your data pipelines. Using Python or Apache NiFi, you can extract, transform, and load streaming data. However, to perform transformations on large amounts of streaming data, data engineers turn to tools such as Apache Spark. Apache Spark is faster than most other methods – such as MapReduce on non-trivial transformations – and it allows distributed data processing.

In this chapter, we're going to cover the following main topics:

- Installing and running Spark
- Installing and configuring PySpark
- Processing data with PySpark

Installing and running Spark

Apache Spark is a distributed data processing engine that can handle both streams and batch data, and even graphs. It has a core set of components and other libraries that are used to add functionality. A common depiction of the Spark ecosystem is shown in the following diagram:

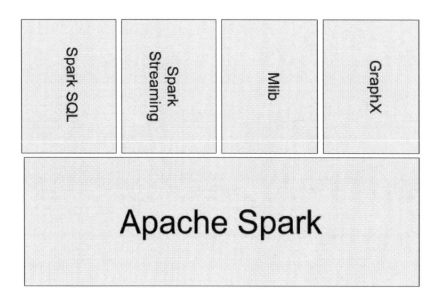

Figure 14.1 – The Apache Spark ecosystem

To run Spark as a cluster, you have several options. Spark can run in a standalone mode, which uses a simple cluster manager provided by Spark. It can also run on an Amazon EC2 instance, using YARN, Mesos, or Kubernetes. In a production environment with a significant workload, you would probably not want to run in standalone mode; however, this is how we will stand up our cluster in this chapter. The principles will be the same, but the standalone cluster provides the fastest way to get you up and running without needing to dive into more complicated infrastructure.

To install Apache Spark, take the following steps:

1. Browse to the website at `http://spark.apache.org`. From there, you can keep up to date with new versions of Apache Spark, read the documentation, learn about the libraries, and find code examples:

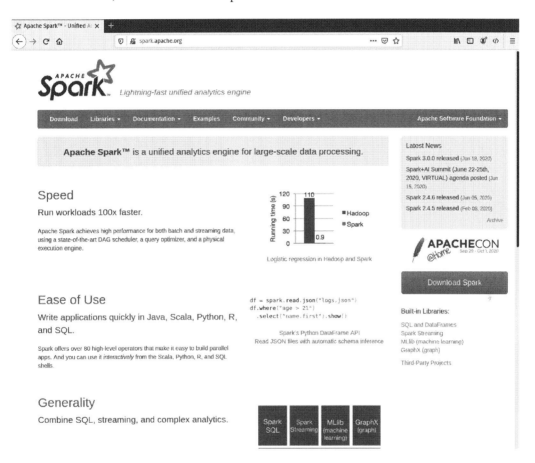

Figure 14.2 – The Apache Spark website

2. From the website, select the **Download** menu option. Choose the version of Spark you want to use – at the time of writing, the newest version is 3.0.0. You will be asked to choose a package type. We will not be using Hadoop, but have to select a version or provide our own. I have chosen **Pre-built for Apache Hadoop 2.7**. On Windows, you may need to trick the operating system into thinking Hadoop is installed by setting environment variables, but on Linux and macOS, this should not be an issue. The download options are shown in the following screenshot:

Figure 14.3 – Downloading Apache Spark for Hadoop 2.7

3. After downloading the file, you will extract it, then move it to the home directory in a directory named `spark3`. You can do this using the following commands:

```
tar -xvzf spark-3.0.0-bin-hadoop2.7.tgz
mv spark-3.0.0-bin-hadoop2.7 ~/spark3
```

4. Next, you will need to make a cluster. As you did with Kafka, you will make a copy of the Spark directory on the same machine and make it act as another node. If you have another machine, you could also put another copy of Spark on that server. Copy the directory and rename it `spark-node`, as shown:

```
cp -r spark3/ spark-node
```

5. To run the Spark cluster, you can use the provided scripts. The scripts to run the cluster use outdated terminology – `master` and `slave`. This language is common in the technology space; however, there have been many voices opposed to it for a long time. Finally, it appears that there is some traction being made in removing this language as GitHub will remove `master` from the branch names. I too have renamed the scripts, using the terms `head` and `node`. To do this, use the following commands:

```
cd ~/spark3/sbin
cp start-master.sh start-head.sh
cd ~/spark-node/sbin
cp start-slave.sh start-node.sh
```

6. To start the cluster, you can now run the scripts as shown:

```
./start-head.sh
./start-node.sh spark://pop-os.localdomain:7077 -p 9911
```

7. You can pass parameters to the scripts, and in the preceding command, you pass the port flag (`-p`) to tell the script which port you want the node to run on. You can also pass the following:

a) `-h, --host`: The hostname to run on. The `i, -ip` flag has been deprecated.

b) `-p, --port`: The port to listen on.

c) `--webui-port`: The port for the web GUI, which defaults to `8080`.

d) `-c, --cores`: The number of cores to use.

e) `-m, --memory`: The amount of memory to use. By default, it is 1 gigabyte less than your full memory.

f) `-d, --work-dir`: The scratch space directory for the worker only.

g) `--properties-file`: This is where you can specify several of these flags in a `spark.conf` file.

The cluster will take a minute to load, and when it has finished, you can browse to the web UI at `http://localhost:8080/`. You will see the details of your cluster and it will look as in the following screenshot:

Figure 14.4 – Spark cluster web UI

With the cluster up and running, you will need to set up the Python environment so that you can code against it. The next section will walk you through those steps.

Installing and configuring PySpark

PySpark is installed with Spark. You can see it in the `~/spark3/bin` directory, as well as other libraries and tools. To configure PySpark to run, you need to export environment variables. The variables are shown here:

```
export SPARK_HOME=/home/paulcrickard/spark3
export PATH=$SPARK_HOME/bin:$PATH
export PYSPARK_PYTHON=python3
```

The preceding command set the `SPARK_HOME` variable. This will be where you installed Spark. I have pointed the variable to the head of the Spark cluster because the node would really be on another machine. Then, it adds `SPARK_HOME` to your path. This means that when you type a command, the operating system will look for it in the directories specified in your path, so now it will search `~/spark3/bin`, which is where PySpark lives.

Running the preceding commands in a terminal will allow Spark to run while the terminal is open. You will have to rerun these commands every time. To make them permanent, you can add the commands to your ~/.bashrc file. After saving the .bashrc file, you need to reload it. You can do that by running the following command:

```
source ~/.bashrc
```

You should now be able to open a terminal and run PySpark, and the result will be the PySpark interactive shell, as shown:

Figure 14.5 – The interactive Spark shell

If you see the preceding screenshot, congratulations, you have PySpark configured. In this chapter, the examples will use PySpark in Jupyter notebooks. There are two ways to configure PySpark to work with Jupyter:

- **Set the drivers**: To set PySpark to run in Jupyter, you can set the PYSPARK_DRIVER_PYTHON environment variable and the _OPTS variable to the Jupyter Notebook using the following commands (add this to ~/.bashrc if you want it to be permanent):

```
export PYSPARK_DRIVER_PYTHON=jupyter
export PYSPARK_DRIVER_PYTHON_OPTS='notebook'
```

- **Find Spark**: You can also use the `findspark` library and add code to your Jupyter notebook that gets the Spark information as it runs. The examples in this chapter will use this method. You can install `findspark` using `pip`, as shown:

```
pip3 install findspark
```

To test whether PySpark runs in a Jupyter notebook, start the notebook server using the following command:

```
jupyter notebook
```

The notebook server will open your browser. From there, you can create a new Python 3 notebook. To use the `findspark` method, add the following two lines to your notebook and run it:

```
import findspark
findspark.init()
```

If the preceding lines ran without error, then the code was able to find Spark.

You can now run PySpark code on your Spark cluster. The next section will walk you through some basic PySpark examples.

Processing data with PySpark

Before processing data with PySpark, let's run one of the samples to show how Spark works. Then, we will skip the boilerplate in later examples and focus on data processing. The Jupyter notebook for the **Pi Estimation** example from the Spark website at `http://spark.apache.org/examples.html` is shown in the following screenshot:

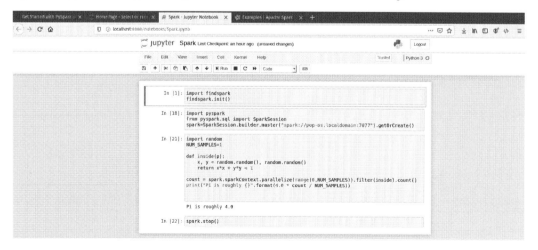

Figure 14.6 – The Pi Estimation example in a Jupyter notebook

The example from the website will not run without some modifications. In the following points, I will walk through the cells:

1. The first cell imports `findspark` and runs the `init()` method. This was explained in the preceding section as the preferred method to include PySpark in Jupyter notebooks. The code is as follows:

    ```
    import findspark
    findspark.init()
    ```

2. The next cell imports the `pyspark` library and `SparkSession`. It then creates the session by passing the head node of the Spark cluster. You can get the URL from the Spark web UI – you also used it to start the worker node:

    ```
    import pyspark
    from pyspark.sql import SparkSession
    spark=SparkSession.builder.master('spark://pop-os.
    localdomain:7077').appName('Pi-Estimation').getOrCreate()
    ```

3. Running the first two cells, you can browse to the Spark GUI and see that there is a task running. The running task is shown in the following screenshot – notice the name of the worker is `Pi-Estimation`, which is the `appName` parameter in the preceding code:

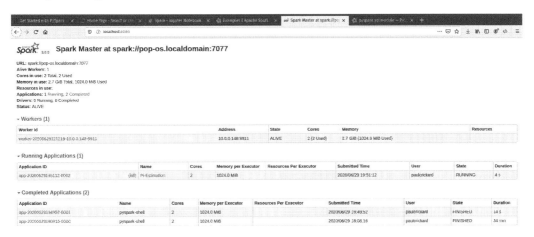

Figure 14.7 – The Spark web UI with a running session and two completed sessions

The preceding code will be used in all of your Spark code. It is the boilerplate code.

4. The next cell contains the work. The code that follows will estimate the value of pi. The details of the code are not important, but notice that the `count` variable uses `sparkContext` and parallelizes a task on the cluster. After the boilerplate, your Spark code will execute a task and get the results:

```
import random
NUM_SAMPLES=1
def inside(p):
    x, y = random.random(), random.random()
    return x*x + y*y < 1
count = spark.sparkContext.parallelize(range(0,
                    NUM_SAMPLES)).filter(inside).count()
print('Pi is roughly {}'.format(4.0 * count /
                    NUM_SAMPLES))
```

5. Lastly, stop the session:

```
spark.stop()
```

Once the session has been stopped, it will show up as a completed application in the web UI. The next section will use Spark with DataFrames and send the data to Kafka.

Spark for data engineering

The previous section showed the structure of a Spark application: we used `findspark` to get the paths, imported the libraries, created a session, did something, and stopped the session. When you do something, it will most likely involve a Spark DataFrame. This section will provide a brief overview of how Spark DataFrames work – it is slightly different than `pandas`.

The first thing you have to do is use `findspark` to set up the environment. Then, you can import the required libraries. Then, create the session. The following code shows the boilerplate to get set up:

```
import findspark
findspark.init()

import pyspark
from pyspark.sql import SparkSession

import os
```

```
os.chdir('/home/paulcrickard')
```

```
spark=SparkSession.builder.master('spark://pop-os.
localdomain:7077').appName('DataFrame-Kafka').getOrCreate()
```

Now you are connected to a session on the Spark cluster. You can read CSV and JSON data just like you did with DataFrames in *Chapter 3, Reading and Writing Files* and *Chapter 4, Working with Databases*, with some slight modifications. When you read in the data, you can use read.csv instead of read_csv in pandas. Another difference between Spark and pandas is the use of .show() in Spark to see the DataFrame. In pandas, you can view dtypes of a DataFrame, and in Spark, you can do the same using printSchema(). The following code reads the data.csv file and prints the top five rows and the schema:

```
df = spark.read.csv('data.csv')
df.show(5)
df.printSchema()
```

The output will be a DataFrame like the one shown in the following screenshot:

```
+---------------+---+--------------------+-------------+--------+-----+-----------+----------+
|            _c0|_c1|                 _c2|          _c3|     _c4|  _c5|        _c6|       _c7|
+---------------+---+--------------------+-------------+--------+-----+-----------+----------+
|           name|age|              street|         city|   state|  zip|        lng|       lat|
|Patrick Hendrix| 23|  5755 Jonathan Ranch|New Sheriland|Wisconsin|60519|103.914462|-59.0094375|
|  Grace Jackson| 36|2502 Stewart Plaz...|  Ramirezville| Arizona|91946|170.503858| 58.1631665|
|  Arthur Garcia| 61|     627 Liu Brooks|  Freemanhaven|  Kansas|97783|-39.845646| 38.689889|
| Gary Valentine| 29|9682 Theresa Vist...|  Allenborough|  Oregon|81537|-30.304522| 81.2722995|
+---------------+---+--------------------+-------------+--------+-----+-----------+----------+
only showing top 5 rows

root
 |-- _c0: string (nullable = true)
 |-- _c1: string (nullable = true)
 |-- _c2: string (nullable = true)
 |-- _c3: string (nullable = true)
 |-- _c4: string (nullable = true)
 |-- _c5: string (nullable = true)
 |-- _c6: string (nullable = true)
 |-- _c7: string (nullable = true)
```

Figure 14.8 – DataFrame from CSV with schema

You will notice that the headers are the first row and there are default _c0 column names. The output also shows that all the columns are strings. You can specify a schema and pass it as a parameter; however, you can also tell Spark to infer the schema. The following code passes that there are headers and tells Spark to infer the schema:

```
df = spark.read.csv('data.csv',header=True,inferSchema=True)
df.show(5)
```

The results are what you expected: a DataFrame with the correct types. The following screenshot shows the results:

```
+---------------+---+--------------------+-------------+--------+-----+-----------+----------+
|           name|age|              street|         city|   state|  zip|        lng|       lat|
+---------------+---+--------------------+-------------+--------+-----+-----------+----------+
|Patrick Hendrix| 23| 5755 Jonathan Ranch| New Sheriland|Wisconsin|60519| 103.914462|-59.0094375|
|  Grace Jackson| 36|2502 Stewart Plaz...|  Ramirezville|  Arizona|91946| 170.503858| 58.1631665|
|  Arthur Garcia| 61|     627 Liu Brooks|  Freemanhaven|   Kansas|97783| -39.845646|  38.689889|
| Gary Valentine| 29|9682 Theresa Vist...|  Allenborough|   Oregon|81537| -30.304522| 81.2722995|
|    Erin Mclean| 23|9349 Williams Lan...|East Markmouth|     Ohio| 4300|-110.860085|  11.476733|
+---------------+---+--------------------+-------------+--------+-----+-----------+----------+
only showing top 5 rows

root
 |-- name: string (nullable = true)
 |-- age: integer (nullable = true)
 |-- street: string (nullable = true)
 |-- city: string (nullable = true)
 |-- state: string (nullable = true)
 |-- zip: integer (nullable = true)
 |-- lng: double (nullable = true)
 |-- lat: double (nullable = true)
```

Figure 14.9 – DataFrame with headers and correct types

You can select a column by using select() and passing the column name as a parameter. Don't forget to add .show() or it will return a DataFrame and not display it:

```
df.select('name').show()
```

You will notice that in pandas, you would have used [] and a column name and also did not need the select method. In pandas, you could also filter a DataFrame by using the df[(df['field']< value)] format. In Spark, you can use select and filter to do the same, the difference being that a select method returns True and False for a condition, and filter will return the DataFrame for that condition. With filter, you can also add a select method and pass an array of columns to return. The code is shown as follows:

```
df.select(df['age']<40).show()
```

```
df.filter(df['age']<40).show()
df.filter('age<40').select(['name','age','state']).show()
```

Notice that in the last line, you didn't use `df['age']` but were able to just pass the column name. When you want to iterate through a DataFrame, you could use `iterrows` in `pandas`. In Spark, you create an array of rows using `collect()`. The following code will use a `filter` method to get all people under 40 and print the array:

```
u40=df.filter('age<40').collect()
u40
```

To get a single row, you can just pass the index. You can convert the row into different formats, and in this example, I converted it into a dictionary. As a dictionary, you can select any value by specifying the key. The code is shown as follows:

```
u40[0]
u40[0].asDict()
u40[0].asDict()['name']
```

The output of the preceding code is a `Row` object, a dictionary, and a string of the value for the key name, as shown:

```
Row(name='Patrick Hendrix', age=23, street='5755 Jonathan
Ranch', city='New Sheriland', state='Wisconsin', zip=60519,
lng=103.914462, lat=-59.0094375)
```

```
{'name': 'Patrick Hendrix', 'age': 23, 'street': '5755 Jonathan
Ranch', 'city': 'New Sheriland', 'state': 'Wisconsin', 'zip':
60519, 'lng': 103.914462, 'lat': -59.0094375}
```

```
'Patrick Hendrix'
```

To iterate through the DataFrame in Spark, you call `collect()`, and then iterate through the array using a `for` loop. You can then convert each of the rows into a dictionary and do what you need for processing. The following code snippet prints the dictionary:

```
for x in u40:
    print(x.asDict())
```

If you are more comfortable with SQL, you can filter a DataFrame using `spark.sql`. To use SQL, you must first create a view, then you can query it with SQL, as shown in the following code:

```
df.createOrReplaceTempView('people')
df_over40=spark.sql('select * from people where age > 40')
df_over40.show()
```

The results will be the same DataFrame as the `filter` method, but just a different method by which to achieve the same result.

There are several functions to perform modifications or analysis on columns or data in a DataFrame. In Spark, you can use `describe()` to get a basic summary of the data in a column. The following code uses it on the `age` column:

```
df_over40.describe('age').show()
```

The output is the common descriptive statistics of `count`, `mean`, `standard deviation`, `min`, and `max`. These five statistics give you a good overview of the data.

You can also group and aggregate your data just like in `pandas`. To group the counts of states, you can use `groupBy()`, as shown:

```
df.groupBy('state').count().show()
```

Aggregation allows you to pass in a dictionary of the field and a method. To calculate the mean of the `age` column, you would use the following code:

```
df.agg({'age':'mean'}).show()
```

For both `groupBy` and `agg`, you can use `mean`, `max`, `min`, `sum`, and other methods that you can read about in the documentation. There is a large number of other functions you can use that require you to import the `pyspark.sql.functions` module. The following code imports it as `f` and demonstrates some useful functions. Again, for more information on all of the functions, you can read the Python API documents at `https://spark.apache.org/docs/latest/api/python/pyspark.sql.html`:

```
import pyspark.sql.functions as f
df.select(f.collect_set(df['state'])).collect()
# Returns a Row of unique states which will be all 50.
df.select(f.countDistinct('state').alias('states')).show()
#returns a single column named states with a single value of
```

```
50.
df.select(f.md5('street').alias('hash')).collect()
#Returns an md5 hash of the street value for each row
# Row(hash='81576976c4903b063c46ed9fdd140d62'),
df.select(f.reverse(df.state).alias('state-reverse')).collect()
# returns each rows street value reversed
# Row(state-reverse='nisnocsiW')
select(f.soundex(df.name).alias('soundex')).collect()
# returns a soundex of the name field for each row
# Row(soundex='P362')
```

When you have finished your data processing, stop the session using stop(), as shown:

```
spark.stop()
```

Congratulations! You have successfully processed data with PySpark.

Summary

In this chapter, you learned the basics of working with Apache Spark. First, you downloaded and installed Spark and configured PySpark to run in Jupyter notebooks. You also learned how to scale Spark horizontally by adding nodes. Spark uses DataFrames similar to those used in pandas. The last section taught you the basics of manipulating data in Spark.

In the next chapter, you will use Spark with Apache MiNiFi to move data at the edge or on Internet-of-Things devices.

15
Real-Time Edge Data with MiNiFi, Kafka, and Spark

In this chapter, you will learn how **Internet-of-Things (IoT)** devices, small computers, and sensors can send data into a data pipeline using Apache NiFi. For computers or devices with little processing power, MiNiFi allows them to be part of a NiFi data pipeline. MiNiFi is a lightweight version of NiFi with a stripped-down set of processors and no graphical user interface. It is built to send data using a data pipeline built into NiFi and deployed to the device.

In this chapter, we're going to cover the following main topics:

- Setting up MiNiFi on a device
- Building and deploying a MiNiFi task in NiFi

Setting up MiNiFi

Apache MiNiFi is a lightweight version of NiFi, to be used in data collection at the source. Increasingly, the source has become smaller IoT devices, sensors, and low-powered computers such as the Raspberry Pi. To incorporate these devices into your data pipelines, you need a way to get the data off the device. MiNiFi allows you to stream the data to NiFi as part of a standard data pipeline.

To get the MiNiFi binary, browse to `https://nifi.apache.org/minifi/`. The following screenshot is of the MiNiFi home page and will provide you with information and documentation for the project:

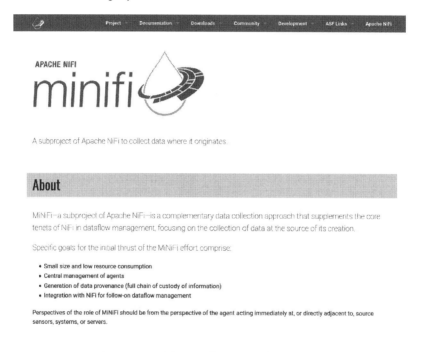

Figure 15.1 – The Apache MiNiFi home page

From the main navigation bar, go to **Downloads** and select the **Download MiNiFi Components** option. You will need to decide whether you want to run the MiNiFi Java or MiNiFi C++ version. Which version is appropriate will depend on the specifications of the device where MiNiFi will live. If you need the smallest footprint and memory usage, then the C++ version is for you. If you have more resources and need to have a wider selection of available processors, then the Java version is your best bet. You can find a list of processors by category, with descriptions at `https://nifi.apache.org/docs/nifi-docs/html/getting-started.html#what-processors-are-available`.

You can always copy the NAR file for any processor in NiFi and put it in the MiNiFi `lib` directory. Some processors will require you to also copy and send the NAR file for the controller service. This chapter will use the MiNiFi Java version.

Download the most current version of MiNiFi (Java), which is currently 0.5.0. Select the `minifi-0.5.0-bin.tar.gz` link and download it. You will also need to scroll further down the page and select the corresponding version of the MiNiFi toolkit binaries. Both the C++ and Java versions use the same toolkit, so you will only need to select the right release – 0.5.0. Download the `minifi-toolkit-0.5.0-bin.tar.gz` file.

Extract and copy MiNiFi and the MiNiFi toolkit to your home directory using the following commands:

```
tar -xvzf minifi-0.5.0-bin.tar.gz
tar -xvzf minifi-toolkit-0.5.0-bin.tar.gz
mv minifi-0.5.0 ~/minifi
mv minifi-toolkit-0.5.0 ~/minifi-toolkit
```

I dropped `-0.5.0` when I moved `minifi` and `minifi-toolkit` to my home directory. In this chapter, I will run MiNiFi on the same machine as NiFi – as I have done with Kafka and Spark – but if you want to run MiNiFi on another device, as you would in production, copy the `minifi-0.5.0` directory to that machine. The MiNiFi toolkit stays on the NiFi machine.

The last step is to set the `$MINIFI_HOME` variable to the location of MiNiFi. You can either export the variable and add it to your path, or the better way would be to edit your `.bashrc` file, as shown:

```
export MINIFI_HOME=/home/paulcrickard/minifi
export PATH=$MINIFI_HOME/bin:$PATH
```

Your `.bashrc` file will look as in the following screenshot. Notice that I have the edits from the previous chapter on Apache Spark just above the MiNiFi edits:

```
if ! shopt -oq posix; then
  if [ -f /usr/share/bash-completion/bash_completion ]; then
    . /usr/share/bash-completion/bash_completion
  elif [ -f /etc/bash_completion ]; then
    . /etc/bash_completion
  fi
fi

export JAVA_HOM=/usr/lib/jvm/java-1.11.0-openjdk.amd64
export SPARK_HOME=/home/paulcrickard/spark3
export PATH=$SPARK_HOME/bin:$PATH

export MINIFI_HOME=/home/paulcrickard/minifi
export PATH=$MINIFI_HOME/bin:$PATH
```

Figure 15.2 – A .bashrc file with exports for Spark and MiNiFi

Now that you have MiNiFi configured and the MiNiFi toolkit ready to go, it is time to create your first data pipeline in Apache NiFi. The next section will walk you through creating one.

Building a MiNiFi task in NiFi

In this section, you will build a data pipeline and deploy it to MiNiFi. The data pipeline will generate flow files and send them to NiFi. The next section will take this further and use a processor that is not included with MiNiFi.

To use MiNiFi, you will need an older version of NiFi. The current tool – 0.5.0 – breaks because of changes to properties output from the `nifi` template. It will be fixed in 0.6.0, but until then, you will need to use at least version 1.9.0 of NiFi. You can get older NiFi versions at `https://archive.apache.org/dist/nifi/1.9.0/`. Unzip NiFi using the `tar` command with the `-xvzf` flags. Place the folder in your home directory using `mv` or your file explorer tools.

You will also need an older version of Java. To install the correct version of Java, use the following command:

```
sudo apt-get install openjdk-8-jre
```

Lastly, you will also need to make sure that NiFi is configured to allow site-to-site connections. In a terminal, go to $NIFI_HOME/conf and open the nifi.properties file. Scrolling about halfway down the file, you will see the Site to Site properties section. In my file, nifi.remote.input.socket.port is blank. If there is not a port specified, edit the file so that the port is 1026, as shown in the following screenshot:

```
# Site to Site properties
nifi.remote.input.host=
nifi.remote.input.secure=false
nifi.remote.input.socket.port=1026
nifi.remote.input.http.enabled=true
nifi.remote.input.http.transaction.ttl=30 sec
nifi.remote.contents.cache.expiration=30 secs
```

Figure 15.3 – Site-to-site properties with input.socket.port set to 1026

Next, start NiFi and create an input port to connect MiNiFi with NiFi. Drag and drop the input port to the canvas and name it minifi. Data from MiNiFi will enter NiFi through this port.

Connect the input port to a data pipeline. The pipeline is shown in the following screenshot:

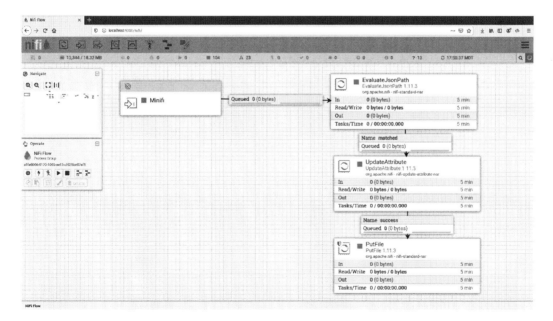

Figure 15.4 – Data pipeline to consume MiNiFi data and write to file on the NiFi host

To build the data pipeline, take the following steps:

1. Drag and drop the `EvaluteJsonPath` processor to the canvas. Configure the
    Destination property to be `flowfile-attribute`. Create a new property named
    `fname` and set the value to `$.fname`. This will be in the JSON received from MiNiFi.

2. Drag and drop the `UpdateAttribute` processor to the canvas. Create a new
    property named `filename` and set the value to `${fname}`.

3. Drag and drop the `PutFile` processor to the canvas. Set the **Directory** property
    to a location on the NiFi host. I have set it to `/home/paulcrickard/output`.
    Leave the other properties as the defaults.

The preceding steps create the connection from MiNiFi to NiFi, but right now, we do
not have a data pipeline for MiNiFi. To create the MiNiFi data pipeline, drag and drop a
processor group to the canvas and name it `minifitask`.

Inside the processor group, drag and drop the `GenerateFlowfile` processor to the
canvas. On the **Scheduling** tab of the processor, set **Run Schedule** to `30 sec`. Set the
Custom Text property to `{"fname":"minifi.txt","body":"Some text"}`.

Next, you will add a **remote processor group**. Drag and drop it to the canvas. The popup
will ask for several properties to be configured. Set the **URLs** property to `http://`
`localhost:9300` and the **Transport Protocol** property to `HTTP`. Leave the rest as the
defaults, or blank. The settings should look as in the following screenshot:

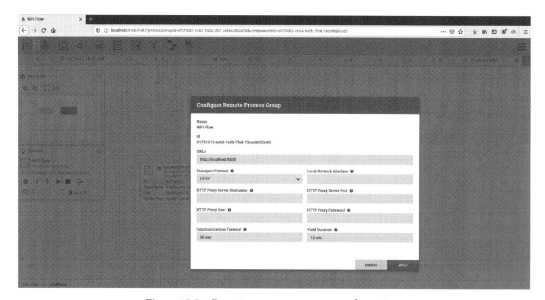

Figure 15.5 – Remote processor group configuration

Connect the `GenerateFlowFile` processor to **Remote Processor Group**. The **Create Connection** popup will allow you to select the input port as **To Input**. It would have guessed correctly and chosen MiNiFi. If not, use the dropdown to select the MiNiFi port you created in the previous steps. Once the processors are connected, right-click on **Remote Processor Group** and select **Enable Transmission**. The icon should now be a blue circle, as shown in the following screenshot:

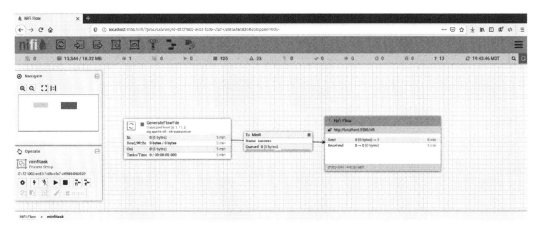

Figure 15.6 – MiNiFi data pipeline to a remote processor group

The MiNiFi data pipeline is complete. To make sure it is runnable on MiNiFi, you need to transform it. To transform it, you will need to export it as a template. To create the template, exit the processor group. Right-click on the processor group, then select **Template**. From the waffle menu in the upper-right corner of the NiFi window, select **Templates** to view all of the available templates. Download the `minifitask` template by clicking the download icon to the right of the table. This will download an XML version of the data pipeline.

To transform the template, you will run `config.sh` in the MiNiFi toolkit. I have made a `minifi-templates` folder in my home directory. Changing directories to `$MINIFI_HOME`, run the following command:

```
./bin/config.sh transform /home/paulcrickard/Downloads/
minifitask.xml /home/paulcrickard/minifi-templates/config.yml
```

If everything worked properly, you should get a message like the one shown in the following screenshot:

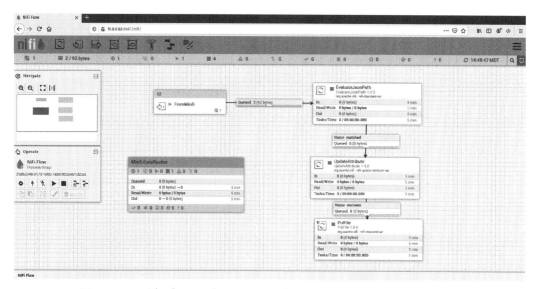

Figure 15.7 – minifi-toolkit transforming the XML template into a YML file

You will now have a `config.yml` file in your `minifi-templates` directory. Copy this file to the `$MINIFI_HOME/conf` directory. You can overwrite the existing `config.yml` file that came with MiNiFi.

From the `$MINIFI_HOME/bin` directory, you can start `minifi` and it will read your `config.yml` file when it does. Use the following command to start MiNiFi:

```
./minifi.sh start
```

Your MiNiFi data pipeline is now running. You can view the logs at `$MINIFI_HOME/logs/minifi-app.log`. But you can also now open NiFi and look at the data streaming in from MiNiFi through the `FromMinifi` input port. Your NiFi data pipeline should look as in the following screenshot:

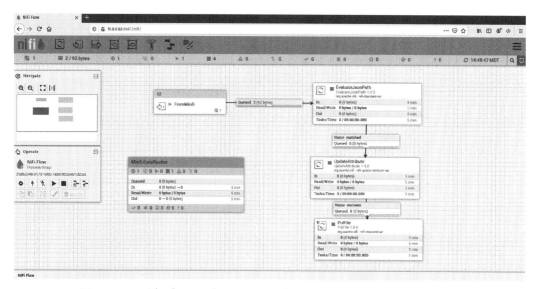

Figure 15.8 – The data pipeline receiving data on the input port from MiNiFi

You will notice that the processor group you used to create the template is stopped. The data is coming from MiNiFi into the NiFi instance and being processed and saved to the disk of the NiFi machine. The MiNiFi machine only sends data, which allows it to not be overwhelmed with trying to run a version of NiFi locally or to have to make remote connections to other machines to write out files at intervals. Streaming data can be sent from the MiNiFi machine to NiFi.

Once the MiNiFi data is streaming into NiFi, you have the full range of tools available to you to process this data. You could send it to a Kafka topic, as shown in *Chapter 13*, *Streaming Data with Kafka*, and make it available to many other tools listening on the topic. MiNiFi opens up the possibility of capturing data from small devices.

Summary

In this chapter, you learned how MiNiFi provides a means by which you can stream data to a NiFi instance. With MiNiFi, you can capture data from sensors, smaller devices such as a Raspberry Pi, or on regular servers where the data lives, without needing a full NiFi install. You learned how to set up and configure a remote processor group that allows you to talk to a remote NiFi instance.

In the *Appendix*, you will learn how you can cluster NiFi to run your data pipelines on different machines so that you can further distribute the load. This will allow you to reserve servers for specific tasks, or to spread large amounts of data horizontally across the cluster. By combining NiFi, Kafka, and Spark into clusters, you will be able to process more data than any single machine.

Appendix

Building a NiFi cluster

In this book, you have built a Kafka cluster, a ZooKeeper cluster, and a Spark cluster. Instead of increasing the power of a single server, through clustering, you are able to add more machines to increase the processing power of a data pipeline. In this chapter, you will learn how to cluster NiFi so that your data pipelines can run across multiple machines.

In this appendix, we're going to cover the following main topics:

- The basics of NiFi clustering

- Building a NiFi cluster

- Building a distributed data pipeline

- Managing the distributed data pipeline

The basics of NiFi clustering

Clustering in Apache NiFi follows a **Zero-Master Clustering** architecture. In this type of clustering, there is no pre-defined master. Every node can perform the same tasks, and the data is split between them. NiFi uses Zookeeper when deployed as a cluster.

Zookeeper will elect a **Cluster Coordinator**. The Cluster Coordinator is responsible for deciding whether new nodes can join – the nodes will connect to the coordinator – and to provide the updated flows to the new nodes.

While it sounds like the Cluster Coordinator is the master, it is not. You can make changes to the data pipelines on any node and they will be replicated to all the other nodes, meaning a non-Cluster Coordinator or a non-Primary Node can submit changes.

The **Primary Node** is also elected by Zookeeper. On the Primary Node, you can run isolated processes. An isolated process is a NiFi processor that runs only on the Primary Node. This is important because think what would happen if you had three nodes all trying to read from a directory, or a single file, or a database. There would be a race condition or a lock. Processors that can result in these race conditions should be run on the Primary Node. The `ExecuteSQL` processor can run on the Primary Node, and then distribute the data to the other nodes downstream for processing. You will see how this is done later in this chapter.

Clustering allows you to build data pipelines that can process larger amounts of data than on a single machine. Furthermore, it allows a single point to build and monitor data pipelines. If you had several single-node NiFi instances running, you would need to manage all of them. Changes to a data pipeline on one would need to be replicated on the others or at least checked to make sure it is not a duplicate. Which machine is running the data warehouse pipeline again? I forgot. Managing a cluster, from any node, makes it much easier and more efficient.

Building a NiFi cluster

In this section, you will build a two-node cluster on different machines. Just like with MiNiFi, however, there are some compatibility issues with the newest versions of NiFi and Zookeeper. To work around these issues and demonstrate the concepts, this chapter will use an older version of NiFi and the pre-bundled Zookeeper. To build the NiFi cluster, perform the following steps:

1. As root, or using sudo, open your `/etc/hosts` file. You will need to assign names to the machines that you will use in your cluster. It is best practice to use a hostname instead of IP addresses. Your hosts file should look like the following example:

    ```
    127.0.0.1    localhost
    ::1          localhost
    127.0.1.1    pop-os.localdomain        pop-os
    10.0.0.63    nifi-node-2
    10.0.0.148   nifi-node-1
    ```

2. In the preceding hosts file, I have added the last two lines. The nodes are
    `nifi-node-1` and `nifi-node-2` and you can see that they have different IP
    addresses. Make these changes in the hosts file for each machine. When you have
    finished, you can test that it works by using `ping`. From each machine, try to use
    `ping` to hit the other machine by hostname. The following is the command to hit
    `nifi-node-2` from the `nifi-node-1` machine:

```
paulcrickard@pop-os:~$ ping nifi-node-2
PING nifi-node-2 (10.0.0.63) 56(84) bytes of data.
64 bytes from nifi-node-2 (10.0.0.63): icmp_seq=1 ttl=64
time=55.1 ms
64 bytes from nifi-node-2 (10.0.0.63): icmp_seq=2 ttl=64
time=77.1 ms
64 bytes from nifi-node-2 (10.0.0.63): icmp_seq=3 ttl=64
time=101 ms
64 bytes from nifi-node-2 (10.0.0.63): icmp_seq=4 ttl=64
time=32.8 ms
```

3. If you do the opposite from your other node, `nifi-node-2`, you should get the
    same results – `nifi-node-1` will return data.

4. Next, download an older version of Apache NiFi, 1.0.0, at `https://archive.
    apache.org/dist/nifi/1.0.0/`. Select the `-bin.tar.gz` file as it contains
    the binaries. Once the file has downloaded, extract the files using your file manager
    or with the following command:

```
tar -xvzf nifi-1.0.0-bin.tar.gz
```

Once you have extracted the files, you will edit the configuration files.

5. To edit the Zookeeper configuration file, open `zookeeper.properties` in
    the `$NIFI_HOME/conf` directory. At the bottom of the file, add your servers as
    shown:

```
server.1=nifi-node-1:2888:3888
server.2=nifi-node-2:2888:3888
```

6. At the top of the file, you will see `clientPort` and `dataDir`. It should look like the following example:

```
clientPort=2181
initLimit=10
autopurge.purgeInterval=24
syncLimit=5
tickTime=2000
dataDir=./state/zookeeper
autopurge.snapRetainCount=30
```

7. In `dataDir`, you will need to add a file named `myfile` with the number of the server as the content. On `server.1` (`nifi-node-1`), you will create a `myid` ID with `1` as the content. To do that, from the `$NIFI_HOME` directory, use the following commands:

```
mkdir state
mkdir state/zookeeper
echo 1 >> myid
```

8. On `nifi-node-2`, repeat the preceding steps, except change `echo` to the following line:

```
echo 2 >> myid
```

    With Zookeeper configured, you will now edit the `nifi.properties` file.

9. To edit `nifi.properties`, you will need to change several properties. The first property is `nifi.state.management.embedded.zookeeper.start`, which needs to be set to `true`. The section of the file is shown as follows:

```
####################
# State Management #
####################
nifi.state.management.configuration.file=./conf/state-
management.xml
# The ID of the local state provider
nifi.state.management.provider.local=local-provider
# The ID of the cluster-wide state provider. This will be
ignored if NiFi is not clustered but must be populated if
running in a cluster.
nifi.state.management.provider.cluster=zk-provider
```

```
# Specifies whether or not this instance of NiFi should
run an embedded ZooKeeper server
```
```
nifi.state.management.embedded.zookeeper.start=true
```
```
# Properties file that provides the ZooKeeper properties
to use if <nifi.state.management.embedded.zookeeper.
start> is set to true
```
```
nifi.state.management.embedded.zookeeper.properties=./
conf/zookeeper.properties
```

The preceding commands tells NiFi to use the embedded version of Zookeeper.

10. You now need to tell NiFi how to connect to Zookeeper in `nifi.zookeeper.` `connect.string`. The string is a comma-separated list of the Zookeeper servers in the format of `<hostname>:<port>`, and the port is `clientPort` from the `zookeeper.config` file, which was `2181`. The section of the file is shown in the following code block:

```
# zookeeper properties, used for cluster management #
```
```
nifi.zookeeper.connect.string=nifi.zookeeper.connect.
string=nifi-node-1:2181,nifi-node-2:2181
```
```
nifi.zookeeper.connect.timeout=3 secs
```
```
nifi.zookeeper.session.timeout=3 secs
```
```
nifi.zookeeper.root.node=/nifi
```

11. Next, you will configure the `cluster` properties of NiFi. Specifically, you will set `nifi.cluster.node` to `true`. You will add the hostname of the node to `nifi.` `cluster.node.address`, as well as adding the port at `nifi.cluster.node.` `protocol.port`. You can set this to anything available and high enough such that you do not need root to access it (over `1024`). Lastly, you can change `nifi.` `cluster.flow.election.max.wait.time` to something shorter than 5 minutes and you can add a value for `nifi.cluster.flow.election.max.` `candidates`. I have changed the wait time to `1` minute and left the candidates blank. The section of the file is shown in the following code block:

```
# cluster node properties (only configure for cluster
nodes) #
```
```
nifi.cluster.is.node=true
```
```
nifi.cluster.node.address=nifi-node-1
```
```
nifi.cluster.node.protocol.port=8881
```
```
nifi.cluster.node.protocol.threads=10
```
```
nifi.cluster.node.protocol.max.threads=50
```

```
nifi.cluster.node.event.history.size=25
nifi.cluster.node.connection.timeout=5 sec
nifi.cluster.node.read.timeout=5 sec
nifi.cluster.node.max.concurrent.requests=100
nifi.cluster.firewall.file=
nifi.cluster.flow.election.max.wait.time=1 mins
nifi.cluster.flow.election.max.candidates=
```

12. The web properties require the hostname of the machine as well as the port. By default, `nifi.web.http.port` is `8080`, but if you have something running on that port already, you can change it. I have changed it to `8888`. The hostname is `nifi-node-1` or `nifi-mode-2`. The web properties are shown in the following code block:

```
# web properties #
nifi.web.war.directory=./lib
nifi.web.http.host=nifi-node-1 <----------------------
nifi.web.http.port=8888
```

13. Lastly, NiFi uses Site-to-Site to communicate. You will need to configure the `nifi.remote.input.host` property to the machine hostname, and `nifi.remote.input.socket.port` to an available port. The properties file is shown in the following code block:

```
# Site to Site properties
nifi.remote.input.host=nifi-node-1
nifi.remote.input.secure=false
nifi.remote.input.socket.port=8882
nifi.remote.input.http.enabled=true
nifi.remote.input.http.transaction.ttl=30 sec
nifi.remote.contents.cache.expiration=30 secs
```

Each node will have the same settings in the `nifi.properties` file, with the exception of changing the hostname to the appropriate number, `nifi-node-#`.

Your cluster is now configured, and you are ready to launch the two nodes. From each machine, launch NiFi as normal using the following command:

```
./nifi.sh start
```

You should now be able to browse to any node at `http://nifi-node-1:8888/nifi`. You will see NiFi as usual, shown in the following screenshot:

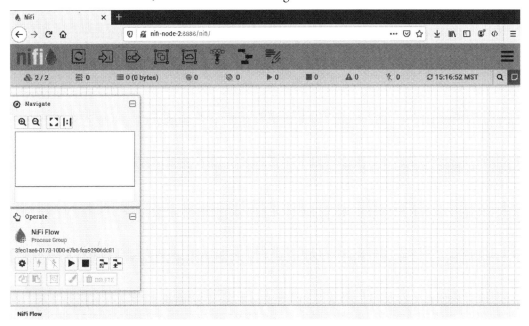

Figure 16.1 – NiFi running as a cluster

Everything looks exactly the same, except for the top-left corner of the status bar. You should now have a cloud with **2/2** next to it. This is telling you that NiFi is running as a cluster with 2 out of 2 nodes available and connected. You can see the events by hovering over the messages on the right of the status bar. The following screenshot shows the election and connection of nodes:

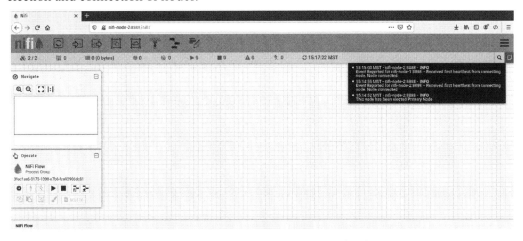

Figure 16.2 – Messages showing events in the cluster

Lastly, you can open the cluster window by selecting **Cluster** from the waffle menu in the right corner of the NiFi window. The cluster is shown in the following screenshot:

Figure 16.3 – Cluster details

The preceding screenshot shows which node is the Primary Node, along with the Controller Node and a Regular Node. From here you can also see details about the queues and disconnect or reconnect the nodes. The cluster is working, and you can now build a distributed data pipeline.

Building a distributed data pipeline

Building a distributed data pipeline is almost exactly the same as building a data pipeline to run on a single machine. NiFi will handle the logistics of passing and recombining the data. A basic data pipeline is shown in the following screenshot:

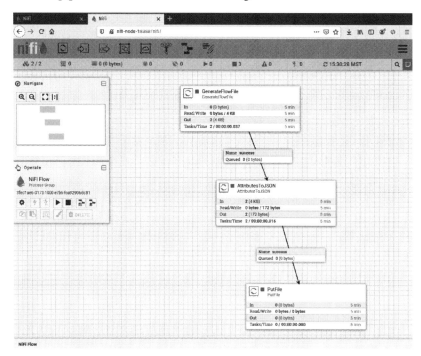

Figure 16.4 – A basic data pipeline to generate data, extract attributes to json, and write to disk

The preceding data pipeline uses the `GenerateFlowFile` processor to create unique flowfiles. This is passed downstream to the `AttributesToJSON` processor, which extracts the attributes and writes to the flowfile content. Lastly, the file is written to disk at `/home/paulcrickard/output`.

Before running the data pipeline, you will need to make sure that you have the output directory for the `PutFile` processor on each node. Earlier, I said that data pipelines are no different when distributed, but there are some things you must keep in mind, one being that `PutFile` will write to disk on every node by default. You will need to configure your processors to be able to run on any node. We will fix this later in this section.

One more thing before you run the data pipeline. Open the browser to your other node. You will see the exact same data pipeline in that node. Even the layout of the processors is the same. Changes to any node will be distributed to all the other nodes. You can work from any node.

When you run the data pipeline, you will see files written to the output directory of both nodes. The data pipeline is running and distributing the load across the nodes. The following screenshot shows the output of the data pipeline:

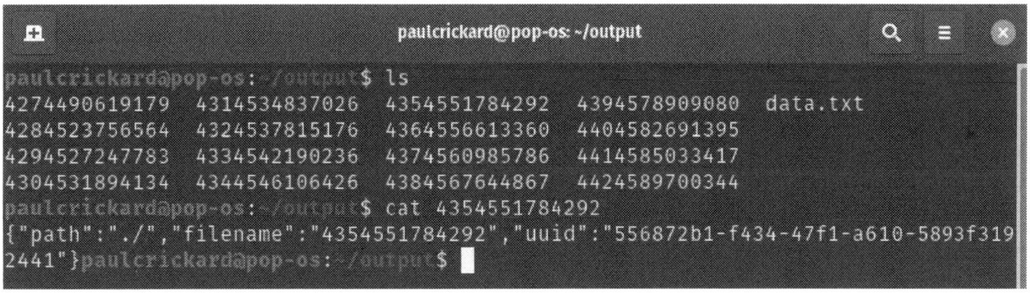

Figure 16.5 – Data pipeline writing flowfiles to a node

If you are getting the same results as the preceding screenshot, congratulations, you have just built a distributed data pipeline. Next, you will learn some more features of the NiFi cluster.

Managing the distributed data pipeline

The preceding data pipeline runs on each node. To compensate for that, you had to create the same path on both nodes for the `PutFile` processor to work. Earlier, you learned that there are several processors that can result in race conditions – trying to read the same file at the same time – which will cause problems. To resolve these issues, you can specify that a processor should only run on the Primary Node – as an isolated process.

In the configuration for the `PutFile` processor, select the **Scheduling** tab. In the dropdown for **Scheduling Strategy**, choose **On primary node**, as shown in the following screenshot:

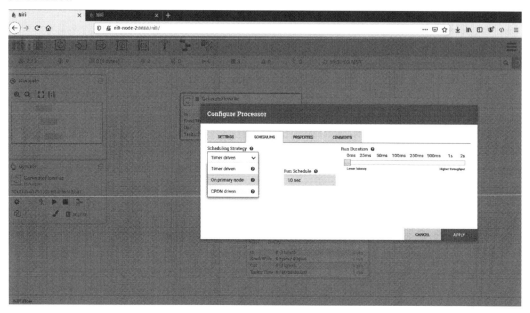

Figure 16.6 – Running a processor on the Primary Node only

Now, when you run the data pipeline, the files will only be placed on the Primary Node. You can schedule processors such as `GetFile` or `ExecuteSQL` to do the same thing.

To see the load of the data pipeline on each node, you can look at the cluster details from the waffle menu. As data moves through the data pipeline, you can see how many flowfiles are sitting in the queues of each node. The following screenshot shows the pipeline running on my cluster:

	Node Address ▲	Active Thread Count	Queue / Size	Status	Uptime	Last Heartbeat	
ⓘ	nifi-node-1:8888	0	4 / 2.25 KB	CONNECTED	07/11/2020 16:11:47 MDT	07/11/2020 16:38:55 MDT	↻
ⓘ	nifi-node-2:8888	0	4 / 2.25 KB	CONNECTED, PRIMARY, COORDINATOR	07/11/2020 16:14:48 MDT	07/11/2020 16:38:54 MDT	↻

NiFi Cluster
Displaying 2 of 2

↻ Last updated: 16:38:55 MDT

Figure 16.7 – Viewing the queues of each node. Each node has four flowfiles

The data pipeline is distributing the flowfiles evenly across the nodes. In **Zero-Master Clustering**, the data is not copied or replicated. It exists only on the node that is processing it. If a node goes down, the data needs to be redistributed. This can only happen if the node is still connected to the network, otherwise, it will not happen until the node rejoins.

You can manually disconnect a node by clicking the power icon on the right of the node's row. The following screenshot shows a node being disconnected:

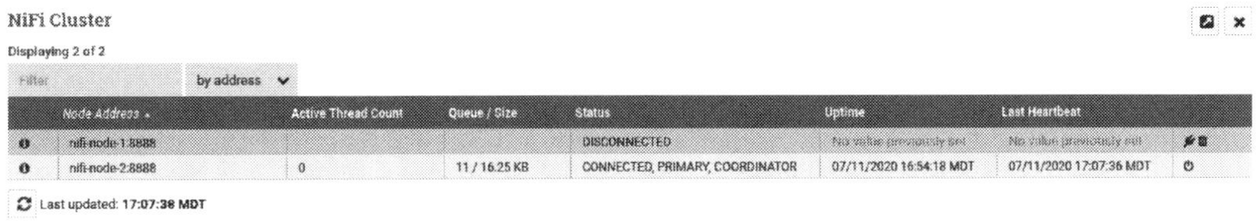

Figure 16.8 – nifi-node-1 has been disconnected from the cluster

In the preceding screenshot, you can see that `nifi-node-1` has a status of **DISCONNECTED**. But you should also notice that it has eight flowfiles that need to be redistributed. Since you disconnected the node, but did not drop it from the network, NiFi will redistribute the flowfiles. You can see the results when the screen is refreshed, as shown in the following screenshot:

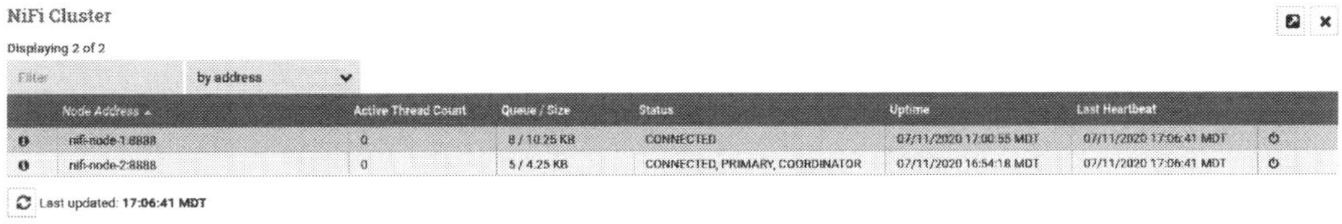

Figure 16.9 – Redistributed flowfiles from a disconnected node

You can also reconnect any disconnected nodes. You do this by clicking the plug icon. When you do, the node will rejoin the cluster and the flowfiles will be redistributed. The following screenshot shows the node rejoined to the cluster:

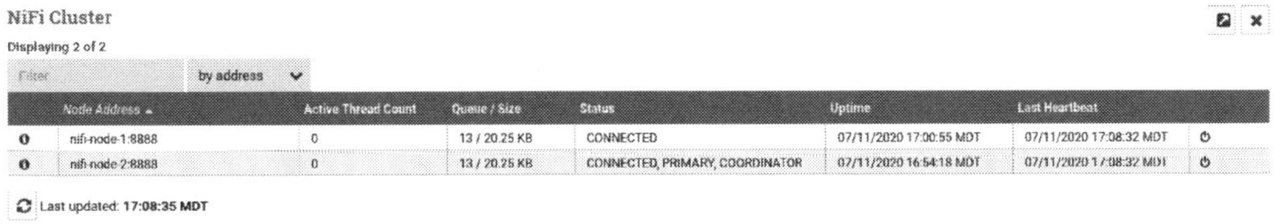

Figure 16.10 – Reconnecting a node and flowfile redistribution

In the preceding screenshot, the flowfiles have accumulated since the node was disconnected evenly across the nodes.

Summary

In this Appendix, you learned the basics of NiFi clustering, as well as how to build a cluster with the embedded Zookeeper and how to build distributed data pipelines. NiFi handles most of the distribution of data; you only need to keep in mind the gotchas – such as race conditions and the fact that processors need to be configured to run on any node. Using a NiFi cluster allows you to manage NiFi on several machines from a single instance. It also allows you to process large amounts of data and have some redundancy in case an instance crashes.

Other Books You May Enjoy

If you enjoyed this book, you may be interested in these other books by Packt:

Practical Data Analysis Using Jupyter Notebook

Mark Wintjen

ISBN: 978-1-83882-603-1

- Understand the importance of data literacy and how to communicate effectively using data

- Find out how to use Python packages such as NumPy, pandas, Matplotlib, and the Natural Language Toolkit (NLTK) for data analysis

- Wrangle data and create DataFrames using pandas

- Produce charts and data visualizations using time-series datasets

- Discover relationships and how to join data together using SQL

- Use NLP techniques to work with unstructured data to create sentiment analysis models

- Discover patterns in real-world datasets that provide accurate insights

The Data Analysis Workshop

Gururajan Govindan, Shubhangi Hora, Konstantin Palagachev

ISBN: 978-1-83921-138-6

- Get to grips with the fundamental concepts and conventions of data analysis
- Understand how different algorithms help you to analyze the data effectively
- Determine the variation between groups of data using hypothesis testing
- Visualize your data correctly using appropriate plotting points
- Use correlation techniques to uncover the relationship between variables
- Find hidden patterns in data using advanced techniques and strategies

Leave a review - let other readers know what you think

Please share your thoughts on this book with others by leaving a review on the site that you bought it from. If you purchased the book from Amazon, please leave us an honest review on this book's Amazon page. This is vital so that other potential readers can see and use your unbiased opinion to make purchasing decisions, we can understand what our customers think about our products, and our authors can see your feedback on the title that they have worked with Packt to create. It will only take a few minutes of your time, but is valuable to other potential customers, our authors, and Packt. Thank you!

Index

Made in the USA
Middletown, DE
18 March 2023

27025614R00199